To Be Real

To Be Real

Truth and Racial Authenticity in African American Standup Comedy

Lanita Jacobs

OXFORD
UNIVERSITY PRESS

OXFORD
UNIVERSITY PRESS

Oxford University Press is a department of the University of Oxford. It furthers
the University's objective of excellence in research, scholarship, and education
by publishing worldwide. Oxford is a registered trade mark of Oxford University
Press in the UK and certain other countries.

Published in the United States of America by Oxford University Press
198 Madison Avenue, New York, NY 10016, United States of America.

Library of Congress Control Number: 2022944652

ISBN 978–0–19–087008–9 (pbk)
ISBN 978–0–19–087009–6 (hbk)

DOI: 10.1093/oso/9780190870096.001.0001

1 3 5 7 9 8 6 4 2

Paperback printed by Lakeside Book Company, United States of America
Hardback printed by Bridgeport National Bindery, Inc., United States of America

To Jackie Lamar Stewart Sr.
Thank you for being a father to me, Daddy. I love you.

Contents

Preface

Let me be real with you, Dear Reader: I can't believe I'm writing a preface for the first book featured in OUP's Oxford Studies in Language and Race series. Sure, I earned a PhD from one of America's premiere linguistic anthropology graduate programs (UCLA). But the truth is that I drifted from my discipline some time ago.

One of the last times I showed up donning my linguistic anthropology cap proper was at the 11th Annual Conference on Language, Interaction, and Social Organization (LISO) held at UC Santa Barbara in May 2005. Even then . . . well, maybe always, my cap was tilted to the side. I facilitated a workshop (Ethnography of Performance: Methodological Insights from an African American Standup Comedy Study) and gave a plenary talk ("[In Pursuit of] 'Truth' and 'Authenticity' in African American Standup Comedy"). Both enabled me to share insights from what was then a four-year study involving hand-written observations of live standup comedy and recorded interviews with standup comics concerning the September 11 terrorist attacks. I remember forcing my own hand in that talk; I had long realized that I couldn't keep writing about live comedy with merely pen in hand—not if I wanted to be taken seriously as a linguistic anthropologist or an ethnographer-proper (and even if that's how long it took for me to convince *most* comics that I wasn't a joke-thief masquerading as a researcher-in-plain-sight). So, I staged my own dramatic challenge and "reveal" by sharing my emailed appeal to Enss Mitchell, owner of L.A.'s premiere Black-owned comedy club, The Comedy Union, to record consenting comics' sets for my "project." Then, I chased it with an exuberant PowerPoint slide that shouted—in real time and marriage-proposal style: "And he said. 'Yes!' " where "he," of course, meant Enss. Which is to say, I used that moment among my tribe to compel myself to do the work linguistic anthropology and Black standup comedy called me to do; I also bracketed that pursuit quite literally with parentheses and apt quotation marks because I knew just how tentative my "pursuit of truth and authenticity" might seem at the time.

After that, I got lost in standup comedy in a delicious way for many years, wandering from linguistic anthropology ever still. My wandering was motivated not just by standup comedy's incessant appeal to me but also given what felt like my unsteady gait on academia's conveyer belt of truth, at least as far as race and authenticity was/is concerned. Which is to say I'd also grown tired and eventually dispirited by the work of centering race-as-social-construction and the analytical options that sure stance afforded. My observations of Black standup comedy routinely suggested a different story or, at the very least, a different valence, one drenched in winking awareness that race is, indeed, a social construction and "winking" only insofar as comics and their discriminating audiences appreciated race as far more dynamic than many scholars concerned with disabling race's fiction were oft willing to concede.

If I listened primarily to precedents within anthropology and beyond, including my second "home," American Studies and Ethnicity, I'd have a few options before me: I could examine live standup comedy if only to deconstruct comics' narratives and jokes about "real" Blackness toward a sure-fire critique of racial essentialism within the jokes. Or I could deconstruct racial authenticity with deference to enduring processes of racialization by pointing out, for example, how the jokes do the handiwork of "making race" and racializing individuals—sometimes disdainfully (yuck!) and, other times, subversively (yay!). This makes sense but it didn't feel like the entire story. I needed to mine the space between these productive options—not woefully because understand, Dear Reader, *none* of these options were "wrong" and, in fact, *all* were "right"! I just needed to figure out how to tell a story that wasn't prefigured or predetermined by the conveyer belt of truth that carries many trained scholars—*tick tick tick*—into the best possible outcomes toward defensible tenure, promotion, scholarly recognition, and maybe even social change one mind at a time. To do this, I took inspiration from Zora Neale Hurston, the famed ethnographer, folklorist, and creative (e.g., novelist, playwright, and Wanderer-Extraordinaire) who inspires my place in anthropology today; I wandered to other fields (e.g., humor studies, disability studies) in search of refuge, however fraught or fleeting, while watching linguistic anthropology from afar.

I am fortunate that in my wandering, a few of my colleagues in linguistics and linguistic anthropology never let me go. H. Samy Alim, the acquiring editor of Oxford University Press's Language and Race series, is among them. I recall vividly the conference he and Marjorie Harness Goodwin hosted at UCLA in February 2012, "Race and Ethnicity in Language, Interaction and Culture," for which he invited me to deliver a theoretical paper on issues of language and race. At this point in my career when I'm less disciplined by the receipt of tenure and can now laugh at the pretension that I could, "would," and, given hard work, *should* become an academic "star" (*Ha! Ha! Haaaaaaa!*—that's *me* laughing), I can tell you that it's nothing short of revolutionary that Alim and others (Alim & Smitherman, 2012; Alim, Rickford, & Ball 2016; Rosa &

Flores 2017; Alim, Reyes, & Kroskrity 2020) explicitly affix race to linguistics (i.e., "raciolinguistics"), affording space for kindred scholars such as Krystal A. Smalls (2020) to break new ground in "semiotics" by adding race to semiotics (i.e., raciosemiotics) in the same volume to examine "the ways race, signs, and the body co-construct one another" (233), as well as Patriann Smith's (2019) "transraciolinguistic" approach, among others.

You know why?

Sometimes, what I'll now call field-specifying is precisely what's necessary to name so as to codify new emphases within established disciplines so they can't be sidelined as a "trend" or eventually cast aside. Sometimes, proclaiming a whole new interdisciplinary area of inquiry backed by cutting-edge and exemplary scholarship is exactly what it takes to keep race on the table, especially if in a more-than-constructivist or constructivist-adjacent way. And sometimes, if not most times, this is what it takes to afford existing and emerging scholars with the theory, methodology, praxis, and will to avoid spending the first decade or two of their careers tiptoeing around the subject by forever-bracketing race's constructedneess lest they be gatekept or publicly admonished for their silly retrograde ways.

Best, these interventions are not merely name-facing or theoretical in nature. Alim and his collaborators (i.e., Angela Reyes and Paul V. Kroskrity [2020] and John Rickford and Arnetha F. Ball [2016]) know that this work has never been easy and sure ain't easy now. They know, too, that such work is most sustainable when it is sustain*ing*—meaning, that scholarly dialogues, collaborations, and publications evince an ethic of sincere care both for individual scholars' intellectual contributions and for scholars themselves so that the hard but necessary conversations around, say, anti-racism, anti-Blackness, and White supremacy, are actually possible. Alim likewise notes in the preface to the paperback edition of *Raciolinguistics: How Language Shapes Our Ideas about Race*, co-edited with John Rickford and Arnetha F. Ball (2020): "Our work must be more than an intellectual exercise. We must draw attention to various forms of racism and dehumanization in order to divulge and disrupt them." He ends with this expressed hope—"that we can create spaces in the academy where future generations of scholars of language and race feel like they have a home, one that is not only institutionalized through conferences, journals, book series, and the like, but a scholarly community that reaches beyond the confines of our current institutional constraints and connects us to our scholarly kin in far corners of the globe" (ix).

At the risk of subverting myself, let me tell how life-giving such race and, I'll add, care-centered work is for me right now. Over a month ago, I submitted what I thought was the final version of this book. After a rigorous perusal,

Alim gently advised me to revisit my book to incorporate most recent work in the field of language and race, and if I'm being honest, preempt some inevitable head-scratching critiques. He shouldn't have had to tell me this, and I'm glad he did: it was the righteous thing to do. Also, when I heeded Alim's wise counsel and did the work I arguably should've done some time ago, I was humbled and shocked.

Turns out that while I was a wanderin', many scholars, some of whom I found myself in the trenches with decades back, have scripted new ways of centering language-and-race in a way that race can no longer be evacuated, bracketed, or otherwise "treated" so as to avoid the risk of re-inscribing race's fictions or worst, becoming a handmaiden of racial essentialism. This more recent work, building upon that of pioneering scholars of language and race (i.e., Smitherman, 1977; Spears, 1999), provides potential ground and scaffold for this book's central hook regarding "a" real Black or that which is decidedly Black about Blackness:

> [Despite pathbreaking scholarship from scholars of color,] the longstanding reluctance to grapple seriously with issues of race in dominant approaches to language persists. This de-centering of race is not simply an attempt to avoid contributing to the troublesome reproduction of racism, **but rather a systematic, cross-disciplinary blind spot that obscures crucial analytical insights regarding the nature of language and social life** [my emphasis]. Moreover, to the extent that conventional research acknowledges race, it too often replicates the limited perspective of earlier scholarship by treating race as a pregiven social category rather than as a focus of inquiry and critique in its own right. **For these reasons, we have chosen to define the field as the field of "language and race." Not only do we view the avoidance of race as unproductive, but by choosing the terms language and race, we are encompassing issues of language and racism and language and racialization. "Language and race," for us, serves as a broad term that pushes back against the scholarly neglect of race as a key area of intellectual inquiry in linguistics and anthropology, and directs future investigations in the field towards a deeper focus on processes of racialization that lead to racist outcomes and multiple forms of social inequality.** (Alim, Reyes, & Kroskrity 2020, 4)

Alim adds:

> **Rather than erasing race, we must work as a collective to produce knowledge that eradicates racism, linguistic or otherwise, at home or abroad** [my emphasis]. Given that race continues to covertly and overtly structure the lived experiences

of millions of People of Color around the world—as well as hegemonically dominant populations (even if unbeknownst to them)—our work must continue to resist and transgress the overwhelmingly White fields of anthropology and linguistics that continue to, at worst, marginalize and, at best, sidestep issues of race and racialization. **While the fields of "language and gender" and "language and sexuality" have long been established, we seek to put forth raciolinguistics as both a field that foregrounds race and as an intersectional project that views race in conjunction with various forms of social differentiation (and urges other scholars to view gender and sexuality as always intersecting with race** (25) [my emphasis].

Whether or not this book manages to reach that sweet spot of reconciliation between what comics are, in fact, doing and what raciolinguistics seeks to amplify and redress remains to be seen. I accept that I no longer rehearse the same chords that would render me 100% comprehensible in the field in which I was trained. I have a written a book that I could only write given where I've landed in the years since that 2005 LISO Conference at UCSB. I likewise won't be surprised if my linguistic anthropological tribe finds in its pages missed opportunities to, say, align my analysis of Michael Richards's racist humor in Chapter 3 with Perrino's (2020) use of "scale" to describe how racialized joke-telling in Northern Italy bears out anti-immigrant politics by erecting boundaries and winks at the level of language and veiled nuance: this undoubtedly is what Michael Richards is dabbling in via his racist anti-Black diatribe cloaked as humor.

I know, too, that one sure oversight would be to miss the chance to underscore the theoretical duet happening between Alim and myself via his discussion of the "transracial subject" and "transracialization" as a political project and my arguments around "a" real Black. Alim's (2016) concept of the "transracial subject" is "transgressive because crossing borders becomes central to disrupting the 'ontologies' upon which definitions of race exist AND because they not only resist race but employ it—*loudly*—*in struggles for racial justice*" (8). In other words, Alim's transracial subject puts Rachel Dolezal's invocation of herself as "transracial" decidedly *out* of mind in deference to, say, how Black queer activists like Alicia Garza, Patrisse Cullors, and Opal Tometi's #BlackLivesMatter network affirms the value of Black life amid widespread police and state-sanctioned violence against Black bodies. As Alim explains, "As long as societies are structured racially, the transracial political project necessitates the alternative subversion and maintenance of racial categorization" (8). And so long as this is true, "the idea that our theorizing should *always* be about destabilizing the idea of race—no matter the context—is naïve at best and counterproductive at worst" (8). He likewise builds on Pollack's

(2005) work to advocate that we begin to "*think transracially*" [by] *recognizing that racially discriminatory contexts require simultaneous/alternating strategies of transracialization with moments of strategic racialization*" (8–9; [my emphasis]).

Now *this*, to me, is what Black standup comedy does on its best and sometimes even its worst day. I see that in comics' relentless and concerted play with race's tell-tale signs and simultaneous insistence on "a" real Black to execute these plays. But to see it and then tell it unapologetically, that's another matter. I had to dwell on the b-side of typical scholarly inquiries around "real" Blackness in linguistic anthropology and beyond to confront what was both "fictitious" (i.e., fake) about race and hence, wrong about racial authenticity by default *alongside* what was palpably, affectively, and sincerely "real" about it in Black folks' humor and lives. I better appreciate how and why Alim arrived at this clearing space on his own terms—within linguistic anthropology proper, and how his arrival makes space for this very book.

For that, I'll happily field any and all collegial hits to come. Frankly, I need to press "send" on this book manuscript in keeping with a deadline suggested by one of the gentlest and most enabling (I mean that in a good way) acquiring editors of all time—H. Samy Alim. I do so in full recognition that all resulting errors, repetitions, unnecessary commas, or random typos and grammatical oversights are all "mine." And I do so in full appreciation that Alim et al.'s vision of what it means to "race language" and "language race" is so encompassing, that a book of this sort from a wandering scholar such as myself can be housed within the Oxford Studies in Language and Race series.

Lanita Jacobs
October 31, 2021

Acknowledgments

Many folks and institutional affordances made this telling possible and I want to shout about it. I'll start by thanking some of Black standup comedy's gatekeepers—and I mean that in a good way. They keep as much as guard the gates of Black standup comedy because they understand that making others laugh even in the midst of pain is nothing short of a gift—at times, a miracle. They appreciate that supporting comics' growth and helping them get onstage in front of an audience is as much about making space for Black creatives as it is sparking the real-time formation of something communal. My heart will always hold gratitude for those I encountered directly or indirectly while researching and writing this book, including Enss Mitchell (owner, The Comedy Union); Anthony Brown and Kathy Westfield (hosts of J. Anthony Brown's comedy show at Lucy Florence Coffee House; Brown hosted and helmed The J Spot in Los Angeles, CA until 2019); Jack Assadourian (owner, Ha Ha Café); Leland "Pookey" Wigington Jr., Sylvia Hillman, and Chris Spencer (promoter, former club manager, and long-time host of The Laugh Factory's *Chocolate Sundaes* show); Bené Benwekere (owner, Mixed Nuts Comedy Club); Michael Williams (founder of the Comedy Act Theatre); Anthony D. Spires and his former wife, Rhonda (producer and founder of the Bay Area Black Comedy Competition and Festival and Full Circle Entertainment); Kenya Duke (long-time promoter of *Phat Tuesdays* at The Comedy Store); "Big Spike" Thompson (long-time promotor of Mo Betta Mondays All-Star Comedy Jam [known now as "MonDeRays" after long-time host DeRay Davis] at the Hollywood Improv); Guy Torry (comic and original host of *Phat Tuesdays* at The Comedy Store); Michael Colyar (comic legend and frequent host at The Townhouse and other LA clubs); standup comic, producer, radio host (i.e., Rennaissance Man) Rushion McDonald; Bob Sumner (VP Talent, Def Comedy Jam); Tina Graham (CEO, Fun Nominal Entertainment); Frank Holder (owner, The Humor Mill Magazine); Stan Lathan (director), among other comedy club owners, hosts, promoters, and standup comedy stewards; without them, this book wouldn't even exist. Thank you for your labor, especially those of you who made literal space for me to scribble notes in the dark recesses of the clubs.

There are also academics and storytellers whose love of humor's nitty-grittiness and wonder inspires this telling in so many ways. They include critic and author Mel Watkins; Distinguished Professor Emerita Judith Yaross Lee; the late comic, screenwriter, producer, and actor Darryl "D'Militant" Littleton; and other scholars and practitioners who take comedy quite seriously as if their very lives, not just their livelihoods, depended on it. Wherever you are, may we continue to dance together in and beyond our respective theory-laden pages with collegiality as our forever-groove.

While writing this book, I benefited from much-needed cash infusions to support research and writing retreats, including USC's Advancing Scholarship in the Humanities and Social Sciences grant, repeat support for writing retreats from the USC Anthropology Department's Visual Endowment Fund from former chair, Dr. Gary Seaman. Dr. George Sanchez, a colleague and mentor in USC's American Studies and Ethnicity Department, also reached into his *own* research coffers to support a much-needed writing retreat elsewhere, something I'll never forget and will always appreciate. Professor Camille Rich Gear who, as then associate provost of Diversity and Inclusion at USC, facilitated my enrollment in the National Center for Faculty Development and Inclusion's "Faculty Success Program," which jump-started additional decanal infusions near the final stretch of book-writing; thank you!

Many friends and colleagues provided words of encouragement as I toiled on this story, especially: Jessica Collett, Stephanie Fitzgerald, Kesha Fikes, Joannie Halls, Carol Everhart, Imani Kai Johnson, Marvin Sterling, Maria Gonzales, Cheryl Mattingly, Sarah Gualtieri, John Carlos Rowe, Colleen Jankovic, Terrion Williamson, "B. B.," USC's Digital Technology Services' team (especially Christopher Huntley, Jason Turbyfill, Corey Clark, Jesse Fair, Damon Jamal Dunbar), Oxford University Press's ever-patient and supportive editorial team: H. Samy Alim, Meredith Keefer, and Macey Fairchild, Sarah Ebel, and Jeremy Toynbee, among others. To all of you (and others I may have missed), I say thank you! Somewhere in the years leading up to this book's publication if not especially near its completion, you said something, shared something, held literal space with and for me while looking me straight in the eye. Please know that your capacity to see me and my writerly intentions in the best way—whether for a moment, a season, or enduringly—made all the difference as I pushed words.

Several former undergraduate and graduate students availed themselves as research assistants, helping me gather additional sources about Black standup comedy and key historical events; thank you, Syann Cromwell, Laura Guzman, Miko Phillips, Forest Trujillo, and Dr. Imani Kai Johnson!

I also need to salute my mother, Gwendolyn J. Stewart, who had a fortitude I didn't quite get when she staged mandatory and impromptu "make me laugh" sessions involving me and my siblings. Thanks, Mom, for nurturing my capacity to laugh to keep from crying, as well as "take" a good joke and dismiss all the rest.

My final thanks are to the comics and their loved ones who availed themselves in ways I still find incredibly gracious and trusting. Without you, this book most certainly would not exist, nor would I have found the will to laugh at and through some of life's most sordid ordeals (or at least try). Thank you for making me and others laugh, think, feel, and remember. May you always be well and find laughter in the storm. May you always know without a doubt who and whose you are and laughingly+lovingly declare it so that others may know too. I . . . *always* see you. Seriously, I do.

To Be Real

Introduction

The Why of Racial Authenticity

I miss Dave Chappelle and his Comedy Central sketch show. I especially yearn for the return of "When 'Keeping It Real' Goes Wrong," one of *The Dave Chappelle Show*'s signature sketches that recounts, in news-like fashion, the tragicomic fate of adults whose personal investment in "keeping it real" (where "keeping it real" = "keeping it [real] Black"), leads them wildly astray.

In one classic episode, a Black woman named Brenda Johnson "keeps it real" by tracking down a woman who calls her, we learn, by mistake. Although Brenda's girlfriend admonishes her to ignore the caller (who promptly hangs up after Brenda answers), Brenda says, "Fuck dat! I don't like people playin' on my phone!" Brenda's anger is fueled by a long-held suspicion that somebody (maybe the caller?) is sleeping with her boyfriend, Jamal. She star-sixty-nines[1] the caller, revealed as an expressly middle-class Black woman named Janice, curses her (and the aunt she claims she was trying to call), and cautions her to stop sleeping with Jamal. Confused and offended, Janice hangs up, inflaming Brenda all the more. "I'm fin-ta [fixing to] ride on this bitch!" Brenda declares, before using the internet to track Janice down and boldly deface what she believes is Janice's car. When the damage is done, Brenda rides off boasting, "'Cuz I keeps it real!" Needless to say, Brenda's final actions lead her to real trouble since the car she vandalizes in fact belongs to Janice's brother, a federal agent. After a "short trial," Brenda earns a six-year sentence in federal prison. She is last seen crouched under the fists of three prisoners who, a narrator asserts, had apparently "kept it realer." Meanwhile, Jamal cavorts with Brenda's friend.

In this and similar sketches, Chappelle and his writers reveal that grown folks can get in serious trouble when they try to be "cool," "hard," or "hip" (just a few euphemisms of "Blackness" to which Black and non-Black folks may at times subscribe).[2] Chappelle's sketches make us laugh and think because they exploit what comedy is best known for—incongruity—while at the same time persuading audiences to consider the stakes and consequences of this quintessential style.

To Be Real. Lanita Jacobs, Oxford University Press. © Oxford University Press 2023.
DOI: 10.1093/oso/9780190870096.003.0001

Thankfully, Chappelle is still here learning and growing and, occasionally, even picking himself up off the stage after being tackled by an interloper during his live show.[3] So is a cadre of Black comedians that I followed over a period of eight years in and beyond Los Angeles's mainstream and Black-owned comedy clubs. These comedians compelled me to think seriously about the ways appeals to "realness" and truth sometimes get cast as cliché, and at other times resonate as a cultural imperative in African American culture, if not American culture writ large. While this book investigates the subtext of the aforementioned Chappelle Show sketch, I'm less invested in its moral hook, which seems to want to admonish Debra, an actress and caricature to be sure, or folks who may share her proclivities. Rather, seeking answers from the realm of comedic play, I ask when, how, and most importantly, *why* Black folks feel compelled to "keep it real"—herein lies the rub, and the opportunity.

The rub is, of course, Who is to say what is real? Aren't "realness" and authenticity subjective? Further, isn't the notion of racial authenticity inherently flawed, or, as my colleague John L. Jackson, Jr. notes, "sure to catch [one] up in their own essentialist trap"? The questions go deeper still. Isn't race a social construction (and shouldn't I, as an anthropologist, already know this)? Hasn't this issue been resolved? If so, why on earth use standup comedy to re-engage this wearying debate? The obvious conclusion to these questions is that if race is folly (since there are no distinct "races" and we're all genetically more similar than distinct), then notions of racial authenticity—however much they preoccupy cultural discourses of the day—are subjective, specious, and should only be critiqued. *Period.*

These questions and answers are poignant. Yet, as sure-fire responses, they often confine in advance the way racial authenticity is discussed in public discourse and, especially, in academic circles. My interest in *why* racial authenticity endures emerged from a longitudinal ethnographic study I conducted on Black standup comedy. This study reaffirmed the need to challenge strict notions of "the" real while recognizing many people's underlying appreciation for "a" real. When I listened with my ears attuned to when comics invoked notions of racial authenticity to make sense of September 11, the war in Iraq, Hurricane Katrina, Michael Richards's [*Seinfeld*'s "Kramer"] infamous outburst at the Laugh Factory, and the election of President Obama, I heard compelling insights about what it means to be Black, as well as the broader stakes of race and claims to nationhood in the new millennium.

An opportunity presented itself. Perhaps by understanding what is at stake in persisting claims about "real Blackness"—which endure despite widely accepted lessons about race's intrinsic folly—we might better understand why generalizations about race matter. Such generalizations inevitably intersect, overlap, and interact with other identity markers, such as gender, sexuality, class; they *matter* to Black folks and, arguably, to all of us, especially, my study revealed, at times when the proverbial –ish hits the fan. Actually, generalizations seem to matter when things are calm and still, too. Social scientists primarily focus only on how racial authenticity gets constructed.[4] Yet my study departs from this approach to aim squarely at when and, most important, *why*, notions of racial authenticity matter. Doing so, I argue, enables a much-needed expansion of the conversations we typically have around "real Blackness."

I'm aware of a second rub; namely, whether standup comedy is the best place to stage a query about racial authenticity. All comics, particularly Black ones, routinely throw shade on race, exploiting stereotypes in the name of fun, provocation, and, as Chappelle so often proves, subversion. To answer this question of *why standup comedy?*, I have to travel back to a few key moments in my own biography: the tragic events of September 11, 2001; my early passion in graduate school; and, further back still, a dark moment in my adolescence when I realized that laughter can truly set you free.

Getting Here

My fascination with Black standup comedy began in the 1990s, during the heyday of HBO's *Def Comedy Jam* and continued with the following decade's explosive ascent of Black standup comedy. I didn't pursue this interest as an ethnographer until over a decade later, however, after the fateful events of September 11, 2001. Tragedy sent me to the clubs; I wanted to hear what Black comics and their predominantly Black audiences were saying about the events of September 11. I (rightly) suspected that a dialogue was taking place that implicated race and complicated the nation's predominant response of mourning, moral outrage, and panic. Sure enough, one of the first jokes I heard was from comic Ian Edwards, who said, dryly: "Hey everybody. There's a new nigger in town. The Arab is the new nigger." The timing (it was October 2001) and sardonic subtext of Ian's joke jolted me, but it was a Black female audience member's equally wry response, "Finally," that piqued my scholarly curiosity. I spent the next year visiting comedy clubs three to four times a week and interviewing comics about their craft. L.A.'s comedy clubs felt like "home" to me—where I belonged. I was also consumed by comics, famous or not, and spent the first four years of this eight-year sojourn using only a pen and pad to chart the real-time evolution of their jokes.

While taking notes in the club's shadows,[5] I gained an appreciation for comics' sets and styles, as well as their use of improvisation to discern well-meaning hecklers from poor naïve (or brave) souls who needed reckoning. I also recorded how comics modified existing jokes in light of evolving social realities such as terrorist attacks, war, natural disasters, and a history-making presidential election. I catalogued the verbal strategies comics used to authenticate themselves as "real" or "real Black" and to coax audiences into endorsing their jokes about what Blackness means. Interviews with comics, club promoters, and some audience members deepened this knowledge by revealing comics' motivations, fears, and inspiration for particular jokes as well as their ideas about comedy, and Black comedy in particular. Ever guided by my discipline (anthropology), I took note of the little things, like the silence that follows a host's initial greeting to their audience, when all you hear is the microphone's hum and the air is thick with audience anticipation and sheer possibility.

I took note of the big things as well, including the fact that Black comics, past and present, have routinely thrown shade on race's assumptions about, say, the presumed differences between Blacks and Whites. They do so in the name of fun and self-definition, which is wrought through exaggerated parody and comparison. More pointedly, many African American comics (and African Americans) appeal to stances around racial authenticity without necessarily vouching for any kind of essentialist understanding of biological distinction. This does not mean their assertions about "real" Blackness are innocent (or "sincere," and thus exempt from incisive critique); still, it warrants noting that prevailing lore around "real" Blackness and racial authenticity are not always suffused with scientific racism.

Just as academics espouse the follies of racial essentialism, comics routinely subject notions of race to endless critique and ridicule—not just reification, as some academic critiques might lead us to assume. Some comics, for instance, flout societal and academic dictates around political correctness, especially concerning race. This is nothing new to comedy, or Black standup comedy in particular. After all, what is comedy but a celebration of the breach—an exploitation of the *ha ha* of incongruity. Black standup comedy is thus fertile ground for deciphering the reasons why appeals to "a" real emerge as a cultural imperative in African American communities. This book is thus less about bracketing or doing away with racial authenticity, conceptually or otherwise, and more about reckoning with the *why* of it. Inspiration for this reckoning came from unexpected blessings.

In my fourth year of fieldwork, Enss Mitchell, owner of The Comedy Union club, and Bené Benwikere, owner of what was once Mixed Nuts Comedy

Club, granted me permission to videotape consenting comics' live sets. I can't tell you how monumental this was for me since it allowed me to systematically collect and vet comics' sets from individual comics who trusted me to provide them (and only them) copies of their sets; many comics agreed because I had interviewed them in previous years. I conducted most of my videotaped observations at these two Black-owned locales from 2005 to 2009. I also observed and, on a few occasions, videotaped comic performances at more "mainstream" locales such as the Laugh Factory, The Comedy Store, Hollywood Improv, Ha Ha Café (in North Hollywood), The Ice House (in Pasadena), and smaller venues, like cafes, coffee shops, fashion shows, outdoor festivals, concerts, soul food buffets (Christian and non-Christian), sports bars, and any other place where Black comics and audiences congregated. In 2002 and 2003, I also observed the Bay Area Black Comedy Competition and Festival spearheaded by Tony and Rhonda (then) Spires of Full Circle Entertainment and featuring such noted comedians as Chris Tucker, D. L. Hughley, Katt Williams, Don "D. C." Curry, rising star "Rod Man" [Thompson], and 2006 winner, the late- Darryl "'D'Militant" Littleton, who wrote *Black Comedians on Black Comedy: How African-Americans Taught Us to Laugh* and *Comediennes: Laugh Be a Lady* (with Tuezdae Littleton).

When I finally looked up and then back on all that I had witnessed, I realized that Black comics had indeed helped me and their predominantly Black audiences make sense of defining moments in the new millennium. Best, I had a story to tell, and its roots ran back to my graduate school days at UCLA in the 1990s. Then, Black standup comedy was "blowing up"—flourishing into the multi-billion-dollar industry that it is today. With popular shows like HBO's *Def Comedy Jam*, BET's *Comic View*, and later, Fox Network's pathbreaking sketch show, *In Living Color*, Black standup comedy provided me, and arguably the nation, critical perspective and comic relief during Washington, DC, mayor Marion Barry's arrest in 1990 for cocaine possession; the (1990–91) Gulf War; the 1992 Los Angeles rebellion; the O. J. Simpson trial, the Oklahoma bombing, the Million Man March in 1995, and other defining events of that decade.

Another reason that comedy followed me beyond my UCLA years, or rather, that I followed it, was because I knew firsthand of its transformative power. During my adolescence, my mother, older brother, twin sister, and I fell upon bad times and were forced to share a motel room at 55th Avenue Motel. The motel sat on one of Oakland's most popular thoroughfares, Foothill Boulevard, and its entrance was next to the bus stop that a few of my classmates and I exited after school. As such, my siblings and I had to find strategic ways to enter the motel undetected, including circling the block a couple of times or lingering until we felt the coast was clear. (We laughed about it then to keep from crying.) One night, my mother sensed our spirits were low, and allowed us to watch Eddie Murphy's (1987) blockbuster comedy special "Raw." (This comedy album, directed by Robert Townsend, still reigns as the top-grossing comedy film of all time.)[6] Eddie lifted our spirits; his colorful quips about his own coming-of-age helped us laugh at ourselves. I remember hearing our collective laughter and thinking, "We are family; we laugh at the same time."

In 1999, when I was finishing up my PhD, my brother DeMarcus died in despair. I compartmentalized my sorrow, but grief demanded a reckoning. Often, while driving to and from comedy clubs, I thought about our shared laughter in that motel room and how sometimes, when my brother laughed, it sounded like he was crying. I mourned that in his final days, he could not find the laughter or faith needed to save his soul. While 9/11 finally sent me to the clubs, I saw vestiges of DeMarcus in the faces and antics of some Black comics. A few, in particular, made me smile through my tears, because even though they struggled with issues that once burdened him, they managed to find relief on the stage. Best of all, when sadness over my brother's death threatened to overwhelm me, Black comics reminded me that laughter can indeed set you free.

Comedy also compelled me because, as a lifelong nerd, I'd missed out on late-night fellowship with people who hailed from working-class backgrounds like me. As a first-generation academic, I maintained some degree of communal fellowship, albeit uneven, through my observations of Black hair salons during graduate school. Later, as an assistant professor at USC, I began my comedy research alongside a separate study of African American families raising children with acquired and traumatic brain injuries (my twin sister suffered a traumatic brain injury in 1994). These studies fueled each other: frankly, observing children in hospitals often made me sad whereas the comedy study made me laugh.

Watching comics closely also helped me appreciate humor's many nuances. Kids and parents contending with a radical and irrevocable "new" in the brain injury study employed self-deprecation, sardonic wit, and physical humor: whether a former track runner now having to negotiate head-starts in playground races, a former A-student transitioning (rather spectacularly) from gifted classes to special education and then back to mainstream and gifted classes, or parents contending with the literal and symbolic loss of the children they once knew. Observing parents try to negotiate empathy for themselves and their Black and mixed-race children also helped me appreciate the ways African American comics appealed to color-blind empathy in the wake of Hurricane Katrina. It was as if each group, parents and comics, asked, "Can you see me?" as if their very lives depended on it.[7] In many ways, and as I discuss in Chapter 2, their lives did depend on being not just seen, but seen as empathetic.

There were other literal connections. Nearly every week in 2002, I'd leave a Los Angeles hospital to interview and dine with a then relatively unknown comic from Charlotte, North Carolina, named Maronzio Vance. Maronzio sank his teeth into Los Angeles's comedy scene, eventually earning spots on NBC's *Last Comic Standing,* Jamie Foxx's *Laughapalooza,* the *Tonight Show with Jay Leno,* Wanda Sykes's *Wanda Does It,* a national Miller Light commercial, and Fox's attempted reboot of *In Living Color.* He was just getting started when our eyes met across a table at the Hollywood Improv's "Mo Betta Mondays" show.

Mike Bonner had joked that night about "bad ass kids," and, in the parlance of standup comedy, "killed" it. This was no small feat. Mo Betta Mondays was a notoriously hard room, and only the bravest comics performed there. Its host, comic/actor DeRay Davis, was a major reason why, given his charm, quick and exacting wit, and frank appraisals of the comics he brought up to what was essentially *his* stage. His loyal audience of regulars came to share his exacting standards and even police the stage themselves. Some would boo any comic, famous or otherwise, if they deemed them unfunny or lazy for recycling material in front of them. I still cringe in memory of some of those Monday night boos; a few folks would set it off by hissing their disapproval, and then others would join in. If the comic onstage couldn't turn things around, those hisses would crescendo into a monstrous, but somehow jovial, "boo!" Amazingly, the room had such a reputation that even unlucky comics viewed their on-stage destruction as a necessary rite of passage—a cold-cock reminding them that they had better stay on their toes if they wanted to play in this game.

Mike, an established comic, was triumphant that night, ripping the room to shreds. He'd even made Maronzio cry. When I noticed tears streaming down his face, Maronzio simply said, "It's funny," and I was right there with him. I thought, "Here's a guy (a comic I'd soon learn) who can laugh and cry at the same time." My subsequent interviews with Maronzio helped me understand what it means to make another comic weep. And also what seasoned comics mean when they describe peers most gloriously as a "comic's comic"— people like J. B. Smoove (or "Leon" from HBO's *Curb Your Enthusiasm*), the late George Carlin, and the legendary Richard Pryor. Maronzio's fine-tuning of his jokes and the work he did to temper his southern accent and earn a spot—any spot—on a club's early show exemplified true "hunger" and ambition. Maronzio's hunger made him risk vulnerability, economic instability, and time with his then two-year old daughter for a chance to be seen by the brokers of Los Angeles's highly competitive comedy scene. He was among several comics whose generosity showed me this hunger and vulnerability, as well as success and failure, up so close that I could catch a feeling of what it means to make a living as a comic. I was thoroughly enchanted by it all.

It would take about nine years for the romance of fieldwork to give way to the task of writing. When I reflected on all I'd witnessed principally from 2001 to 2008, I realized I'd heard comics muse about monumental occurrences, such as terrorist attacks and natural disasters, and the landmark election of President Obama—in short, defining moments of the new millennium. I thought it fitting to stop there and hone the hook that had been gnawing at me ever since I set foot in the Comedy Union in October 2001. But committing to this "hook"—the "why" of racial authenticity—wasn't an easy thing do. In fact, once I'd named it, I had to hold onto it for dear life. For one, I didn't think racial authenticity would be something I'd revisit—certainly not as former adolescent whose racial authenticity or "real" Blackness was routinely called into question during the how-real-art-thou trials of high school. (Once, as a newspaper columnist at Fremont High School's Media Academy in Oakland, California, I cribbed someone's column title to proclaim "I don't talk white! I talk right!" in my weekly editorial. . . . Oh grace for the younger me!)

Years later, in my graduate training in linguistic anthropology, I'd learn not to rush so quickly for the legitimacy of respectability codified through language choice. Naw; there was no need to discount the grammatical and phonological systematicity of what I and my colleagues call African American Vernacular English (and some still lovingly call "Ebonics"). Rather, it was imperative that we acknowledge how one's fluency in African American English and African American discourse styles—including styles of *indirectness* and *signifying* so central to African American standup comedy—mark racial consciousness and affinity; in essence, one's presumed racial authenticity and communicative competence.[8]

Which is to say, I'm attentive to, but not bound by, the politics of respectability that has disciplined (and arguably continues to discipline) research in African American studies, shaping what we study, the scholarly verses we contribute, and sometimes even how we deem research participants as productive or "representative." Likewise, I am equally conscious of but not beholden to a similar politics of representation governing Black standup comedy, which renders some forms of humor (e.g., hyper-physical, bawdy, or "blue") as suspect, and others as "smart," "productive," and refreshingly "universal" in the minds of comics and Black audiences alike. (This is one reason that legendary comic/actor Bill Cosby reportedly chastised Eddie Murphy for being "too dirty," and also why Murphy defended himself, dissing Cosby in the process, in his [1987] comedy album, *Raw*.)[9] Given the stakes of racial stereotypes and the cumulative effect of racist and fetishized representations of Black bodies, language, sexuality, and even laughter, Black humorists are expected to debunk stereotypes and are called to task for jokes that reinforce them. Their jokes, to say nothing of their individual successes and failures, can reflect back on their broader communities in positive or negative ways with palpable effects. (Think again of veteran comic/actor Bill Cosby who has been both a moral voice and the subject of ardent critique given the ever-mounting sexual abuse charges leveled against him—with consequence.) As such, Black audiences and Black comics themselves sometimes weigh in with a sense of entitlement on whether or not Black comedic work (e.g., Tyler Perry) is "good" or "bad" for the Black community and society at large.

This binary focus on "good" versus "bad" comedic representation may be short-sighted, strangle-holding comics' artistic license and obscuring their subversive play with and *against* early racist tropes. But what often motivates such dualistic thinking and policing of comics' delivery and sets are the perceived stakes of these representations for shaping the way Blacks are seen and treated by others and among themselves. This was true historically when Black leaders such as W. E. B. Du Bois and Booker T. Washington and influential Black southern women of the Black Baptist church felt "respectable behavior" would help "uplift the race" while offering similar protections under the law as those extended to Whites.[10] It remains true today among anti-racist activists who proclaim via hashtags that #BlackLivesMatter, #IamTrayvonMartin, #IamMichaelBrown, #IamSandraBland—sadly the list grows and grows—to decry the premature deaths of respectable (e.g., "college-bound," "honors student") African Americans in police custody.

Seducing/Disciplining the Subject

In navigating the terrain of authenticity, it is ethnography, anthropology's modus operandi, that grounds me. Anthropology requires researchers to observe with their whole heart, mind, body, and senses open to insights, regardless of whether these insights offend, unsettle, or disturb the very hypotheses that instigated their queries.[11] Ethnographers must therefore devote sufficient time to build trust and rapport with research participants, if only to observe their everyday talk and interaction unfettered. Such work requires consummate reflexivity—that is, thinking critically about our own (and others') cultural assumptions in order to check our insights and stances against any hidden proclivities, personal, political, or otherwise that might unduly influence our bourgeoning insights. Ethnography also requires a professional commitment to remaining open, since you never know what seemingly mundane occurrences might shine a light on the cultural significance of "the everyday."

That's why I'll always appreciate the day my department's former office manager, Rita Jones, called me into her office and offered unsolicited advice about "not getting caught up" in this research. What she meant by "not getting caught up" was losing myself, professionally or otherwise, in the excitement of the research. As a former dancer who had also married an entertainer, she knew all too well just how alluring entertainers could be; she didn't want me to fall prey to comics' allure and screw up my gig (and marriage) at the time. Although she didn't say it explicitly, Rita was talking about seduction.

Seduction ran through my work like a serpent, suffusing my ethnographic fieldwork, if not my very topic—*racial authenticity*. Maybe that's also why one of my dear African American colleagues called my topic "sexy" when he heard my early ramblings on this subject. Inwardly, I bristled, but increasingly, the specter of seduction bore increasing relevance to my research. Standup comedy is the ultimate seduction—an aphrodisiac harnessed to enthralling effect by many a comic. Comics endear themselves to audiences by their own exquisite design with various tools of their trade: precise timing, carefully leveraged color, physicality, artful self-deprecation and raw vulnerability, and acute observations about the oft-invisible but shared aspects of our humanity.

My very means of inquiry, ethnography, is also, I'd argue, a seductive endeavor. If it is to be fruitful, ethnographic fieldwork relies on exchanges of vulnerability and a rapport built via shared experiences over time. Ethnographers are sincerely trying to get in people's business; we want to occupy their personal space and lives as "participant" or "distant," but ever-present, observers—often for no less than a year—witnessing weaknesses (as when comics "bomb" [do poorly]) and triumphs (as when comics "kill") with notebooks or digital recorders in hand. When we gain people's trust and they begin to act "freely" or "truthfully" despite our presence over time, it is a precious gift.

Fieldwork thus also warrants critical reflexivity (i.e., thinking about how we think), checking our cultural baggage (so it doesn't taint our ability to see people's diverse cultural practices in their own right), and pursuing scientific "objectivity" that never loses sight of just how intersubjective (think "interdependent") our research actually and already is—always. Which is to say, in a post-colonial era wherein the natives gaze and talk back,[12] anthropologists increasingly acknowledge that our fieldwork and resulting insights are *always and already* produced by an interaction of various subjectivities, including our own and those of the folks we study, not to mention shaped by the contexts in which we study and the disciplinary and ontological questions and traditions that guide us. Ethnography also warrants strict ethical stances because love, fear, anger, hope, and other human emotions are often, if not always, further implicated in that mix.

While I can safely say that no professional comics were shagged during my fieldwork and writing, I must admit that they may have been unwittingly seduced by my conversations with them on the page. To assure comics that I was not a low-down-dirty joke thief, I shared excerpts of my ethnographic notes with select comics. This was unprecedented for me[13] and certainly a rarity among my professional clan. Most anthropologists don't share their notes with research participants for perhaps obvious reasons; we want to avoid unduly influencing their behavior, and we're still trying to figure out what we're seeing on those sometimes diary-like pages. When I reviewed my ethnographic notes in preparation for this book, I didn't recognize myself. I wrote with consummate passion and an easy knowing—like a woman in deep flow. I wrote as though I was falling, if not already deeply in love with my topic and research participants.

The tenor of my observations, at least the redacted ones I shared with them, were largely wide-eyed and celebratory; I highlighted their good sets and noted the creativity in their mediocre or bad sets. I paid close attention to their gear, a significant aesthetic component of their onstage personas. I took note of comics' pre-performance rituals (e.g., Nick Cannon prays before he goes onstage) and acknowledged when comics like Don "D. C." Curry, Kevin Hart, and Jeff Garcia commemorated their mothers and grandmothers with comedic send-offs that most audience members did not know were eulogies. I paid attention when they weren't aware: comics' backstage banter about road opportunities and shady promoters; which comics "bucked the light" signaling the end of their set; ways to enhance a joke; post-show critiques of their own or others' sets on the sidewalk under the night sky; flirty engagements with fans and groupies. My notes took on a life of their own; I learned much later that my notes traveled well beyond the select group of comics and club promoters I sent them to. Comics, including those who performed and those who didn't, looked forward to reading my excerpted notes and, in fact, began to expect them. Soon, some even called me a "writer"! This designation won me access to some of L.A.'s most popular comedy clubs[14] and further wrought my seduction.

"Black" nights, such as the Laugh Factory's *Chocolate Sundaes,* Hollywood Improv's *Mo' Betta Mondays* [now *MONDERAYs* after its host, DeRay Davis], or The Comedy Store's *Phat Tuesday* show were often their club's top-selling nights (the reason, some comics joked, for why the club finally got a new stage); crowds lined up behind a red rope and some were even turned away. But women, especially ones deemed attractive, were sometimes immune. Promoters maintained a guest list that privileged ladies, who constituted the primary audience of most comedy clubs, and let them in for free before a certain hour to draw larger audiences that included men. At the time, I donned an inconspicuous and steady uniform of baggy jeans and a UCLA hoodie that likely did not do me any favors in this regard. I fear I would have likely been turned away had comics, promoters, and doormen not recognized me as "the writer" and ushered me in gratis. This was no small gift. In fact, it was catalytic in ways I couldn't imagine.

Being seen as a writer flattered me and made me want to write more accessibly—that is, in ways that reflected the hearty ease of my ethnographic notes and in ways my mother (and comics) might want to read. Bigger still, I realized that I didn't need to pit my concern for the "why" of racial authenticity against sound analyses and critiques of this very subject. This realization took an additional six years to sink in, but after it did, my hardest work yet entailed figuring out how best to say it. Ideally, this book will speak to those who have been burdened by the imperatives of Black authenticity (e.g., Blacks excluded from the realm of "real" Blackness for their sexual preferences, ways of speaking, class, mixed heritage, hair texture, skin color, etc.). On its best day—and I say "best" because quite soon and elsewhere in this book, I'll need to call some scholars by name and parse their theoretical gifts—this book will compel scholars who deem social constructivist approaches to race as the best way to dismantle its fixity to sit with what comics taught me: that there is more yet to be said about racial authenticity in African American culture that neither abnegates important truths about the socially constructed nature of race or coalesces Black masses into a homogenized whole. There is more still to be said about "real" Blackness that stresses the ways comics use humor and comedy's inherent intersubjectivity[15] to tease out the politics of identity and the cultural imperative of racial solidarity, and shore up communal boundaries in critical and calm times. And there is more to be said by anthropologists about race and Blackness, in particular, that neither collapses race into culture or race into racism such that we ignore the ways race has served and still serves to create African American culture that is, in parts, distinct and ever-robust, ever-shifting and evolving, and a creative and collectivizing force in the lives of African Americans.[16]

Authenticity and Sincerity

This resulting book thus focuses on the topic of racial authenticity but in a way that hasn't really been done in academic scholarship. In one sense, we scholars already know quite a bit about racial authenticity's essentialist assumptions, scripts, and exclusions. We may, in fact, think we know too much, which can obscure other ways of approaching the problem—since of course the research often casts authenticity as a problem (or "as problematic" in academic-speak). For approaching these oft-noted "conceptual paradoxes of authenticity (it's fixidness and essentialist assumptions)," Dimitrios Theodossopoulos[17] offered a useful suggestion that aligns well with my own belief that we must appreciate, rather than condemn or bemoan, racial authenticity's complexity. Namely, he advocates that we "pay increased attention to the multiple and overlapping meanings of the authentic . . . [because] acknowledging authenticity's flexibility might necessitate an engagement with its non-flexible, very specific, local conceptualizations, which . . . often co-exist—and reveal themselves simultaneously—within the same processes or negotiations."[18] With my interest in the political and everyday stakes of "authenticity" in the lives of African Americans in the United States, the comedy club space, much like humor itself, provides the frame and specific local contexts for insights into commonsense understandings of race that are paradoxical, contradictory, and equally valid and helpful in understanding racial authenticity. Race and authenticity are always fraught, contested, and, for many, intensely felt.

Japtop and Jenkins (2011) concede as much in their edited volume, *Authentic Blackness,* and issue one of the boldest critiques of authentic Blackness I've yet to read. They chart a historical lineage of notions of "real" Blackness emerging within and outside the African American community that were not merely injurious to the souls of Black folk, but also delimiting, in enduring and oft-violent ways, who "real" Black people could be. For example, European colonizers were among the first to distinguish enslaved Blacks as "house niggers" or "field niggers," determining their oppressive and interconnected fates under the tyrannical system of slavery. During the Harlem Renaissance, Black literary icons situated the rural South and later, urban ghettos, as the epicenters of "real" Black "folk" culture, which positioned the Black bourgeoisie as racially inauthentic or "race-traitors" by comparative default.[19] During the 1980s, African American (largely male) rappers' assertions about "real niggahs" centered Black males (oft-hypermasculine poses) and sidelined Black women out of the revised category of "niggahs," perpetuating the Black-male centering discourse of the Black Power Movement and exacerbating Black women's invisibility given their similar marginalized place and iconicity in the Feminist Movement.[20] Other scholars in and beyond anthropology have argued that historical and contemporary representations of authenticity[21] and "real Blackness," in particular, in pop culture, are now commodified, over-determined, if problematically defined by outsiders.[22] How does one concede such realities but nonetheless remain invested in unpacking the "why" of racial authenticity in the commodify-able realm of standup comedy, no less? How does one pursue a path that veers from a primary and, for some, moral concern for "how racial authenticity is performed, constructed, and enacted" to "*why* racial authenticity is performed, constructed, and enacted"? Let me be clearer: couldn't the question of the "why" be beyond the best point? How and why have I stubbornly honed this unpopular hook in my undergraduate and graduate courses, conference presentations, and essays to this book?

Beyond the convictions afforded by my own research, I drew inspiration from wherever I could—whenever I could—beginning with Matthew Pasevich's aptly titled 2009 dissertation, "Why Authenticity Matters." Pasevich became a comrade in my push to interrogate the "why" of authenticity from a place attuned with how people use language—comedy—to fitfully engage in authenticity's presuppositions, tenets, provocations, and imperatives. Understanding that "authenticity exceeds its supposed death in postmodernity," Pasevich instead asks, What makes authenticity such a durable and flexible discourse? What does the rhetorical lens offer the study of authenticity that other lenses do not? He is not naïve to the ways his rhetorical and discursive framework acknowledges the socially constructed nature of authenticity and its claimants. (Nor is he invested in a swift retort highlighting the circular nature of social constructionism; as William James and other philosophers of pragmatism point out, constructivist stances, by their very nature, participate in and instantiate the very truths they seek to unpack.)[23] Still, he asks productively, "Given the theories of how individual subjects are constrained by institutions and power, can real world speakers actually do anything when they mobilize authenticity in their speech" (Pasevich 2009, 6)?

Having unearthed a chorus of support from like-minded scholars with a similar appreciation for the "why" of racial authenticity, I was encouraged that anthropologists were part of this small inspirational choir. Given their stalwart appreciation for people's everyday actions and heartfelt beliefs, they, quite naturally, could not dismiss the "why" of racial authenticity. In fact, they wrestled with its import despite a seeming "anthropological correctness," as Theodossopoulos (2013) called it, that would abnegate its significance because it can neither see nor hear claims of authenticity as anything but a cultural construction. Instead, Theodossopoulos (2013) offered ways to and through authenticity's trappings to something bigger; that is, understandings of the local, and authenticity's inherent complexity: "Understandably, there is some wariness about authenticity's static and exoticized connotations and a fear of falling in its trap; but there are also great opportunities for further analysis focusing on deciphering authenticity's local binary logic and application in everyday life" (347). As Charles Lindholm (2013) acknowledges:

> None of the critics or theorists of authenticity have had much to say about the way authenticity is *actually* pursued in concrete cultural circumstances. Investigating these aspects of authenticity has been more or less left to anthropologists, sociologists, and folklorists, who demonstrate that the drive toward authenticity is a cultural construct coincident with the rise of possessive individualism, the development of late capitalism, and the appearance of nationalism, among other factors. . . . However, like arguments disproving the existence of God, demonstrating the contingency of faith in authenticity does not alter the power of that faith over the hearts and minds of men and women today. Whether we like it or not, authenticity, as a motivating force in the modern world, is here to stay. (390)

Since I was interested in studying folks' fascination with a cultural real or a racial real, and what this says about real folks' common sense notions of race, I also couldn't ignore David Livingston's (1998) fiery and, for me, generative retort to scholars who'd interpreted his use of images to indict and interrogate early instances of scientific racism as complicit in reproducing the very racism he'd sought to critique. (The critique Livingston confronts can just as easily be directed my way since many might view my emphasis on the "why" of racial authenticity beside the best point; meaning, instead of chasing Black folks' investment in "a/the" real Black, I'd do best to dismantle race and debunk the very notion of racial authenticity vis-à-vis a constructivist analysis that boldfaces race as a biological fallacy and human invention.) For his part, Livingston charted a line through what he calls the discourse of high modernity (and I call postmodernism's certainty of uncertainty) to instead center courtesy, trust, and experience. In wishing to recognize people's experiences as one reason to trust the value inherent to authenticity, Livingston drew from George Steiner's (1989) own strategic deployment of the notion of "cortesia"— the courtesy of listening to others and to the text in order to engage in "an initial fundamental act of trust" so that we then "*feel*" (Livingston's emphasis) the claim to human suffering or *experience* what is repugnant about injustice. Livingston (1990) implored: "I want to urge that we require a notion of authenticity so that we can speak of degraded or debased representations of difference" (16). While acknowledging "that we can't ever get to a 'perfect' representation of 'others' or ourselves," Livingston argued that "we can surely say that some representations, like some maps, are more or less adequate, more or less authentic, than others" (18).

Thus, instead of preemptively vetting local claims of authenticity with "anthropological correctness," anthropologists might do well to engage ethnography to unearth what Van de Port (2004) calls "registers of incontestability" that disrupt normative disciplinary explorations of "authenticity" in academia and beyond. Like Livingston, Van de Port highlighted what constructivist approaches to authenticity tend to overlook: people, more or less, manage to transcend the constructedness of their life worlds by realizing what Lindholm (2002) calls an "authentically felt grounding" of their views and understandings.[24] In standup comedy, this emerges through laughter, jokes, hisses, and boos.

These authors added fire to my embers until I encountered yet another way to conceptualize these everyday experiences and feelings of a/the real from my dear colleague John L. Jackson Jr. Jackson's (2005b) book, *Real Black: Adventures in Racial Sincerity*, stopped my pen for a second. After reading it, I had lost certainty about whether there was anything more that needed to be said about authenticity. Jackson's book is full of gifts, not the least of which is his accessible scholarly voice, deference to his research participants who speak almost as much as he does, and, perhaps most important here, his concept of "racial sincerity." Racial sincerity is not just a conceptual innovation (as I once prematurely argued—for shame!); it's both an ethnographic achievement and intervention that recognizes "realness" as a mantra among Black Brooklynites and African American culture more broadly. Sincerity displaces the focus from "authenticity"—where essentialism rests—to people's subjective accounts, and even their psychic investments, in a "real," without necessarily lending credence to the essentialist tenets undergirding authenticity. If authenticity relies on rendering a verdict on whether or not something or somebody is real, racial sincerity aims to put that restless feckless dilemma to bed by giving me and, arguably all of us, a way to talk about the relentlessness with which Black folks and other folks subjectively determine their own or others' presumed "realness," while fully acknowledging that their efforts (and indeed our own evaluations of them) are collectively derived assessments. Racial sincerity thus allows us to acknowledge and appreciate that "real Blackness," revised as "racial sincerity," matters to people, and that Blackness is as performative as comics such as Key and Peele—through sketches like "The Phone Call" (where two Black guys "blacken" their speech on a corner to avoid getting mugged by one another)—suggest it is.

Still, I wasn't convinced that sincerity mapped neatly onto authenticity, or that they shared the same provocations and politics in regard to race. Authenticity is arguably the explicit disavowal of sincerity, since one can be earnest in attempts at "realness" but still be deemed "fake" albeit sincere. Authenticity, by contrast, does not quibble about earnestness; it's clear about its terms and mandates. Authenticity requires, per Pasevich (2009), a self-conscious analysis in order to determine its presence or absence. Less invested in exploring the philosophical roots or ontological status of authenticity,[25] Pasevich maps authenticity as a discursive phenomenon and rhetorical tool, and, moreover, as a potential commonplace reinforced by the doxa of the everyday. Authenticity, he argues, "maintains such durable force because it offers a sense of stability and an assurance of our access to the real and the truth. This effect, however, is constantly shadowed by the continual threat of the unraveling of that stability. Authenticity . . . is a stabilizing force leveraged against indeterminacy in its many forms, a way of battening down the hatches" (Pasevich 2009, 25).

We can again be reminded of Theodossopoulos's (2013) call to appreciate authenticity's complicated and contradictory nature—this is precisely where its power lies. Authenticity is worth something and, as such, it is worth fighting for, especially, scholars tend to agree, in the case of music (e.g., the "blues"), art, and instances of cultural appropriation.[26] Conversely, sincerity, especially when deemed "successful," can blanket sins with a soft cover of grace because it privileges an individual or item's earnestness. This grace factor does not extend to authenticity; this is because authenticity, while equally subject to performance and subjective evaluation, is presumably more rigid, fixed, and intuitive.

It bears noting too that authenticity relies on sincerity. According to Jackson, "One of the time-tested mechanisms for deeming authority inauthentic is to first prove it insincere" (2005b, 12). In other words, sincerity often has to go through authenticity, thus alluding to the ever-presentness of authenticity in Black folks' deliberations about "real" Blackness. Sincerity is often also a measure of authenticity, insofar as being true to yourself is also a way of being Black to some;[27] Blackness, in this ideation, is the "truth." (Authenticity doesn't require the sincerity test, though sincerity does come in handy in extolling grace for those deemed "inauthentic"—as, say, a Rachel Dolezal or perhaps Black Lives Matter activist Shaun King who once purported (or, in the case of King, still claim) that they are "Black" because they "feel Black" despite "genetic evidence" that might prove otherwise. Yet, lest we sleep on sincerity's power, let's remember, too, that the question of earnestness can make or break hearts, win or lose wars and elections, and change the mind and the world.

And so, I wondered, must authenticity and sincerity remain distinct? If, per Jackson (2005b, 12, authenticity is "what is most constraining and potentially self-destructive about identity politics," might they ever be reconciled versus collapsed in potentially generative ways? Answers to these questions rolled in from unexpected blessings, further cementing my investment in the "why" of racial authenticity.

Some years after reading Jackson and after more fits and starts academically and personally, I received much-needed lab space and help with digitizing my data, affording me the means to vet the comedy shows and interviews I had conducted. Around this time, I also had a dream, in which Authenticity and Sincerity sat side by side, on a shared foundation, in two distinct houses—both oozing with laughter. Upon their common foundation, I reasoned, sincerity and authenticity bespeak one another, sharing affective space and possibilities; both move something in people and make them laugh. They are co-dependent and mutually reliant, beckoning equal appreciation for the ways people's valuation of "a real" enables them to underscore "the real." I staged a crude sketch of the two houses against an emboldening soundtrack that necessarily included such hits as Cheryl Lynn's debut single and disco jam, "Got to Be Real"; The Tower of Power's "What Is Hip?," which interrogated the soul-rock divide of the 1970s to chart-topping success; Roberta Flack and Donny Hathaway's enchanting ode to Black love, "Be Real Black for Me"; and Meshell Ndegeocello's fraught treatise on the "a real"/"the real divide" if ever there was one, "Akel Dama" (Field of Blood) featuring Gil Scott Heron. (The playlist continues to grow.)

Meditating on my verse-serving dream, I determined that both authenticity and sincerity have a place in people's ideations and lives. Even jokes that lampoon static and homogenizing notions of "real" Blackness rely on it as a subtext. It's the ground that makes room for the critique. I learned, then, to see the utility in both concepts with a palpable if not concerted deference for authenticity's dictates, intersubjective workings, and stakes. Like Jackson, I was invested in the interaction of various subjectivities informing my and my research participants' (chiefly comics but also audience members, promoters, club owners, journalists, etc.) dialogues around race, realness, and truth both on- and offstage, and I was especially compelled to sit with what these enduring dialogues about "real Blackness" and truth might reveal about the "why" of racial authenticity. I also excavated additional reasons to stay the course from scholars who do not necessarily share my investments in the "why" of authenticity but nonetheless inspire it in their own attempts to wrestle a conviction from a caveat. A few warrant special mention given their insistence on the enduring significance of race and, by extension, Black folks' investments in identity politics implicating "a/the" real.[28]

Again, it's understandable that authentic Blackness and its critique have been thoroughly entrenched with a sense of caution and danger, lending a heavy sense of seriousness to any academic or comedic exploration of these ideas. Many scholars have been greatly concerned with decentering notions of authentic Blackness, seeing the value in subjecting our work and ideas to theoretical and empirical scrutiny across the Black Atlantic and trans-hemispheric, in light of the modernist, postmodernist, and more recent neoliberalist turn, to say nothing of sound provocations in queer studies and beyond.[29] Still, as Darnell Hunt (2005) asserts, "Blackness remains," fitfully tied up in a Black-White binary that remains stubborn, stalwart, and impactful; this is true despite compelling calls for hemispheric/transatlantic comparisons, queering, and even relational ethnic studies that have resounded in recent years as a way to decenter the United States, its stalwart Black-White dichotomy, and African Americans as a homogenized beacon of Blackness. John L. Jackson Jr. (2005) likewise notes elsewhere, "The rhetorical avoidance of race does not automatically buttress its anti-essentialist cause. In fact, taking away race's vocal chords, the acoustic concreteness of its explicit bark, does not mean that one has defused its bite. If anything, race becomes more compelling in silence, when unspoken. . . . When race and racism work best, we don't even think to talk about them; they cannot really be seen. We noddingly eschew any and all public policy implications" (394). Visweswaran (1998, 79) cautions, too, that deracialization might actually be the sign of a more pernicious racialization."[30]

Harrison (1998a, 616; citing archaeologists Orser 1998 and Epperson 1990) likewise advocates learning to analyze race with a "dual vision" that denaturalizes race without failing to recognize the hard social fact that race consciousness, in some form (and it often assumes a multiplicity of forms) has been and continues to be a salient basis for survival, resistance, and opposition.[31] Hunt (2005) adds that deliberations about representations of Blacks, whether on TV or, I'd add, standup comedy, are "wrapped up in our ongoing efforts to establish who we are, who we are not, and who we hope to be. As a consequence, we each regularly affirm and police the boundaries of race in our own little ways, as a means of bringing necessary order to our social experience" (3).[32] Viveros (add date) adds this provocative point in an essay celebrating Dave Chappelle's parody of race:

Racial authenticity is built on the one foundational experience that no person of color can escape: A legal and social tradition that has set the person of color as a thing apart, an object of consideration, inquiry, legislation, contempt. Even barring direct encounters with people who harbor especially racist attitudes, the society in which we live is populated by countless folks—many with various kinds of bu- reaucratic, academic, judicial, and social authority—who do not grant us the same premise in humanity as their own. Further, we live knowing that in a previous age, we would have been even more unlike our peers: more vulnerable than others to disease and weather and other privations, and superadded to this, subject to harm, and persecution, to the point of death, by the general citizenry. . . . This knowledge is . . . the essential ground of racial authenticity. Perhaps such a proposal seems perverse in that it suggests that such authenticity is a negative effect of a thing set in motion by the dominant culture. But I would argue that this irreducibly per- sonal encounter with history and the intersubjective ground of racism—with the fact that sociohistorically, at least our bodies can never be more or less purely a form of self-expression, that they mark us . . . as those whose humanity is or has been diminished by our group membership, by our very bodies—is the founda- tional, universal, and therefore authentic experience of the racially subordinated subject. (142)

These and other assertions compel me as much as the late Marlon Riggs's (2004; see also Riggs 1987) collaborative and penultimate documentary, *Black Is . . . Black Ain't.* In this distinctly in-group film, which also grapples with Riggs's end of life, he uses the collective pronoun "we" to lovingly im- plore African Americans to abandon rigid and oft-heteronormative and male-centered notions of "real Blackness" that deny their gumbo-stew variety. Less preoccupied by hegemonic definitions of "real" Blackness" and pur- posely focused on Black folks' deliberations around "real" Blackness, Riggs also underscores individual complexities and cultural nuances (e.g., educa- tion, class, gender, sexuality, education, language) that serve to define indi- vidual "I's" *always* within a collective "we." This collective "we" is the African American community whose members are intrinsically diverse yet in many ways bound by interconnected histories, fates, and lived experiences.[33] In other words, Riggs understands that ideas and feelings about race and authen- ticity matter as indices of individual identity and communal belonging, (sadly) sometimes in toxic ways, even as he celebrates cultural aspects he deems distinctly " Black" (e.g., southern dishes like "gumbo," African American English, Black dance and music). His film thus not only indicts racial authen- ticity but celebrates and acknowledges what is arguably "Black" about African American culture. I linger in the space of these two assertions and along- side concessions by Angela Davis and the late bell hooks, both of whom ac- knowledge in the film that strong stances around racial authenticity can be a redemptive and even a subversive form of self-definition among people (e.g., African Americans) who have been defined by others. At the height of post-modernism, hooks (1990) wrote similarly (and with considerable care) that

> the postmodern critique of "identity," though relevant for renewed black liberation struggle, is often posed in ways that are problematic. Given a pervasive politic of white supremacy which seeks to prevent the formation of radical black subjectivity, we cannot cavalierly dismiss a concern with identity politics. Any critic exploring the radical potential of postmodernism as it relates to racial difference and racial domination would need to consider the implications of a critique of identity for oppressed groups. Many of us are struggling to find new strategies of resistance. We must engage decolonization as a critical practice if we are to have meaningful chances of survival even as we must simultaneously cope with the loss of political grounding which made radical activism more possible. (26)

Concerned about the postmodern critique of essentialism, especially regarding identity, hooks was citing nothing less than survival (again) in her caution against the mounting popularity of such a critique.

Also, much like the *Dave Chappelle Show* sketch, "When 'Keeping It Real' Goes Wrong," we can lampoon authenticity all day onstage, off stage, in private corridors and know we're being cheeky, petty, subversive, or even plain old wrong or funny while doing so. We also can and should critique it in academic halls and corridors in the spirit and tenor of Marlon Riggs and other like-minded scholars. But our good work does not stop the relentlessness by which authenticity is shored up, played out, performed, and adhered to ever so nonchalantly and second-naturedly by Black folks of all class backgrounds. My intervention, if I dare call it that, is really just a matter of emphasis on why racial authenticity endures.

This emphasis makes all the difference in how one interprets Riggs et al.'s film (*Black Is . . . Black Ain't*) and the relevance of W. E. B. Du Bois's (1990 [1903]) seminal concept of "double consciousness" to explain how African Americans perceive and negotiate their fraught citizenship in America given the enduring significance of race and dogged persistence of racism. This emphasis also informs how I vet recent analytical imperatives across such diverse fields as anthropology, humor studies, African American studies, gender studies, and further, even shapes how I tell this story. I have found it necessary (though not always easy) to stay behind the energy that authenticity often provokes in me and others in order to unearth deeper lessons and insights from Black humor and laughter. I need to keep it loose or at least as loose as

Black comics whose incessant play with notions of authenticity motivates this telling.

Duly armed with a sense of humor and tasked with unpacking it, I aim for a serious reckoning with the motives behind racial authenticity claims. Forgetting, if slightly and only temporarily, the scholarship that already knows what's wrong with racial authenticity, I make space to let speak, and listen to, African American comics who deigned to say something about racial authenticity at critical moments in the new millennium. After all, serious and sardonic takes on "the real," in comedy, everyday life, and academic scholarship, will likely abide with us for quite some time, especially in regard to race. Comics who dared to say something about "the real"—rooted in both a universal appreciation for "a real," as well as in contextual provocations of the day—open the door for some insights that beckon our renewed consideration for how race's steady functions throw shade on presumptions of a post-racial moment, as well as steady shine on the fraught imperatives of racial authenticity—itself nuanced by other complexities such as gender, sexuality, class, education, and so on—in African American communities.

In Chapter 1, I return to the 9/11 joke that re-ignited my passion for Black standup comedy as a cultural laboratory and communal space, which helped me appreciate the intersubjective subtext of racial authenticity—anew. In Chapter 2, I explore Hurricane Katrina humor, in particular comics' critical rewrite of who gets to be "authentic" American worthy of empathy and intervention versus refugees warranting exile for their own good sake. Chapter 3 examines how empathy and authenticity informed Black comics' public and private responses to Michael Richards's infamous rant at a Los Angeles comedy club. Chapter 4 excavates Kevin Hart's comedic archive to evidence his trickster acuity and delineate the fraught and, at times, costly work he does to "keep real" and legible to an expanding fan base that includes African Americans and other communities. My final chapter (Conclusion) wraps up this telling by reconciling the strange and teachable convergences between my research and personal and professional life during the final years leading up to this telling, with lessons in tow regarding the "why" of racial authenticity and the imperative of "a" real Black in Black standup comedy if not everyday life.

Let's go, in faith that laughter might set us and pre-demarcated notions of "real Blackness" free.

1

"The Arab Is the New Nigger"

African American Comics Confront the Irony and Tragedy of September 11

> "Black people, we have been delivered. Finally, we got a new nigger.
> The Middle Easterner is the new nigger."
> Comedian/writer Ian Edwards
> "Finally!"
>
> **(African American female audience member)**

The September 11 attacks killed the muse of America's most popular humorists for a spell.[1] As Jay Leno and David Letterman expressed their personal grief onscreen, I wept while wondering how African American comics and their audiences might respond to the unfolding crisis. To what extent did African American and other urban comics find humor in the wake of such wide-scale tragedy and loss? What might their shared laughter say about matters of race, identity, and nationalism post 9/11? Given my lust for laughter, story, and communion, and like other writers before me,[2] I could do nothing in the months and years following 9/11 but give steady chase.

I began, tentatively at first, by listening to Steve Harvey's morning radio show. Sobered by the loss of American lives in New York City; Arlington County, Virginia; and Stonycreek Township near Shanksville, Pennsylvania, he still staunchly opposed sending his son to fight in the Iraqi war given enduring racial inequalities in America. In October 2001, I finally built up the nerve to visit the Comedy Union, a Black-owned club in Los Angeles, California. There, I heard the joke by Ian Edwards that serves as this chapter's epigraph: "Black people, we have been delivered. Finally, we got a new nigger. The Middle Easterner is the new nigger." Since 9/11 was still very much the elephant in the room, Ian's willingness to broach the subject allowed us all—his audience and certainly the club's owner[3]—to heave a collective sigh of relief. One Black female audience member's emphatic reply—"Finally"—struck me,

To Be Real. Lanita Jacobs, Oxford University Press. © Oxford University Press 2023.
DOI: 10.1093/oso/9780190870096.003.0002

too, precisely because it was *not* laughter. After all, humor scholars typically take laughter as "proof" that a joke has "fired" successfully and that the audience is indeed "co-author," especially, if not necessarily, in the intersubjective playground of standup comedy.[4] Audience co-authorship remains true, of course, even when audiences don't laugh, and instead boo, hiss, stare blankly, sip audibly, or return other might-as-well-be-sighs—but as comics repeatedly told me, the slow steady horror is an apathetic un-speaking crowd.[5] In this case, the audience's empathetic reply to Ian's joke did not just feed and stoke my curiosity about 9/11 humor; that give-and-take signaled the promise of Black standup comedy writ large to ignite communal dialogue about events as radical as 9/11 and as mundane as Shaq's shoe size.[6]

I visited local comedy clubs four to five times a week in the first year of this eight-year study, taking field notes and interviewing comics in cafes and restaurants all the while. In time, I amassed a wealth of jokes highlighting such topics as the war on terrorism, patriotism, racial profiling, and (then) President George W. Bush. September 11 humor seemed to provide much-needed catharsis as well as a comedic "call back" to Du Bois's notion of "double consciousness," inviting critical meditation and not just time-stamped critique. While certainly sympathetic to the victims of the 9/11 attacks, including one of their own (comic David Williams, a.k.a Dogface), many comics maintained an unabashedly critical stance toward American foreign policy, presidential rhetoric, and frenzied flag-waving, belying popular claims that America had become more unified and its citizens more patriotic as a result of the national tragedy. Shang Forbes, a comic and poet, vehemently opposed President Bush's post-9/11 war rhetoric and the nation's heightened and reactionary patriotism. In a typical rant, he asked a Hollywood Improv crowd, "Why were there no flags being displayed before 9/11? Where was the patriotism? . . . Look at the flag—*it was made in China!*" Other comics condemned simplistic and ahistorical accounts of U.S.–Middle East conflict that conveniently absolved America from culpability in past and present tragedies.

Forbes ended his set by revealing how race continues to qualify the experiences of African Americans in the United States, alluding to the then-pending police brutality case in Inglewood, California,[7] which sadly resonates today: "They [critics] always say (*stereotypic southern accent*), 'Don't make fun of the flag you fucking . . . nigger boy. It's America!' Well [then] stop slapping [Black] teenage heads against the hood of motherfucking police cars!" Race, notions of real Blackness, and the [real] truth of 9/11 all proved pervasive undercurrents in 9/11 humor, beckoning renewed attention to why racial authenticity might matter to Black folks, especially when the ish hits the fan and they need to assert who they *are* and, tragically, given anti-Black racism within the United States and around the globe, *are not.*

Tracing ambivalent patriotism, the cynically hailed arrival of a "new nigger," and jokes that expose the lie of post-9/11 unity given enduring racial injustice, this chapter explores how 9/11 humor served as both a balm and critique for African American comics and audiences. African American humor, from slavery to the present, has proven to be a balm in times of trouble, as well as an indirect means of confronting racial injustice. As a genre characterized by expressive "lies," poignant "truths," and lively call-and-response, Black stand-up comedy has also offered a formalized and communal mechanism for commenting on daily and monumental tragedies, often in contrast to mainstream accounts. Laughter and applause from African American audiences can thus serve to endorse comics who are perceived to "speak truth to power" about the war on terrorism and other political matters. For many ethnic minority audiences, 9/11 jokes "work" as political commentaries that resist pro-war rhetoric and implicate a larger shared history of racial marginalization. These jokes also work because they invoke problems of race in America, particularly comics' ongoing struggles against violations of their and others' civil liberties. Even the at-times out-of-sync exchanges between comics and audiences underscore comedy's capacity to push the limits of the "too soon" joke/political critique. Ultimately, Black comics' 9/11 jokes reveal African Americans' precarious belonging in an American collectivity, even or perhaps especially when national tragedy strikes and calls for unity dominate. Collective laughter at the lie of post-9/11 unity becomes its own form of belonging for African American audiences, whereas heckling, booing, and discordant responses serve as a reminder that when it comes to the Black comics in this study, balm and critique are in constant interplay.

The Arab as the "New Nigger"

The Arab or Middle Easterner as the "new nigger" theme echoed like a riff in many urban comedy rooms. Much like Ian's joke, which tags Middle Easterners in America and beyond as "new niggers" to highlight Blacks' newfound reprieve from "DWB" (i.e., Driving While Black) or racial profiling (herein lies the sardonic rub!), comic/actor Don "D. C." Curry remarked at the Ha Ha Café, "It's a good time to be Black. If you ain't got no towel wrapped around your head, your ass is in the game!" Glenn B. speculated that "good things come out of bad things," since racists now deflect their hatred from Blacks to people of Middle Eastern descent. At the Comedy Store, he reported meeting a skinhead in the post office who sought to reassure him by saying, "We don't hate you. We hate the Arabs." Similarly, "A. C." acknowledged that while the national tragedy was "messed up," it had fortuitous consequences as well. He told a crowd at Mixed Nuts, "I haven't been a nigger for a month! Everyone's like, 'Hey Brother!'" Before he disavowed the use of the n-word (something I'll discuss further in Chapter 3), the late Paul Mooney also quipped, "They [the United States] done with the land niggers and moved on to the sand niggers." Mystro Clark, who is also a Navy vet, waited awhile to process 9/11 humor in order to say something fresh, albeit critical. He ended his 2003 comedy CD ("Mystro Clark: Sexy Funny Bastard") with this: "I feel sorry for the Arabs that was born and raised here though 'cause them the ones that got it hard. They was cool; they was just 'Akbar The Friendly 7/11 Owner' before. Now, they're 'Suspect Number 12'. . . . They're trying to blend in, make their turban look like a baseball hat, painting stars and stripes on that shit. . . . They tryna lose their accent. (*In stylized "Middle Eastern" accent*) 'What is happening, my nigger?'"

Comics noted that racial profiling post-9/11 was largely deferred to Arab Americans, or those perceived to be Arab or Muslim, and for a time, they celebrated waning antagonism toward African Americans. Tony Rock evoked contentious relations between African American passengers and Middle Eastern cab drivers in New York City when he quipped, "It's a good time to be Black. Afghanis are the new niggers. Cab drivers pick me up and let *me* drive!" Similarly, New York native Frantz Cassius invoked a history of conflict between Blacks and the New York Police Department when he joked, "There's one good thing that came from the terrorist attacks. For a good while, the police left Black people alone. [Recently] the police stopped me. I had some weed in my hand and some cocaine in the trunk. They asked me if I'd seen anything out of the ordinary. I told them (*puffs an imaginary blunt*), 'I just saw two Arabs walking down the street, and they looked suspicious. You may want to go check 'em out.'" In this exaggerated plot, Cassius turns the notorious DWB, or "Driving While Black," phenomenon on its head—in the face of a perceived Arab threat after September 11, driving over the speed limit while smoking marijuana becomes an excusable offense.

Cassius's joke also acts as a veiled critique by underscoring African Americans' newfound "rights" consequent to Arab Americans' waning civil liberties. But the story behind the joke is more compelling than the punch line: in an interview, Cassius revealed that his joke was inspired by an actual interaction with a New York police officer just days after the terrorist attacks. Accustomed to aggressive police action during routine traffic stops, Cassius was surprised when the officer simply admonished him to stop speeding and released him without issuing a ticket. Cassius explained the irony of his good fortune, noting, "Now, the focus is on something bigger than the Black man—someone who's *really* after White people, and not some imaginary enemy." In a similar play on this premise, comic/actor Ralph Harris alleged that first-class passengers now gladly welcome rap artists into their exclusive cabin space. Using hyper-standard diction, he impersonated a passenger issuing a rather unorthodox request: "Excuse me, stewardess? That gentleman who walked by with the gold chains and baggy jeans—do you think he could have a seat next to me? You can just take it off my tab." This joke sardonically expounds on the ways racist stereotypes about Blacks have evolved since the terrorist attacks. In Harris's world, the harrowing events of 9/11 did not necessarily absolve Black men of the stigma of being dangerous so much as it temporarily recast them as potential allies in America's new war on terrorism.

Comic Courtney Gee went so far as to frame the September 11 tragedy as a great equalizer. At the Ha Ha Café, he joked that everyone, including the most privileged and unquestionably American (i.e., White men), are subject to heightened scrutiny under new airport security laws: "[Now] White men . . . get to be suspects too. They get to see what it feels like." Gee then performed his interpretation of an angry White male passenger at an airport security checkpoint: "What?! Take off my shoes? What the fuck for?! I don't own a 7-Eleven or have a fucking dot on my head!" Here, Gee exploits multiple stereotypes to highlight the seeming dissolution of racial profiling in the wake of 9/11. Collectively, he and other comics depict a new day wherein non–African Americans—for example, Whites, Pakistanis, Indians, and particularly Arab Americans—are vulnerable to indiscriminate searches and police harassment. Read as political commentaries, these and other jokes also suggest that despite such generalized vulnerability, 9/11 was not a great equalizer since not all Americans, and certainly not Blacks, experience equal footing with regard to their civil liberties.

An Ambivalent Patriotism

Overwhelmingly, the 9/11 jokes I heard in "urban" comedy clubs offer cautionary perspectives on America's war on terrorism and its sociopolitical ramifications. As complex political commentaries, these and other jokes offer important, racially nuanced insights on what it means to be an American in the aftermath of the terrorist attacks—perspectives too often lost when our nation rallies in the face of so-called new vulnerabilities. As Ian Edwards told me during a 2002 interview, "Blacks understand why this is happening. White folks are in a fog. . . . They feel vulnerable but we've been feeling vulnerable for quite some time." Many comics highlighted how America's war on terrorism disproportionately affected minorities in adverse ways, including Godfrey (C. Danchimah Jr.) who said, "There's a war going on. . . . I like it when they show the white soldiers and not the 800 blacks and Latinos on the front lines."[8]

What may be perceived as new vulnerabilities are not new for ethnic and racial minorities in the United States, as revealed by a prior riff on the "Arab as new nigger" premise from a Richard Pryor joke. In his (1974) comedy special, "Is It Something I Said?," a year before the end of the Vietnam War, Pryor mused:

White folks tired of our ass too. They getting them some new niggas: the Vietnamese. [*audience applauds at length*] [They're like] "Bring 'em over. Bring all of 'em over! Niggas won't mind.'" They didn't ask us shit! We the motherfuckahs that got to give the jobs up for 'em. [*audience applauds at length*]. . . . They [Whites] was funny man pleading for the orphans and shit: [*imitates crying woman*] "God, we've got to do something. The little orphans, oh my goodness!" Bitch almost had me go and gettin' an orphan! People in Mississippi, white folks in Georgia and shit adopting babies. Shit gon' last about a year then that racism gon' come out. [*southern voice*] "God damn! What in the hell we got here Margo? [*to Vietnamese adoptee*] Ain't your eyes ever gonna round out? Look like one of the neighborhood coons!" And I'm for orphans, now you know, don't get me wrong. I like orphans but shit, they got 10 million niggas here need to be adopted. [*audience applauds*] They got a show in L.A. on TV, they be selling niggas for adoption on the TV. You ever see those shows? [*imitates a plaintiff newscaster*] "Get one of these niggers, *please*? This big head one here, he's alright. I'd take him home, but I have a dog." . . . [They] got all the Vietnamese in the . . . army camps and shit. Taking tests and stuff. Learning how to say "niggah." So, they can become good citizens. . . . They got classes, you know they have 'em. [*imitates American drill sergeant*] "Alright, let's try it again troops." [*imitates Vietnamese cadet*] "Nigga-nigga-nigga! Nigga-nigga-nigga-nigga!" [*as drill sergeant*] "Well that's close. . . . You get your ass kicked, you know you made it." [*audience applauds at length*]

Pryor brilliantly introduces a caveat that is in many ways similar to another 9/11 joke by Eddie Griffin:

All of sudden, on 9/11, I'm an American! White people run up to me [saying],
"Mr. Nigger! We love ya! Come here. Welcome to the family. Come here nigger!'"
That shit lasted 30 days. But I made a "come-up" in them days . . . all my loans
got passed. Nigga got credit cards. I knew what it was to be a white American
for 30 days! [I] walk in a bank, [*imitates White bank officer*] 'Nigger come in. We
got ya. Need a house loan? Right here! Give it to him! He's an American!" Nigga,
[after] 30 days, they want they shit back. [*stylized "White" voice*] "Um, nigger we
figured it out. We thought we were gonna need your help, but we've bombed them
so it's cool. Give us our shit back. Back to being a nigger. Go ahead. Go ahead."
(*Dysfunktional Family*, 2003)

Pryor and Griffin underscore the primacy of race and Blackness, in particular, in determining American citizenship even, if not especially, in times of
crisis. It bears noting that even Pryor's subsequent disavowal of the n-word,
which I discuss further in Chapter 4, does not nullify his larger critique about
African Americans' enduring marginalization and displacement, nor his implicit stake in the Black-White binary governing race relations in America.
Racism against Blacks, Pryor pointedly suggests, can even be a pathway to
American citizenship.[9]

As forms of political critique, jokes such as these do more than serve as
fodder for divisive identity politics; rather, they beg us to consider what comics
and audiences gain from soulful and resonant calls to "realness" during critical moments as they contend with the sobering realities of anti-blackness.
As actor/comic Evan Lionel solemnly notes, recurring instances of racial profiling, fatal police brutality, and racism broadly complicate expressions of loyalty to America, even in the face of war:

We all love this country, but a lot of folks think that Blacks don't support the war
on terrorism. That's bullshit. It's just hard for me to get behind the war on terrorism
over there when we haven't done it here. Blacks and Jews are like, "Can we stop
off in Alabama and hunt the terrorists there before [we go to] Afghanistan?!" The
number one terrorist ain't [Osama] Bin Laden. It's the grand wizard [KKK] and he's
right here. Let's go get him [first] and *then* let's go to Afghanistan. . . . People say,
"Well if you don't like it then go back to Africa." What African tribe I'm-a go back to?!
Plus, Black people helped build this country! . . . I love America.[10]

As political columnist Jonetta Rose Barras wrote in the *Washington Post* on
October 28, 2001, African American responses to 9/11 encompass sadness,
fear, and grief as well as doubts concerning the meaning of the American flag
and how far civil liberties extend in times of crisis (A6; A19). The laughter

I observed arguably reflects more than the ideological idiosyncrasies of African American comics and their audiences. Instead, the nature of 9/11 humor reflects a widely shared ambivalence among African Americans concerning the nation's response to the attacks and their collective identity as Americans at this critical historical moment.

Nation-building and recuperation, especially in times of crisis, often require authenticating citizenry who work to police the boundaries of their beleaguered communities, distinguishing insiders from outsiders or, as President George Bush declared, an "us" versus a "them" (see also Benson 2013). Eddie Griffin likewise joked in "Dysfunctional Family" that he'd assembled an impromptu huddle of American citizens—themselves a multi-cultural cohort of racial tropes—to confront a man with a "towel on his head" at the airport shortly after 9/11. Then, he confessed, "I know now how white people look at niggahs. [*in standard English*] 'White people, I understand.' 'Cause I never thought I would be racist, but I see that towel, a nigga nervous now." "Dominique" (Whitten)[11] took a different turn, coalescing America's populace of color under a collective (and decidedly "Black" rubric):

I like everybody. But if you ain't white, you black. I don't care what you call yourself. "Mexican," "Jamaican," we all the same. 'Cause George Bush don't see nothing but "us" and "them." And if you ain't "us," you "them"! 'Cause if they pulled up a bus right now and said we was going back to slavery, *ese* [Spanish for "dude," "bro," "man"] that mean you too. Jamaican rude boy, you come on too. Asians, bring the computers, y'all come on too. This [is] a new slavery: "www.slavery.com." They just punch your picture up, and you come up grinning.

The "Arab as new nigger" premise is itself a telling exemplar of the paradoxical impact of September 11 on the lives of many African Americans. While many comics adopted this premise as a sardonic celebration of their newfound privileges resulting from the curtailment of Arab American freedoms, others invoked this premise, directly or indirectly, to critique America's diminished attention to racism, poverty, and other social ills plaguing African American communities following September 11. Ray Chatman alluded to the tenuousness of the "Arab as new nigger" thesis in light of past and recent high-profile cases (e.g., the O. J. Simpson trial) in which the alleged sins of one Black person serve to stigmatize African Americans as a whole. Referring to the Washington, DC, sniper case, and almost a year to the date of Ian Edwards's joke about the "Arab as the new nigger," Chatman inspired raucous laughter at Mixed Nuts Comedy Club when he joked:

Hell. if we had placed bets on whether or not the [Washington, DC] sniper was Black or White, we would've all lost money! I couldn't believe it was a brother! He [sniper] done set us back *again*! After September 11, we wasn't niggers no more. We had *new* niggers! Now, we niggers again.... How you gon' be niggers *again*?!"[12]

In speculating on the new dangers facing African Americans, given the disclosure of the snipers' ethnicity, Chatman's joke challenges the very premise on which it is based. In essence, he suggests that the post-9/11 framing of the Arab as "new nigger" was a bittersweet outcome at best, since it afforded African Americans only basic freedoms as US citizens (e.g., temporary reprieve from indiscriminate racial profiling and police brutality). Moreover, his conclusion—"How you gon' be niggers *again*?!"—is strictly rhetorical, suggesting that African Americans are ever vulnerable to disparaging labels and perceptions.

Authenticating "Real Niggahs" in 9/11 Humor

When I showed a few comics a draft of an essay-version of this chapter before its initial publication, some of them scoffed. While Don "D. C." Curry and Brandon Bowlin both acknowledged the plight of Arab Americans in their jokes, they nevertheless found the "Arab as new nigger" comparison to be an inappropriate, if not insulting, metaphor to endorse verbatim. Curry, in particular, felt that my use of this metaphor as both a title and (then) hook failed to problematize the slur "nigger" and falsely equated the recent hardships experienced by Arab Americans with the chronic struggles faced by African Americans—to say nothing of its complex usage among Black comics. For example, many other comics qualified their frequent use of the slur "nigger," distinguishing it from their colloquial use of the term "niggah" as an in-group and affinity marker. Comic/actor Chris Spencer echoed the general consensus when he discouraged Whites from using the word in any context. Spencer added, "[Plus] when we [African Americans] say it, it's 'nigg*ah*' not 'nigg*er*.' Avoid the '-e.r.' if you want to stay out of the 'E.R.' [emergency room]."

Comics also used "niggah" to reference African Americans as a whole and valorize streetwise—essentially "real"—Black folks who would sneer at the threat of a box cutter, thus invoking racial difference to vouch for the valor of African Americans in the face of terrorist threats. Often, comics portrayed "ghetto" sensibilities, cunning, and urban combat skills as authenticating descriptors of Black culture and identity. Such attributes contrast the generalized vulnerability undergirding the ambivalent patriotism of the "Arab as new nigger" premise. Consider both the timing and success of Scruncho's joke: "If three real niggahs had been on the plane, It-Wouldn't-Be-No-War-Right-Now! Because you can't hijack niggahs with a knife." Scruncho's joke "ripped" (i.e., garnered thunderous applause and even standing ovations) before primarily Black and diverse crowds at a time when the nation had been hit and was struggling, vis-à-vis political rhetoric, to promote bids to patriotism through shopping, and other forms of flag raising, to shore up its ranks.[13] He wasn't the only comic or audience member thinking along these lines; many comics expressed a common suspicion that if Blacks had been on the doomed flights, or if the terrorists had merely opted for Southwest Airlines (a low-cost airline), the terrorist attacks might not have happened. Michael Colyar likewise speculated, "There must not have been a lot of brothers in first class the day that the planes were hijacked. I'm sorry, but you can't hijack no niggahs with a knife!"

Earthquake, a particularly gifted comic, repeatedly roused diverse audiences to hysterics when he mused that Blacks wouldn't have played the role of terrorists either, no matter how persuasive Osama Bin Laden was. At the Comedy Store, he joked: "'Sama Bin Laden is a hell of a motivator. He [lives] in caves while others blow shit up. Ain't no niggahs gon' go along with that. If I worked for him, it would be a whole 'nother story. He'd be like, 'Go do that [stage a suicide bombing]!' I'd be like, 'Where you gon' be?!' Hell, I know a pimp when I see one!" While hosting the Comedy Store's legendary Phat Tuesday show, comedian Geoff Brown jested, "God rest the souls of those who died. But them must've been some passive Whites on the plane. What happened to those nigger-killing, Indian-land-stealing White folks? Where's the Aryan when you need him? . . . We needed some big niggahs to guard the plane. They would've made the terrorists change their minds." Brown fearlessly flirts with the forbidden by daring to question how the victims aboard the two fateful flights allowed themselves to be overtaken. His provocative query further pushes the envelope by highlighting America's complicity in a contentious history of slavery and conquest; arguably, this tactical maneuver of revisiting tragic histories within the United States complicates an "America-as-victim-*only*" response to 9/11.[14] Earthquake similarly mused, "Many people wonder why I'm not tripping after the terrorist attacks in New York and DC. I'm a niggah—I've been dealing with [White] terrorists all my life!" and, in a pseudo-patriotic rejoinder that further lambasts post-9/11 calls for unity, "*Still*, I'm glad the White man came over to Africa and got *me*!"

However, Brandon Bowlin, one of the most political comics I observed, threw copious shade on notions of "real" (stoic) niggahs when he joked before a small primarily African American crowd at the Ha Ha Café:

Black folks been living off the fumes of the Black Panther movement for far too long. Thinking you the shit just *'cause* you black. . . . Stop looking for rappers to be hard. You ain't hard just because you can snarl and say some dope ass lyrics. . . . [*snarls and imitates rappers*] "I'm hard niggah!" No. No, you're not. The . . . lunatics who blew up the World Trade Center took "hard" to a whole new level. You try that hard shit [with them], . . . they'll [terrorists] look at you [and say], [*stylized Middle Eastern accent*] "No you're not hard. No, I'm sorry. . . . No sir. . . . Okay yeah okay rap okay. [*mockingly waves hand as if frightened*] I'm scared motherfucker. Oh, you come in here to rap for me? Oh noooo! My heart is beating so ever fast sir.'[15]

When I first shared these and other jokes in that essay bearing the same title as this chapter, I didn't fully appreciate how deeply and pervasively notions of racial authenticity and truth framed many of the jokes I'd heard.[16] But after its publication, Scruncho's joke about the obvious lack of Black folks on the fated 9/11 flights kept gnawing at my craw. It wasn't just that his joke earned standing ovations from Black and diverse audiences alike; it was that his un-abashed allusion to Black authenticity (via the popular premise "if Blacks had been on the hijacked planes") had occurred to several comics and even occasioned a few rebuttals (recall Brandon Bowlin and Godfrey's jokes about the terrorists' valor of self-sacrifice with thugs as a comparative foil).

These jokes, to say nothing of their post-9/11 timing, hinted at the "why" of racial authenticity and audiences' willingness to accept premises that centered questions of identity and Black authenticity at a time when national rhetoric was calling for something quite different. Consider, for example, that Scruncho's joke "worked" in part given Blacks' ironic privilege as the "niggers" of the United States. For many audiences, their marginalized racial positionality and the primacy of anti-Blackness throughout the world grants them a "right to speak" and the privilege to push the supposed boundaries of what's "too soon." Which is to say, many audiences, diverse and primarily Black, were willing to presume Black comics' empathy with leftist concerns and accept their audacity given Black comics' license and penchant for truth-telling.

Yet, although Black audiences were willing to go down some political paths that were antithetical to mainstream rhetoric, all audiences, regardless of race, scoffed if jokes did not display sufficient empathy with American victims of 9/11—or perhaps if they lacked the right mix of empathy *and* incisive critique. For example, one amateur Black comedienne met silence before a predomi-nantly Black crowd when she jested that the tendency of African Americans to run first and ask questions later had contributed to the death of Blacks on the upper floors of the World Trade Center. Another White male amateur comic aroused jeers from audience members and comics, including the show's host, when he told a nearly all-Black crowd:

> You are NOT from Africa. That's for sure. You are American. Can you just see some [White] guy saying, . . . "I'm American. –No wait. I'm *Swedish* American"? That's not important right now in a time of national crisis. . . . Political correctness will die with the souls in New York. We need to be together, especially now. I want to help to make that happen through comedy. Good night!

Boon Shakalaka, another (Black) comic who performed that evening, delivered the first of several retorts when he took the stage next, asking rhetorically "We're all American ya'll? Why weren't we Americans back then? When we were singing, 'We Shall Overcome'?" (Additional retorts came from the show's Black female host, several groaning audience members, and one who'd warned, "Watch it"). Overwhelmingly, comics and audiences needed the right balance of balm and critique to laugh at 9/11 jokes; thus, jokes that were heavy on in-group caricature but light on empathy (as in the first case), as well as sets that sounded more like correctives than jokes (as in the second instance), failed.

Comparatively, rants, like Chris Rock's infamous distinction between Black folks and "niggahs," more successfully won Black audience's investment, likely because he situated his comments as a personal issue and won Black crowds' support on the basis of his right to speak his truth and his audacity in doing so. Rock routinely peppered his diatribe with the phrase, "I'm tired of this shit!," at one point ratcheting up, "I'm tired of this shit! Tiiiiii-eeerrred!" Like another Black comic, the late-great Bernie Mac, Rock was not "scared." But veteran and White comic Ralphie May also successfully pulled off this premise at The Comedy Union.[17] In an audacious rant punctuated with the rejoinder, "I'm tired of this shit," May told his primarily Black audience, "Fuck the 'African' in African American . . . and I'm not saying it cause ain't none of ya'll been to Africa," earning a smattering of wry laughter. Ralphie May routinely poked fun at his humble class origins while lambasting all things "PC," so it was no surprise to his audience that he'd go here.

Jokes that waged critiques, but did not immediately empathize with the victims of 9/11, sometimes simply required more time and effort to coax agreement from audiences. While hosting the 2002 Bay Area Black Comedy Competition, Don "D. C." Curry ranted like a fired-up preacher against America's war on terrorism and defended his remarks with this decree: "America ain't been no angel!" Eventually, he won the audience's buy-in; throughout Oakland's Paramount Theatre, Black fans uttered comments like, "That's right!," "He's right!," "Mmm hmm," and "Preach!" In a much smaller club setting, Corey Holcomb managed to salvage a joke that initially questioned America's vilification of Osama Bin Laden. When he said, "Bin Laden, that's my niggah," and his primarily Black audience bristled, Holcomb countered, "Ya'll don't know him! We just saw him moving his mouth, but he could've been saying, 'Hey, I ain't done shit. I don't know what they been saying about me but hell.' . . . So, what we need to do is figure out why those folks who drove into them buildings was so upset about," earning a few claps. He told yet another crowd who'd hissed, "Fuck all ya'll. I ain't talking about what happened to them folks [9/11 victims] but ya'll act like this was the worst thing ever to happen. The Indians got slaughtered *in* America and 5,000 folks die and we act like it's the end of the world." This example further suggests that comics have to balance empathy and critique, implying that times of crisis call for comedy that can serve as *both* balm *and* biting political commentary at once, which makes sense considering the ambivalent, precarious belonging and patriotism afforded to Black audiences post-9/11.

Jokes that marked a racial divide in the ethnic group(s) targeted by terrorists and traced the perceived impact of September 11 on Black versus White Americans were particularly successful in predominantly Black rooms. In his (2000) one-hour comedy special, Killin' Them Softly—one year before 9/11—Dave Chappelle presciently remarked on the disproportionate impact that a terrorist strike would seem to have on White versus Black Americans. In the punchline of one joke, Chappelle remarks: "Terrorists don't take black hostages. That's the truth. I have yet to see one of us [where "us" means Black folks] on the news reading a hostage letter. . . . Terrorists are smart. They know what they're doing. . . . They know us black people is bad bargaining chips. . . . They [terrorists] call up The White House (imitates terrorist making phone call), 'Hello. We have got five black— Hello?'" The White House hangs up the phone at the mere mention of "Black," underscoring Chappelle, Spears, and Vidale's collective point about the seeming triviality of Black lives in the United States and beyond (and hence the tragic necessity of movements such as #BlackLivesMatter). Further, when heard alongside prior jokes about "real niggahs" (recall the "'real Blacks are heroic" premise underlying Scruncho's crowd-killing joke: "If three real niggahs had been on the plane, It-Wouldn't-Be-No-War-Right-Now! Because you can't hijack niggahs with a knife"), laughter becomes more somber. "Real niggahs" could not be terrorists be-cause their "ghetto sensibilities" would kick in, but they can't be hostages ei-ther because they *aren't even strategic or viable targets to begin with.*

Many Black and diverse crowds seemed hip to both subtexts. When sev-eral comics asked Black audiences to indicate, by show of hands, their lingering trauma after the terrorist attacks, audiences responded, in line, with more chuckles than raised hands.[18] Chris Spencer, a longtime host of the Laugh Factory's *Chocolate Sundaes* show, observed, "It's a damn war going on and Black folks are the only ones going out [and] having a good time!" Comic Loni Love similarly joked that she was angry with the terrorists for interrupting her hair appointment, but even more perturbed with White Americans for not preventing the September 11 attacks. With hands on her hips, she chided, "White people?! Why y'all let this happen?!" Chappelle won laughs after wearily informing a crowd at the Hollywood Improv, "White folks done got us into some problems *again*." Toby Hixx likewise quipped, "Fuck a war. It' a war right here. I drove over here with my check engine light on. . . . Bill collectors would be calling me on the front lines." Freeze Luv, along with other comics (e.g., Jay Phillips and Joe Claire) impersonated President George W. Bush as a modern day thug, adding, "You want to really fuck them [Taliban] up? Send 'em TV, crack, and come back a week later." Earthquake offered his own suggestions for finding Osama bin Laden (who was then still alive): "Send Child Support. He'll [bin Laden] be in court on Monday!" Later, he identified White males in his audience and quipped, "My vote is on you ['White boys']. You always fuck the minorities up." And Mike Epps reminded a diverse crowd, "America *been* on attack. Every time I talk to the police, they're like, 'Can you step out?' I just go ahead and lock that motherfucker [his car] (imitates the sound of a car alarm being activated) 'cause I never come home." (Epps gets routinely arrested in such instances.)

The successful examples are many but jokes that underscored 9/11's racially unequal impact, despite national calls to the contrary, also generated notable controversy in wider venues, suggesting differences in audience's willingness to parse through the thicket of race to conjure sense from 9/11 and other tragedies in the new millennium. Comic and actress Thea Vidale provoked a surge of protest letters after an appearance on National Public Radio's *Tavis Smiley Show* when she quipped:

White people, I love you dearly. I do. But Osama bin Laden—he ain't mad at us, he mad at y'all. Y'all got a problem. . . . I don't know what you did to him, made him mad, but y'all got a problem. . . . America was shocked 'cause it's not so much that we got bombed; it's <u>where</u> they bombed us. They bombed us at the World Trade Center. That's the World Bank in this country! You know 'cause if it had . . . been bombed in Compton . . . or Harlem, they would've been saying (*upbeat reporter voice*), . . . 'Osama Bin Laden has bombed Compton, California; and Harlem, New York. *Next*, Jim with sports.'

Comic/actor Arie Spears presented a similar theory, "A lot of people don't know it, but the safest place to be right now is the ghetto. Osama and them not worried about niggahs. Can you imagine Al Qaeda trying to convince bin Laden to bomb Black people? They'd be like, 'Osama, we have found a target!' Osama would be like (*highly agitated*), 'What is this Compton?! Look, I don't have time for this . . .'"[19] In Spears's comedic reality, the reason that Blacks are spared from greater casualties is not because of their cunning or combat skills. Rather, the fate of Compton and other poor minority enclaves is predicated on their marginal status in the United States, and hence their negligible currency as American targets in the terrorists' imagination. Spears's impersonation of a weary bin Laden exposes his devaluation of the ghetto as a strategic American target, much like Vidale's parody of an impassive American news reporter reveals the media's disregard of a potential terrorist strike (and, presumably, other tragedies) in the ghetto. Yet many listeners found Vidale's comments to be distasteful, divisive, and anti-White, compelling Smiley to devote a subsequent segment to responding to listener comments and stress his support for freedom of speech. The controversy surrounding Vidale's joke is itself a commentary about the way audiences police the boundaries of tragic humor, as well as how race can constrain or facilitate laughter at such comedy. It's worth mentioning, for example, that the sentiments expressed by Vidale were not only echoed by other comics (as seen above) but were also overwhelmingly endorsed by predominantly Black and brown audiences throughout Los Angeles. These audiences recognized that Vidale's humor included a poignant critique of how African American lives are treated as less valuable, a problem that a national crisis like 9/11 not only doesn't erase but can in fact deepen.

Double Consciousness and 9/11 Humor

There's so much here indicting the enduring "color line" identified rather presciently by W. E. B. Du Bois that makes repeat invocations of a Du Boisian "double consciousness" not only politically expedient but responsive to his intellectually generative legacy. As dutiful scholars ruminate on the contextual nuances of Du Bois's conceptual proffering, some alleging that his varied use of the concept at the turn of the 20th century was not or could not be relevant in the way I and many scholars and writers use it today[20], Du Bois's allusions to "the [invisible] veil" that precludes Whites and some mentally colonized Blacks from seeing even "Talented 10th" (i.e., "successful" and professionalized) blacks as citizens and empathetic humans, grounds my use of his concept as surely as black comics' continued allusions to black people's enduring struggle for legibility, rescue, and, frankly, life regardless of class, nationality, gender, and so on. The concept of "double consciousness," despite its class-steeped origins and elitist optimism, thus resonates as a way to explain Black folks' enduring struggle to be Black *and* American with psychic and affective ease; as African American novelist Gloria Naylor notes, being Black in America remains a "political construct" (at best) since "we have yet to feel within this country that we are home."[21]

Pryor enacted such double consciousness in his 1974 joke (above) about "new niggas" after the Vietnam War, which his Black audience routinely corroborates. They clap when he speaks of Vietnamese child adoptees and soldiers as "new niggers," much like Black audiences today endorse Ian Edwards's and other comics' claims about the "Arab as the new nigger" and Blacks as negligible hostages. Pryor's audiences also applaud at length when he reveals Vietnamese child adoptees, in particular, as "new" and empathetic "niggahs," more empathetic than America's Black children needing adoption. Pryor's crowd is also right there with him when he declares the recitation of a racist slur ("nigger") as a precursor to American citizenship, throwing shade all the while on the surety of his prior claim about the status of the Vietnamese as "new niggers." Pryor's joke and, indeed, Pryor himself, likewise provide a through-line for understanding how Black standup comedy acts as both a balm and a critique, particularly when the proverbial –ish hits the fan, and then again, when things seem calm and still before the next (quite literal) and inevitable storm.

Postscript

During a recent guest lecture[22] on 9/11 humor wherein I riffed on the "why" of racial authenticity and the significance of 9/11 humor in light of Blacks' continued struggle to be seen as empathetic citizens and Americans, a Black male student named "Alex" approached me after class to say this: "It's funny and you laugh because it's just so true today still . . . and you're like . . . you're like (quietly) . . . 'Help?!'" His slow move from light-hearted remarks to somber observation got to me. I stammered my way through a recitation of how Black comedy—even if/when seemingly self-denigrating (Dance 1998) or speculative and rumor-ful (see Turner 1993)—can function as a form of resistance, shared witness, and a balm in times of duress. But I sensed that he was wanting comedy to do more than just incite laughter that soothes; depressed by videos documenting the deaths of unarmed African Americans by police, he wanted Black comedy to spark action in the nation and perhaps among his peers, and he was struggling, as many of us are, with what laughter can and cannot do. I imagined, too, that he was asking another question that often emerges around racially and politically charged humor—a question that plagues audiences and comics alike. (Recall, for example, that Dave Chappelle famously walked away from his hit TV show (*The Chappelle Show*) and a $50 million contract in 2005, in part because he couldn't tell whether one of his crew members was laughing *with* the implicit critiques of a stereotype-laden racial sketch or merely *at* the stereotypes. Similarly, this student (as have others I've worked with and taught) wondered, was everyone laughing *with* the critiques encapsulated in 9/11 humor, or were they merely laughing *at* the racial stereotypes and authenticity tropes deployed by comics to critique xenophobia, debunk ahistorical accounts of America's innocence, and mark shared communal identities and ideologies? This question haunts me, and especially comics who play in the messy field of racial and political critique, because laughter can say "yes, I agree!" as surely as it can raise questions by occurring to comics and Black audiences at the "wrong" place. That ambiguity can transform laughter's cathartic release into a cynical sigh.

The student's expressed despair *and* hope still linger in my mind, recalling the humor I observed about Hurricane Katrina. Like my student's plea, Black comics' quips seemed to cry, "Help," while, at the same time, coaxing resilience akin to Kendrick Lamar's anthematic chant, "We gon be alright!"[23] Comics' appeals to a collective "we" through pronoun references that signal in-group conversations and shared stakes, "Black" impersonations bespeaking cultural stances and ways of seeing the world, and political critiques that bespeak a decidedly and unapologetic "Black" perspective, are additional indicators of the way comedy marks shared experiences and truths, and begets feelings of hope and resilience. These jokes that straddle racial despair and Black resilience also struck me as what comics *needed* and, thus, *could only* say: Blacks and others who were abandoned by the state post-Katrina were not refugees but, rather, authentic and "real" American citizens who remain worthy of much more than they got.

2

"Why We Gotta Be Refugees?"

Empathizing Authenticity in African American Hurricane Katrina Humor

> A niggah gets a little water in his house and now he's a . . . *refugee*? Why we got to be refugees? Why can't we be evacuees? We're American citizens!
>
> **Comic/Writer/Actor Joey Wells**

Joey Wells's quip above epitomizes the rage and despair felt by many Black Los Angelenos after Hurricane Katrina devastated the US Gulf Coast, leaving over 75,000 largely poor and Black residents awaiting aid in the port cities of New Orleans, Louisiana; Gulfport and Biloxi, Mississippi; Mobile, Alabama, and in Florida's southern and panhandle regions. Told in August 2005, Wells's joke is an even more sobering riff than the "Arab as new 'nigger'" premise discussed in Chapter 1. Lest you forget, comic Ray Chatman quipped *How you gon' be niggers again?!* in 2002, arguing that Americans of Middle Eastern descent are *not* "new niggers" post-9/11, at least not so long as anti-Blackness runs amok, damning Blacks overall for the sins of two Black snipers in Washington, DC, Maryland, and Virginia. Hear if you will the formulaic similarities in Chatman's and Wells's jokes—"How you gon' be niggers *again*?!"/ "Why we got to be refugees?"—as both comics exploit rhetorical query to expose the life or death stakes of anti-Blackness in America. Taken seriously, their time-stamped riffs bookend a despairing tale: whereas Chatman's quip post-9/11 is rife with sardonic speculation (i.e., How you gon' be niggers *again*?!), Wells's joke post-Hurricane Katrina (i.e., "Why we got to be refugees?") is its most-tragic coda. Further, in Wells's imagination, Blacks are not just America's perpetual "nigger" in only the most damning sense of the term; they can also be un-empathetically written off even in their most vulnerable hour (e.g., as lawless "looters"). They are thus subject to premature death and evacuation from the realm of

To Be Real. Lanita Jacobs, Oxford University Press. © Oxford University Press 2023.
DOI: 10.1093/oso/9780190870096.003.0003

American citizenship and rescue, if not literal evacuation from New Orleans proper as "refugees" and not evacuees.

In this chapter, I discuss how Black comics and audiences wrestled laughter from yet another tragedy.[1] This tragedy bore a decidedly racial and classed face, as most of the Katrina storm victims were poor African Americans without the financial means to evacuate when ordered. As storm victims struggled to "make do" atop rooftops, bridges, and in the crowded New Orleans Superdome, they were dealt additional blows when early media reports depicted some Katrina victims as more dangerous than desperate. As Chatman's joke suggests, this designation didn't just have consequences for those deemed to be "looters"; it also cast a pall over all Black Katrina victims, including society's most vulnerable—elderly women dying in wheelchairs while draped in American flags, and crying babies whose moms were so desperate that they tried to hand them off to people who were evacuating on buses.

Many comics scoffed in rage at these disturbing sights by openly acknowledging the overwhelmingly Black and poor face of Katrina victims. They also marshaled empathy—a seeing and holding onto as if one's own—for Black Katrina victims to varying degrees. For example, some comics' jokes seemed to cry out to storm victims, "I see you in my laughter and tears, and I'm not letting you go because your survival is also mine." Other comics held onto Black Katrina victims as if they were family members, but nonetheless shamed select Black "looters" and/or Katrina victims overall—as if they were kin—for not leaving. As I'll soon show, these intimate "tough love" caveats involve more than mere chastening; by appealing to Black respectability politics—the tragically necessary but oft-futile belief that Blacks must exhibit "model behavior" (even in dire straits) for the benefit of their *always and already* unempathetic collective—Black comics recuperated Black storm victims as empathetic subjects. They also debunked discourses that unfairly pathologized them as "looters" and otherwise normalized their plight (e.g., Figure 2.1). However, at least one comic I observed, Rod Man Thompson, eschewed Black respectability altogether or, rather, redefined it anew by reframing Black Katrina victims' so-called "bad" behavior as emblematic of "real Black" resilience and ingenuity in the face of White privilege, duplicity, and apathy. In essence, he flipped the script of respectability via an artful play on the trope of Black-White differences and Black one-upmanship by whatever means possible. Finally, a few brave Black and non-Black comics seemed to ditch respectability and empathy altogether by merely lampooning—with mixed success—Black Katrina victims, if not African Americans overall,

Figure 2.1. Barbara Bush's Tone Deaf Assessment of Black Katrina Victims' Good Fortune. Readers may recall Marie-Antoinette as the last Queen of France before the French Revolution. Described as frivolous and extravagant, she came to symbolize the people's hatred for the old regime. Legend has it that when she was informed that poor people had no bread to eat, she responded, "Let them eat cake." In her editorial cartoon, Shelley Matheis situates former First Lady Barbara Bush's remarks (as mother of then-sitting President George W. Bush Jr.) toward Katrina evacuees who'd been relocated to Houston, Texas—("So many of the people in the arena [Houston Astrodome] here, you know, were underprivileged anyway, so this is working very well for them")—as equally tone-deaf, patronizing, and offensive, likely fomenting a regime change in the United States that ushered in Barack Obama, America's first black president.
https://www.cartoonstock.com/cartoon?searchID=CS365471 Shelley Matheis/www.cartoonstock.com.

for either not evacuating or expressing a strong desire to help rebuild New Orleans post-Katrina. Storm-related humor, especially Thompson's joke, kept me tethered to comedy clubs, albeit in a slightly different way than before. Whereas I had theorized, observed, and "felt" my way through 9/11 humor (where again, there was so much loss), Katrina humor forced me to feel and later write through engulfing racial despair. This affective path to knowing occasioned many tears. Tears I sometimes could not, per the title of Michael Eric Dyson's unapologetic book-length "sermon to White America," stop given the spectacle of unabated Black suffering, then and now.[2]

Unearthing a Hook from a Storm

Comedy's ability to trick tears into laughter lit into me during this tumultuous time. I'd been searching for a hook in comedy clubs for about four years then, swimming in ethnography's inductive pull. But racial despair overwhelmed me, and I found myself again asking the painful question: How can comics make *this* funny? Since Hurricane Katrina occurred amid enduring reports of racial profiling and state-sanctioned violence against Black and brown bodies—backing up Chapman's sardonic post-9/11 quip ("How you gon' be niggas *again*?!") like a cruel joke—I was also asking a more personal question: How can I live and love in a racially stratified world while holding dearly to those I've lost?

As I listened to comics' laments and appeals, I learned again what it means to "laugh to keep from crying." I felt Wells's anger and disbelief down deep in my soul. I also knew what comic Tony Young meant when he joked that he'd "always wanted to see more Black people on TV, just not like *this*." And Melanie Comarcho too; when she assumed her signature hand-on-hip pose and deadpanned, "We 'refugees' now after we done built this motherfuckah?!," I dropped my pen and cried, "Yaaasssss!" When I heard comics invoke notions of "a" real Black to critique Katrina victims' designation as "refugees" and "looters," I got more than cathartic release. My hook shape-shifted from a shadow into a bold prompt and eventually won me over riff by riff. I recalled 9/11 humor that made decisive play of "real" Blackness, including Scruncho's slam-dunk joke: "If it had been at least three <u>real</u> niggahs on that United Airlines flight, it wouldn't be no war today because you can't hijack niggahs with [just] a knife!" This joke roused Black and diverse crowds to their feet just months after September 11, piquing my curiosity about *how* such jokes were told and *why*. Satisfying this curiosity meant paying close attention to jokesters and their comedic styles (i.e., the *how*), as well as the contextual, political, personal, and other motivations underpinning the jokes they tell (e.g., the *why*).

To follow this path of inquiry, I could never forget comedy's inherent intersubjectivity: namely, the incessant back-and-forth between comics and audiences that expresses itself through laughter as well as silence; Black comics' steady dance with each other both onstage and off; and the racial, cultural, and political milieus sparking Black humor in the first place (i.e., the *how* and the *why*). My mounting curiosity about the *hows* and *whys* of racial authenticity surprised even me since I was acutely aware of racial authenticity's limiting scripts, both as a former adolescent who'd been teased for "talking White," and, chiefly, as an anthropologist ever-sure that race—this notion that we humans are biologically distinct from one another—is a falsehood of the highest order. But this conviction receded as a prevailing and disciplining hook when comics' storm-related jokes about "real Black folks" managed to soothe my despairing heart.

Comics' no-holds barred stance toward Katrina's racial contours also occasioned my own surer stance as a scholar—a stance I'd surely need to tell this story. Before Katrina, I was necessarily attendant to respectability politics, both as an African American woman and a scholar (then) seeking tenure at a top-tier university. This meant that I was more likely to scan for evidence of racism's pall, despite its glaring presence, lest I be accused of "race-baiting," as were those who flagged racism and racial inequality as decisive factors in Katrina's tragic aftermath. Looking back, I fear I sacrificed my own authenticity so as not to go unheard in academia's literal and proverbial classrooms.

Fortunately, comics gave nary a care to respectability politics when they lambasted then-president George W. Bush, who didn't physically touch down in Mobile, Alabama, until September 2, 2005, five days after Katrina made landfall, or visit New Orleans until September 11, 2005, despite the city's considerable death toll, devastation, and media coverage. Nor did a few hold back when they excoriated then-secretary of state Condoleezza Rice who regrettably vacationed and shoe-shopped while Katrina raged,[3] and even took aim at storm victims who did not heed evacuation orders and/or nabbed TVs instead of food before and during Katrina, respectively. They inspired me to do the same in my career by asking whether my hyper-bracketing of "racial authenticity" during lectures as an African American female professor, likely the first many of my students had ever had, was serving me and my students best.[4] My investments in Black folks' investment in "a" real steadily deepened, as did my belief in comedy's potential to bespeak truth, if not life itself.

Laughing alongside comics and audiences, I absorbed additional lessons in the "why" of racial authenticity and empathy's blessed affordances: both were sorely needed given Katrina's destructive toll. I saw how notions of sincerity (i.e., saying what one means and meaning what one says) represented a flip-side or scaffold for racial authenticity, insofar as being "true" about what one says and means is oft-perceived by African Americans as a marker of "real Black folks," if not an idealized personal trait. Incidentally, some comics say this trait is woefully lacking among White Americans who remain blind to their racial privilege and silent about its affordances and preclusions.[5] I also recognized that comics' bids to authenticity often implicated sincerity, while others bore an unmistakable and unapologetic investment in what I call "a" Black real for reasons I'll explain soon. Observing comics with both my heart and my mind over time thus served to nuance my question and boldface my analytical investments in when, how, and especially, *why* Black comics and their audiences endorse notions of "a" real Black while remaining fully cognizant of the diversity within Black America and the broader Black diaspora.[6]

It bears repeating that my concerted focus on "racial authenticity" versus, say, Jackson's seminal concept of "racial sincerity" is (again) a matter of emphasis, a *choice*. In making this choice, I in no way mean to imply that scholars who place "dismantling race" high on their analytical agendas are drinking some kind of respectability Kool-Aid. To make or even imply such a claim would be unfair, inaccurate, and frankly, plain stupid (especially if one considers as but a start Jackson's scholarly archive to date). Plus, who needs such tit-for-tat theorizing in *these* days and times, especially since social constructivist approaches reveal the performative, fluid, "imagined," and, when contextually and analytically apropos, debunk-able nature of authenticity, sincerity, race, gender, and other taken-for-granted notions and positionalities. My stalwart fascination with "a" Black real likewise appreciates these lessons, even as it places explicit emphasis on the "why" of racial authenticity. I need readers to appreciate how and why Black comics and audiences harnessed notions about "a" Black real when a storm of unprecedented proportions rocked their world, if not their very sense of themselves as legitimate American citizens. Equally, I want readers to understand what many Black folks find redeeming about "a" Black real (versus "the" real Black) beyond Hurricane Katrina—that is, when things are calm and still. But first, let's revisit Hurricane Katrina's dastardly toll.

Hurricane Katrina's Destructive Toll

Hurricane Katrina remains the single most catastrophic and costliest natural disaster in US history.[7] In New Orleans, Katrina's twenty-foot surge collapsed levees meant to withstand a Category 3 hurricane (Katrina was a Category 5), flooding the port city in twenty feet of water in some spots. While New Orleans received the most attention as a historic port city and popular tourist destination, Mississippi bore the brunt of Katrina's damage; in Pass Christian, storm surges—the highest ever recorded on the US coast—were as high as 27.8 feet. Alabama's port cities and Florida's southern and panhandle regions were also ravaged by the storm.

Tragically, Mother Nature was not the sole culprit of the devastation wrought by Hurricane Katrina. Miscommunication and, in some cases, failed communication between local, state, and federal officials compounded the storm's devastation. For example, New Orleans's mayor at the time, Ray Nagen, ordered a mandatory evacuation just a day before the storm made landfall despite frantic warnings from the National Hurricane Center of Katrina's inevitable destruction several days prior. But more than a quarter of the New Orleans population lived below the poverty line and did not have the resources to leave. Twenty-seven percent of New Orleans residents didn't own a car, making evacuation all the more difficult and costly.[8] Once Katrina hit, those who could not leave found themselves stranded on their roofs or sheltering in the city's overcrowded Superdome. There, they awaited at least five days for federal aid, resorting to all manner of survival tactics amid premature media reports of excessive violence, rape, pillaging, and murder.[9] These reports overshadowed any sign of aid to come and even served to keep it at bay; one of the more gross examples of negligence include the rejection by Federal Emergency Management Association (FEMA) of 300 dump trucks and vans, 300 boats, 11 aircraft, and 400 law enforcement officers offered by the Department of Interior so as to not expose workers to "looters, snipers, and felons." Comics like Ron G. couldn't help but milk humor from the government's horrific pause. When an audience member at The Comedy Store laughed a bit late at his jokes in October 2005, he quipped, "You FEMA? You was kind of late on that laughter."

The US government's gross mishandling of the storm proved fatal, literally choking up several comics onstage and off. While the storm's final death toll remains unclear, estimates range from as few as 1,833 to more than 4,100, with most fatalities occurring in Louisiana and Mississippi. Most who died were senior citizens. Over 700 people are reported as still missing post-Katrina. Katrina's survivors, some 15 million, were also affected, having had to evacuate their homes and confront rising gas prices, a crippled economy, and a host of emotional problems. Poor individuals, mostly Black, felt these effects the hardest. Hurricane Katrina also proved costly, causing $81 billion in property damage in New Orleans alone, and over $150 billion in Louisiana and Mississippi collectively. Most recent (2019) expert reports elevate Katrina's overall fiscal toll, including both the damage and economic impact, to $161 billion.[10]

Shocked by this shameful spectacle, aid poured in from America's "first-world" allies and poorer nations alike. When Mexico's president at the time, Vicente Fox, shipped troops—the first ever on US soil since the Mexican-American War in 1846—along with rescue experts and a naval vessel full of medicine, food, and water, comic KACE joked, *"You know things are bad when Mexico sends aid!"* Additionally, Kuwait made the largest single pledge of $500 million in oil and cash, while Qatar, India, China, Pakistan, and Bangladesh pledged very large donations as well. By late February 2006, over seventy countries had pledged money, oil, and other assistance totaling

$854 million, which, according to the Associated Press and a 2011 report by the Heritage Foundation,[11] went largely unclaimed by the US government due to a tragic lack of political will to galvanize resources.

American citizens also donated in record-breaking fashion. The American Red Cross received nearly a billion dollars for Katrina aid, the highest amount ever donated for a single cause in US history. Nearly half of this amount came from funds raised by NBCUniversal's "A Concert for Hurricane Katrina" on September 2, 2005, where rapper and fashion mogul Kanye West stunned audiences, as well as co-host comic Mike Myers and follow-up performer comic Chris Tucker, when he ignored the teleprompter's script to decry the media's representation of Black Katrina victims and their gross treatment by their government and military. West's heartfelt and off-the-cuff remarks below shocked viewers too but are now celebrated as his bravest use of what linguistic anthropologists call "breaches"[12]—a breaking of socially-accepted scripts—to speak truth to power.[13] Here's what he freestyled:

> I hate the way they portray us in the media. You see a black family, it says, 'They're looting.' You see a white family, it says, 'They're looking for food.' And, you know, it's been five days [waiting for federal help] because most of the people are black. And even for me to complain about it, I would be a hypocrite because I've tried to turn away from the . . . TV because it's too hard to watch. I've even been shopping before even giving a donation, so now I'm calling my business manager right now to see what is the biggest amount I can give, and just to imagine if I was down there, and those are my people down there. So, anybody out there that wants to do anything that we can help — with the way America is set up to help the poor, the black people, the less well-off, as slow as possible. I mean, the Red Cross is doing everything they can. We already realize a lot of people that could help are at war right now, fighting another way — and they've given them permission to go down and shoot us! [*West's co-presenter, comic Mike Myers reads from the teleprompter; when it's West's turn, he again ignores the teleprompter to famously declare:*] George Bush doesn't care about Black people!

West's rant is powerful, not merely as a breach of protocol that disrupts and likewise exposes the mismatch between the congenial tenor of the televised fundraiser and Katrina victims' living hell on American soil; he also filled the airwaves with an uncomfortable truth, one calibrated and potentially endearing given his own willingness to be accountable to fellow Black citizens in duress. His shaky voiced sincerity aroused empathy for Katrina victims, for whom he advocates as if they are his own blood kin. His most provocative indictment is of then-president George W. Bush, whom he describes as hostile toward Black Katrina victims, if not the chief architect in the "They" (e.g., federal government) that belatedly authorized the US military to momentarily turn their guns away from post-9/11 terroristic "threats" toward domestic victims.[14] (West would later retract his description of Bush as "racist," even though he never in fact used those words.) West would go on to commit additional, if not infamous, televised breaches, with mixed responses, but this one in particular eventually won him empathetic recognition from his startled co-host, Mike Myers, fellow telethon presenters, and several comics who channeled West's impromptu provocation into comedic bits.

Alex Thomas, a former choreographer turned comic, actor, writer, and philanthropist, was one of them. Visibly angry, he told a crowd at The Comedy Union in September 2005, "Is it comedy time? I'ma vent! Did ya'll see Kanye (West)? Audience members laughed, a few said "Yes!" and Thomas re-enacted, or better, yet revised, West's impromptu comments during the telethon and preserved West's deadpan delivery for comic effect. " 'Bush don't give a fuck about niggahs.' "

Thomas's joke, or "vent" as he called it, parlays West's indignation into comedic truth-speak and cathartic release; namely, he embodies the quiet comportment with which West concluded, "Bush doesn't care about Black people," but exaggerates it, too, by incorporating the racially charged signifier, "niggah," the expletive "fuck," and African American Vernacular English grammatical structure (i.e., "don't" instead of "doesn't") into a shout-worthy punchline: "Bush don't give a fuck about niggahs." In Thomas's hands, "niggah" is a communal signifier, as opposed to a merely controversial racist or classist qualifier, that mirrors West's loving hold of Black Katrina victims while encompassing Black folks overall. Both West and Thomas likewise suggest that what happens to Black Katrina victims implicates Black Americans writ large. Moreover, although physically removed from New Orleans, Black L.A. audiences' affirming laughter and shout outs suggest that they nonetheless feel Katrina victims' pain and fully recognize the neglectful fuckery at hand.

West's remarks sparked bits at an after-hours spot in Los Angeles wherein "Luenell" (Campbell) praised West for raising her consciousness about Hurricane Katrina, as well as Sierra Leone's exploitative diamond mining industry (in which children are forced to mine for "conflict diamonds" and die in civil wars financed by them). Luenell then told her small crowd:

I tried denial for two days. Comic Review taped there [New Orleans]; now it's gone! People who laughed there [at Comic Review] is fucked! I thought, 'Well, I got to do something!' So, I donated to the Red Cross at Krispie Kreme [Donuts] and went to church. . . . They had a telethon . . . whites singing, tryna pacify a nigga. They need to have Jill Scott Herron and Malcolm X playing. It's time for niggas to raise up! After the tsunami, they was over there in two days. [With us, they say], "Let the niggas drown" . . . I'm pissed! We all gon' suffer from this! What they gon' find when they pump the water out? Where they gone pump it to?

Luenell's set begins with high praise (for West), a confession of her own inability to reconcile Katrina's devastation with the government's sub-par response, and steadily builds to a rant akin to West's televised remarks. Like a comic using the stage as a form of comic relief, she works through a crushing sense of racial despair, suspicion about the US government's uneven response to domestic and foreign tragedies, cynicism toward White domestic aid, and a fraught declaration of Blacks' intersubjectivity and collective suffering (i.e., "We all gon' suffer from this!"). Her grief, ever-palpable, colors her attempt at self-deprecation (e.g., "So I donated to the Red Cross at Krispie Kreme [Donuts] and went to church") and further stokes her despair, mounting anger, and, finally, her call to political action more dramatic than any existing televised telethon, and as unapologetic as Malcolm X and American soul and jazz poet, Gilbert "Gil" Scott Heron (e.g., "It's time for niggas to raise up!"). Ending her set, Luenell admitted that the spectacle of Katrina made her think of her own daughter and the precarious future facing young Black girls and boys these days.[15]

Luenell's expressed shade toward hurricane relief telethons wherein "whites [sing], tryna pacify a nigga" reveals a broader cynicism among Black comedians post-Katrina. Similar jokes spilled out from both televised and comedy club fundraisers, sometimes with a cadence as bold as West's and as sincere as Thomas's and Luenell's rebuttals and reprisals; at other times, comedians issued the slickest (i.e., barely perceptible) jokes or counternarratives to interrogate White liberal sincerity and espouse empathetic love for Black and other Katrina victims.

By speaking openly and unapologetically about the racial dynamics of the storm and the disproportionate hyper-visibility of Black vulnerable citizens, comics like Luenell and Thomas, as well as rapper West marshal their own sincerity (e.g., vulnerable admissions of grief, despair, embarrassment, confusion, and rage) to abet their audience's laughter and recognition of the storm's racial disparities. Their jokes thus afford the audience's cathartic release, and even, per Luenell, invite their politicization via a call to bold action. This call to action chiefly entails keeping "real" and true about the storm's tragic revelations concerning race and class and bestowing empathy, a feeling for Black Katrina victims as if their suffering were one's own, such that rescue, intervention, and recognition of their shared humanity is only natural. Luenell was not alone in her demonstrable call to give, see, feel, and act; her and other comics' bids to collectivize, to hold onto Katrina victims as if their own amid the government's incredulous neglect, ran through much of the humor I observed in the storm's wake. Empathy remained a relentless subtext in the Hurricane Katrina humor I'll now discuss; comics both enacted and appealed for it in all sorts of ways, at times resorting to "tough love" appeals to respectability given its occasional capacity to save imperiled Black lives or jokes that eschewed respectability altogether in favor of something a bit cheekier and b-sided. Many comics also leveraged the "n-word" strategically in their calls for more empathetic recognition and classification of Black Katrina survivors. I pay close attention then to comics' verbal stylings in hopes that by unpacking their joke's artful structure, affective tone, and stance, I might gain additional lessons in the comedic affordances of empathy, sincerity, and racial authenticity.

Hurricane Katrina Humor

"Why We Got to Be Refugees?"

Joey Wells's disbelief and rage as host at The Comedy Union remain as palpable to me now as they were just weeks after Hurricane Katrina. Before the storm, Wells was purposely refashioning his then largely jocular and self-effacing shtick into something more personal and revealing. He "grew [it] up," so to speak, by divulging more of himself onstage, including his travails as a first-time single father to his then-teenage son. But Katrina shook Wells to his core, disrupting even this valiant stretch of his set. Offstage, he suffered a mild depression over Katrina that threatened to uproot him onstage; while warming up the crowd at The Comedy Union in September 2005, nearly two weeks after the storm (9/13/05), he admitted, "I'm not a political comic but this Katrina thing has got me worked up!" Wells added:

> I must admit, I ain't really cool with white people this week.... [They're] fuckin' with us over there man. . . . Real quick! Real quick! Tomorrow we are having a benefit FOR the victims—not the "refugees"! We are having a benefit for the victims of the thing 'cause they been calling niggahs "refugees" all week! [*Audience roars, a few women yell, "OKaaay!"*] God Damn! [*Wells caricatures a news reporter pointing to an imaginary TV screen.*] "As you can see the refugees. Just look at the refugees. The refugees are just walking in the water. There's feces everywhere and the refugees are all behind me." [*Drops caricature.*] God Damn! They're victims!"

Wells's lament bespeaks a resonant trope post-Katrina that fiercely rejects the "refugee" label for reasons he soon reveals and apparently shares with his vocally empathetic audience. He gets there by staging an especially loaded teaser or invitation that ultimately services his subsequent and quite pointed observation about Hurricane Katrina's racial dynamics.[16] Wells disavows the term "refugees" as an apt description for Black storm victims, blaming Katrina's devastating aftermath not on natural disaster (or climate change) but rather on "White folks" (arguably White apathy and indifference) and reporters who appeared indifferent at worst and pitying at best. Reporters' blanket descriptions (e.g., "refugee") detached Black Katrina victims from the realm of US citizenship and protection, effectively writing them out of house and home while refusing to use their rightful names (i.e., American citizens and "victims" versus "refugees")—effectively giving them a double-slap.[17]

Wells's aggrieved invitation and lacerating caricature of news reporters also affectively leverages the n-word, much like the comics discussed previously. His use of "niggah" to reference Black Katrina victims is empathetic, not derisive, in part because it lacks the "-er"— that combustible and punishable suffix that another comic, Chris Spencer, warns can send its sayers to the "E.R." (Emergency Room). In Wells's hands, "nigga/niggah" is multivalanced— that is, capable of signifying multiple meanings and is thus, context-dependent. Wells uses "niggah" as an in-group marker of Black folks writ large in a manner that *sees* and *feels* Katrina victims as empathizable and intrinsic to a collective (Black) "we." Further, in Wells's affective leveraging, "nigga/h" indexes Blacks as both a racial collective *and* a stigmatized group; "niggah" marks and holds the racist critiques made of Blacks (as in, *They* say we are "refugees"), and disavows this singular read of "nigga/h" at the same time (as in, "Damn what they say! Black Katrina victims and Black folks writ large are empathetic human beings and victims, in the case of Katrina survivors.") Many staunch critics of the term miss this complexity in meaning, as do those who acknowledge the n-word as an in-group recuperation of a stigmatized and brutalizing term but still overlook the ways the term's racist antecedents might imbue it with additional meaning, if just a trace, in contemporary use. This trace may likewise fuel staunch resistance to the term's deployment in whatever regard, especially among older African Americans who, given their personal experience with the n-word's caustic sting in prior eras, see no redemptive appeal in its use today. This trace is arguably always present, requiring special attendance, then, both to comics' affective uses of the term and audiences' reception. Looking again at Well's joke above, we see that unlike the media's shoddy attempts at sympathy, which Wells re-enacts via caricature as pitying and offensive, Wells's joke empathizes and humanizes

Black Katrina victims, even as he revises understandings of the n-word as merely a racial epithet—something I'll revisit in Chapter 3.

As show host, Wells's introductory remarks set a decisively political mood; his rage caught afire, igniting what linguistic anthropologists call "agreement expletives" (e.g., "OKaaay!," "Yes!," "That's right") and humor scholars appreciate as "evidence" (e.g., enthusiastic applause) of a successful joke. Other comics who performed that night and in subsequent weeks issued their own riffs on the "Why we got to be refugees?" trope, again, with empathy as a central goal and stake since its affordance often determined whether folks displaced by the storm got classified as a "refugee" versus something many comics and Black folk deemed more empathizable: "'victim," "survivor," or bona fide American "citizen." Alex Thomas, discussed earlier, bristled with outrage as he recalled news clips depicting Katrina victims as "refugees" versus "evacuees" or "survivors." Thomas also felt the media was an instigator (i.e., shit starter) and, this time, impersonated CNN commentator Larry King's seemingly cavalier description of Black Katrina victims as "refugees" as a problematic case in point:

> [*impersonating Larry King while looking into an imaginary camera*] "We'll be right back with the New Orleans refugees." [*to audience*] What the fuck?! Couldn't it be "evacuees"? [*audience applauds wildly*] But I have to admit that when I turned this on, I was like, is this Africa? If it was Utah, Iowa, the U.S. would've dropped like 19,000 jet skis. Instead, we see footage of a niggah on a Frisbee talkin' 'bout, "We can't swim!" I didn't see no whites and the ones they found was Black! [*Thomas then performed a White female storm victim with a White name "talking Black" to reporters.*]

Thomas invokes race slyly here through his use of the n-word to reference Black Katrina victims before a predominantly Black crowd ever-sensitive to the politics of this word. He also invokes race, or Whiteness, in particular, by imagining how the US government might have responded had Hurricane Katrina damaged the predominantly White states of Utah and Iowa; here, Utah and Iowa are code for "White," and Thomas presumes that this Whiteness affords state protection, rescue, and acknowledgment. Thomas's pointed observation also marshals sincerity via his reluctant (i.e., caveated) confession: "But I have to admit that when I turned this on, I was like, is this Africa?" Thomas performs reluctance here, signaled by the preface "But" in "But I have to admit," and his self-conscious admission about what he and many others, myself included, deemed downright surreal about images of Katrina victims stranded atop roofs and dying in the streets and flooded homes. To Thomas, these images conjured "third-world" realities that, tragically, seemed atypical in the United States. A different kind of normalization—a new normal tolerant of explicit and violent anti-Blackness—seemed to be re-inserting and re-asserting itself in the African American and American imagination. This struck many—including those who believed the government intentionally blew up the levees that compounded Katrina's devastation, obliterating NOLA's nearly all-Black ninth ward—as a case of state-sanctioned, premature Black death. His impersonation of a White female storm victim with a "White name" talking as if she were Black to reporters also exploits incongruity to comically signify on the way Blackness was figuratively evacuated in the media's coverage. Black victims, Thomas quips, were not always deemed empathetic subjects, whereas Whites somehow managed to marshal unconditional empathy and coordinated rescue given their presumed innocence and legitimacy as US citizens.

D. L. Hughley, among several Black comics featured on Comic Relief 2006, also had trouble reconciling the images he'd seen of Black Katrina victims in utter despair on US ground:

> I was actually in Japan when Hurricane Katrina hit, and I don't speak Japanese, but I was watching the news and I saw Black people running and they kept saying "refugees." I'm like, " 'Refugees'! What the fuck happened in Haiti? Them wasn't refugees; them was American citizens! 'The Refugees' was a hip-hop group that I'm glad . . . got back together. Fuck that shit!"

Whereas Hughley (and Thomas above) chiefly centered Black Katrina victims in their jokes in Black comedy clubs and on TV, respectively, Katt Williams, pitched the storm as an equalizer of sorts between poor Blacks (i.e., "niggahs") and Whites (i.e., "rednecks"). In his televised set on Comic Relief 2006, he joked:[18]

> The one thing [the hurricane] did do was make white people and Black people the same in Louisiana in that hurricane. White people, we love you. Black people love you white people. I want to take this opportunity on this stage to say, "Please send some money." ' Black people, I know that tippin' is not our thing. We don't like to tip. We are heavy budgeters. If we have $12, we only expect to spend $12. Give you $2 and that would mean $14. We didn't have $14. We had $12. But I . . . would just like to urge all Black people watching right now to please send some money. Whatever it is, it's very important. . . . [T]his message for the weather service. Uhh, just instead of showing the graphs and shit and all the charts could you please just say, "Leave." Just tell motherfuckahs to leave because niggahs and rednecks do

not ever want to leave a crisis. Y'all seen rednecks on national television when the hurricane coming. They just right there in front of the trailer . . . [*impersonates a "Redneck" holding a microphone*] "Is this thing [microphone] on? Leaving?! I ain't never gawd damn leaving! My gawd damn mother grew up here! My gawd damn grandfather grew up here!" They'll never leave. Then after the hurricane, they'll show 'em again. The whole trailer's upside down. [*flips onstage stool upside down to resembled up-turned trailer*] And they're just like, "I don't know why Jesus would do this to me! I really don't!"

In setting up this joke, Williams deploys racial comparison, a canonical trope in American ethnic humor, in ways similar to the joke that got comedienne/actress Thea Vidale in trouble with some non-Black listeners on Tavis Smiley's former public radio show; readers may recall that shortly after 9/11, Vidale quipped, "White people, I love you dearly. I do. But Osama bin Laden—he ain't mad at us, he mad at y'all. Y'all got a problem. . . . I don't know what you did to him, made him mad, but y'all got a problem," effectively marking, via the emphatic pronoun "ya'll" (versus "we"), the fact that she and other Black Americans do not constitute a global terrorist threat or even collateral damage, given their role as negligible (i.e., unempathetic) American targets. (Sadly, Katrina seemed to reaffirm her satire's sobering subtext.) Although similar, however, Williams's joke manages to subvert the trope of Black-White racial differences and even yields empathetic voice to poor Whites, albeit cheekily by holding the fates of poor Black and White New Orleanians as mutually intelligible, even if racially distinct. In mining for underlying commonalities—the universal subtext of most "successful" (i.e., ha-inducing) jokes—Williams's cheekiness also affords laughter in multiple places; that is, on both an a-side and a b-side, or a foreground and a background—so long as one listens closely to what he said beforehand.

Williams actually begins this portion of his set by lampooning Blacks, a diplomatic move, by suggesting that they, as a collective, do not tip but might want to reconsider that seemingly cultural or stereotypical practice and donate to the Katrina relief effort (see endnote xvii). Here, race or Blackness, in particular, absorbs class by framing service-related frugality as a "Black [cultural] thing"; also, Black folks and he, himself by association, get taken down a peg via this self-deprecating maneuver. Then, he turns his loving chide on poor Whites who ignored evacuation warnings but were nonetheless shocked by the storm's predicted and actual devastation. His use of "rednecks" and "niggahs"—racial and class-marked slurs on the a-side— are lovingly flipped as geographically and blood-tie-loyal foils on the b-side; Williams's deft play thus marshals a critique that endears and appreciates both groups' disproportionate racial and economic vulnerability in the wake of Katrina while privileging his right to speak as a fellow marginalized [Black] man). Perhaps another reason his joke "works" is because not too many of us can argue with his comedic depictions without seeming classist or elitist; roots matter, he affirms, especially when one considers NOLA as a historic port city and internationally renowned tourist site in America, as well as "home" to such die-hard New Orleanians as the ones he caricatures.

I actually think Williams's play on Black-White differences and similarities has yet another b-side, one that winks toward "a" real Black under the cover of Black humor—the dark kind. Before he launched into this ingratiating part of his set wherein no one, not even Black Katrina victims, are immune from tough-loving critique, he'd told his predominantly White and often uncomfortable-looking audience, "Some of ya'll have never seen a nigga excited before. So I'ma just show you. I'ma make you honorary niggas tonight so you can see what—Here's a niggah happy," and did a quick iteration of the 1980s "running-man" dance. Williams then segued into a joke about White folks' fearlessness of wild animals, a familiar premise in Black standup comedy. For me, this moment in Williams's set hints yet again at an a- and a b-side, one that daringly flirts with racial caricature; in essence, he leverages himself as a petite, agile Black man dancing quite well before a predominantly White audience to stage a more explicit tease of White folks who he (and many other Black folk) fears are way too comfortable around wild animals. I read his dance break as an angst-riddled wink to the behind-the-scenes dynamics of hurricane relief efforts[19]—the very ones lampooned by Luenell—if not a snide performance of Black folk's ability to dance in the midst of a storm (or, at least in this very telethon replete with its own set of subjective "hit and misses"). Said another way, while seemingly self-deprecating insofar as he enlists his own body and physical agility to literally "dance for White folks," Williams's "running man" may have also been a sly way of thumbing his nose at the stark disparity between this Katrina fundraiser's racial demographics (i.e., primarily White, comics inclusive) and the storm's predominantly poor Black victims. To me, back then and especially now, in the wake of Trump's presidency, all of these reads exemplify the prospective ha's and aha's of Katt's jokes—where the "ha" gives us something we all can laugh about and the "aha" beckons us to consider laughter's limitations—all while begging the question: and the joke, now, is on whom?

Namely, the racial and classed fault lines exposed by Hurricane Katrina risk foreclosing Williams's expansive appeal, or abets yet additional interpretations of his joke. For example, it might well be argued, with tragic irony of course, that poor Whites suffered by association with poor Blacks insofar as their

Whiteness alone could not save them. "Niggahs" and "rednecks" suffered together post-Katrina not only due to their shared impoverishment but chiefly given anti-Blackness. What an ironic trick bag race presents, such jokes suggest, often followed by rueful laughter and applause. Ah; but even here, the specter of false equivalency rears its ugly head with sobering truths: while poor Whites, whom Williams labels "rednecks," were adversely affected by Katrina, they were not impacted to the degree that Blacks were. In fact, some Whites in neighboring parishes, ones whom outsiders might even call "rednecks," shot Blacks and threatened Black neighbors who they assumed were looters—with impunity no less—when they (Blacks) sought refuge and aid beyond the Superdome.[20] Studies also show that NOLA has become both White and richer, that Whites of all socioeconomic backgrounds say they're "better off" after Katrina, and that poor Blacks have not returned to the city to the same degree as have White residents, poor or otherwise.[21] In *We Were Eight Years in Power: An American Tragedy,* famed author and social critic Ta-Nehisi Coates vigorously dispels the myth we seem loath to concede: poor Blacks and poor Whites are aligned less by class and more accurately distinguished by poor Whites' claim and purchase of White supremacy. Williams's hyper-performed set inflects all of these realities and potentialities, animating the racial anxieties underlying this televised benefit.

Why We Got to Be "Looters"?

Other riffs flowed in accord with the storm's dictates and revelations, including the media's description of some Black New Orleanians as "looters" in explicit contrast to media depictions of Whites as "finders," photographed in identical poses (see Figure 2.2); editorial cartoonist Keith Knight (and several comic TV hosts at the time, including Carlos Mencia and Jon Stewart) satirized the Associated Press's contradictory briefs by reproducing the images and pointedly asking readers, via caption, "Can you spot the difference between looting and finding?" (see Figure 2.3). His strictly rhetorical caption invites readers to see and explicitly name race, even if in their minds, as an unnamed logic behind the AP's racially discrepant depictions.

Black comics hastened to ask and answer Keith Knight's meta-rhetorical and sartorial question in their own way through comedic counternarratives or jokes that exposed the "looters versus finders" trope in mainstream media as fundamentally racist—with life or death consequences for those deemed unempathetic as "looters." They also marshaled empathy for Black Katrina victims via decidedly in-group critiques of alleged looters, sometimes

A young man walks through chest deep flood water after *looting* a grocery store in New Orleans on Tuesday, August 30, 2005.

Two residents wade through chest-deep water after *finding* bread and soda from a grocery store after Hurricane Katrina came through the area in New Orleans, Louisiana.

Figure 2.2. Associated Press, 2005.

https://www.apimages.com/metadata/Index/Associated-Press-Domestic-News-Louisiana-United-/01519ba441e1da11af9f0014c2589dfb/11/0 AP Photo/Dave Martin (top); https://www.gettyimages.com/detail/news-photo/two-residents-wade-through-chest-deep-water-after-finding-news-photo/53509740 Photo by Chris Graythen/Getty Images (bottom).

Figure 2.3. Editorial Cartoon Satirizes AP's Transom, 2005.
https://kchronicles.com/store/buy-reprint-rights.html The Official K Chronicles.

delivering their chides like "tough love" discipline, and other times flipping the script entirely via masterful turns of play.

For example, Wells offered up empathy with a "tough love" chaser at a subsequent show in October 2005 wherein he channeled angst into hope by dismissing the media's charge of "looting" and calling forth Katrina victims' (and arguably Black folks' overall) resiliency like an agentive prayer:

[looking down at the floor while shaking his head woefully] It's fucked up right now . . . but they [Katrina victims] gon' make it. . . . They just gon' make it. . . . The majority of them people are Black. We know that and it's fucked up. And it's some White people out there too but it's some bullshit going on. . . . But . . . they not looting; they're surviving. . . . You gotta do what you gotta do. . . . [*rhetorically and emphatically*] "Niggah, I'm hungry?! I ain't ate?! . . . Niggah, it's a Walmart?! Niggah I steal NOW and it ain't even nothing going on. Niggah, I'm not gonna NOT EAT! . . . I'm crashing windows just like them." . . . And so, they're just tryna survive. . . . But at the same time, the niggah with the TV should be shot right here [*points at his neck*]. . . . This niggah is in Walmart like this [*picks up stool onstage and totes it gleefully*] . . . Niggah, you ain't even got no where to shit and you got a big screen TV?!

Wells's joke merits further unpacking if only to best appreciate how he and other comics explicitly invoke an "us/we" versus "they/them" to empathize poor Black Katrina victims, or, in the case of at least a few comics, entirely re-brand the apathetic subject of the Black "looter"—those stealing questionable items like TVs and, sadly, fishing poles—as empathetic indeed. Wells begins his joke with a hopeful lament (i.e., "It's fucked up right now . . . but they [Katrina victims] gon' make it. . . . They just gon' make it.") and not-so-veiled reference to the racial dynamics of the storm (i.e., "The majority of [Katrina victims] are Black. . . . And it's some white people out there too, but it's some bullshit going on"). This transitions into an indictment of media logics that help legitimate Black storm victims' subsequent exile, both figuratively through the label "refugee," and literally via their dispersal to other parts of the nation with little chance of return. His declaration, "It's some bullshit going on," is but another way to say, "It's some <u>racist</u> bullshit going on" to an already knowing Black crowd. Most important, Wells also forefronts empathy by identifying with so-called looters at the level of "I" and "we" by literally placing himself within a comparable scene; in doing so, he is in no way apologetic and, in fact, employs double-negatives to underscore his point (i.e., "Niggah, I'm not gonna NOT EAT!") and potentially damning confession (i.e., I'm crashing windows just like them); his joke all but declares: "I would've done the same thing too and maybe even worse!"

Wells's alignment with the seeming foils of Hurricane Katrina illustrates one way comics can soften the tenor of their impending critiques of vulnerable subjects, as well as identify and empathize with them. His ability to see Katrina victims in terms of himself without co-opting their experience, though, is an ultimate act of empathy.[22] Additionally, his shifting use of "niggah," marked by his emphasis on the deictic "this" signals Wells's most-calibrated empathy, and likewise requires his audience's diligent attention, and ours too, in order to decipher when his use of "niggah(s)" is all-encompassing, empathetic, or critical.

If we keep looking closely, staying with him as he mines humor from tragedy in real time, we'll see that Wells's initial use of the term is all-encompassing, gathering him, his audience, and Black Katrina victims into a collective. Here, the n-word does double-duty as a collective signifier of a "we" that forever hints at the term's more racist connotations. Still, his use of this highly charged and arguably more capacious term is less an endorsement of the n-word's racist logics and antecedents that it is a wry wink or signal to Black audiences who are ever-cognizant of how they are viewed by racist or otherwise ignorant others. Audiences (and readers like you) must likewise "keep up" with the n-word's multiple significations, especially since, later in his set, Wells sets up a more charged and critical iteration of the n-word; that is, he deploys "niggah" in a disciplining "tough love" kind of way, thus calibrating empathy for Black Katrina victims who engaged in cost-free scavenging.

Wells's emphatic and shifting uses of the n-word also usher in a decidedly in-group tenor that suggests, "Let's talk on a communal level," given both his audience's demographics (i.e., Black) and existing social mores governing who can and cannot use the n-word with impunity. Having established this intimate frame, Wells then castigates select "looters" through his artful, "tough love" deployment of the deictic "*this*" to reference "*This* niggah" in Walmart. Audiences must again keep up to properly decipher who "niggah" is *affectively* and further realize that "niggah," in the early part of this joke, encompasses everyone in his predominantly Black audience but becomes more isolating and critical when prefaced by the deictic "this" to castigate "real" looters who happen to be Black.[23] Wells closes by way of a caveat—"But at the same time, the niggah with the TV should be shot right here" [*points at his neck*]—effectively distinguishing "good" versus "bad" [Black] looters here, but with a trace of grace that was harder to see in newscasters who did the same thing.

If we stay with Wells (and you a bit longer with the linguistic anthropologist in me), we can further unpack the "how" and "why" of his artful comedic labor: namely, Wells deploys pronouns to signal both his personal identification with Black "looters" in New Orleans, and the interconnectedness of him, his audience, and Black Katrina victims. The joke travels from a "they" to a "we," to a "you," and, eventually, to an "I," ultimately concluding from these various collectivizing and personal vantage points, and pivots: "So, they're [Black "looters"] just tryna survive." His pronominals (e.g., they, we, you) further aid as reference points in this joke, helping audiences affectively determine which "niggah" is being invoked and also their relationship to them. As an African American man, Wells is ever-aware that the questionable looter occupies the same proverbial boat as the so-called moral looter; in Wells's mind, both affect one another at a pragmatic and heart level. They are in the same proverbial boat. It might be said that he throws the "niggah with the TV" in the flood waters as an unrespectable casualty since they, by virtue of their recorded "sins," threaten to capsize the whole boat. But his contempt for this looter is leavened by a rhetorical first-person appeal (i.e., "Niggah, you ain't even got nowhere to shit and you got a big screen TV?!") versus a top-down third-person critique. Said another way, he directs his reproof, rhetorically at least, *to* the questionable looter versus dissing him in the third-person (e.g., "THIS niggah ain't even got nowhere to shit and he got a big screen TV?!"); in this oh-so-subtle way, his first-person scold enacts tough love that is, in many ways, attendant to the imperative of respectability when (or since) White people and the world are watching. Moreover, Wells's use of "niggah" lubricates his appeal to respectability given its enduring rewards for Blacks, especially those who are deemed "looters" and "refugees," if not "niggahs again" per Ray Chatman's joke about the Washington, DC, snipers in Chapter 1. And this makes all the difference—keeping "tough" love and empathy afloat in even his comedic caveat.

Like Wells, D. L. Hughley also distinguished "real" looters from industrious Katrina victims during his televised set on Comedy Relief 2006:[24]

And if he [a Katrina victim] was stealin' clothes and food, he wasn't lootin'! That was survivin'! However, that one motherfucker that was pushing that plasma TV through six feet of water?; he was lootin' like a motherfuckah. . . . I'm like, "How the fuck you gon' steal a TV while you on TV? . . . And where are you gon' plug it in at? . . ." [*laughs*] And the biggest question [*parodying an agitated White person*],[25] "How come they didn't leave? They had plenty of warning. They should have left!" Well, in addition to the fact that that's the poorest place in the country, Black people . . . we really have a special relationship with God: [*impersonates Black person*] "God gon' give me a sign. God gon' let me know." And He will. But you got to stop looking for the big shit like the burning bushes and the rumbling clouds. Sometimes God just send a weatherman saying, "All this shit right here, is about to go down the street. . . . That's from the book of Doppler radar number 9-1-1. Get in the god-damned car."

Hughley's joke publicly scolds Blacks who took things that, according to conventional wisdom, might not serve them best in the context of their displacement. Still, like Wells, his critique is calibrated insofar as he issues it only after debunking the "refugee" label outright and rhetorically asking and then answering the question that, for many critical onlookers and the ever-astute Katt Williams, precluded empathy toward Katrina victims stuck on roofs and in the Superdome: namely, why didn't they leave New Orleans and other vulnerable areas along the Gulf when instructed? His disciplining critique thus makes his bid to respectable behavior a caveat, rather than a pre-requisite, to his broader call to love and save. In essence, by fronting empathy, he doesn't make rescue contingent on Black Katrina survivors' "good" behavior, nor does he silence his own voice by critiquing some spoils of the hurricane as suspect. The fact that Hughley issues this corrective on television also serves to discipline a wider and diverse audience toward another perspective, a counternarrative, that recuperates unempathetic Black storm victims to a place of lovability so that they might be saved not just by donations but something more priceless and enduring: empathy.

Other comedians appealed to notions of racial authenticity or "real Blackness" with nary a care about matters of respectability and with utmost concern for empathy. Rod Man Thompson, bless his heart, is one of them who hilariously recast Blacks deemed "looters" as astute, resilient, industrious; in essence, "real" Black. His joke made me cry laughing but for its resonance and redemptive holding, further coaxing my (and perhaps his audience's) appreciation for the promise of "a" real Black. Both the "looters" charge and the "refugee" label threw many Black folks for a heart-crushing loop, especially when the media seemed to embrace and use it repeatedly, sanctioning both decrees as actual and factual. In this way, the "looters" designation (or, rather, symbolic "charge") seeds the conditions of possibility for their forced exile—being rooted not only in natural disaster but also in unrespectable and consequential behavior: unempathetic subjects don't get to be citizens.[26] Thompson seemed especially hip to this trick bag during his set at The Comedy Union in October 2005, just weeks after Hurricane Katrina made landfall in New Orleans and Mississippi, when he confessed:

> I wish I was in Katrina. I need to go through a nice ass flood. These niggahs bout to do the best in life. We don't do well in water. That shit depressed me. I cried listening to Hardy L. Jackson (who'd lost his wife in the flood). Katrina, that's a Black ass name.[27] It's a Black thing. We resilient. This too shall pass.

Just as Wells's and Thomas's jokes strategically weave their way toward comedic punchlines with funny revelations about themselves, their foibles, and comic sensibilities in order to empathize themselves and their comedic subjects (e.g., Katrina victims), Thompson deftly flirts with danger via his candor but calibrates it toward comic gold with well-placed empathetic stances. Namely, his feigned desire to have been in Katrina may, at first blush, appear as callous as Barbara Bush's controversial speculation that Katrina survivors might in fact fare better in exile than they had in Louisiana (revisit Figure 2.1) or other callous and patronizing jokes that emerged in Katrina's wake (e.g., "Why did the Black man jump? To get to the next roof.") Yet, by centering empathy, he avoids making a joke purely at Katrina victims' expense by situating himself as in need of a "nice ass flood"—an oxymoron at best. He also makes generalizations, a la Alex Thomas, D. L. Hughley, and another comic I'll soon discuss (Paula Bel), about Black folks' discomfort in water, tricking racial essentialism—this idea that ALL Blacks do xyz—toward comedic recognition of some Blacks' discomfort in water. Moreover, he also outs his own depression and empathy for Hardy Jackson, a Katrina victim whose wife was taken by the flood when he lost hold of her hand,[28] even as he observes the racial nature of the hurricane's racialized name and Black' folks penchant for resilience and faith. In this way, Thompson bestows empathy before launching a counternarrative to the "looters versus finders" trope. In the parlance of my Millennial/Generation Y students, his joke gives "zero fucks" about respectability (despite its life-saving capacity) and compels his audience to feel the same; listen:

> [They] was tryna say we was looting. . . . Cause White people like to use code words for stealing. . . . I don't know where they get this "looting" shit at. . . . Just regular ass. [*assumes voice of a Black so-called "looter"*] "We going in here and get some shit." That's all it is. You know yeah, "I ain't got no shit. I need some shit." . . . Yeah but they tried to give us approval on certain things that we can get you know. Like a niggah could see a TV [and thus hear news reports]. We couldn't see a TV; we didn't know what was approved. . . . 'Cause they was like, [*impersonates an earnest White TV reporter*] "If you're getting water or Pampers for your babies, that's cool . . . but tennis shoes and T.V.'s, that's out." You know. "That's . . . gon' be stealing right there." [*drops caricature*] Niggah don't care 'cause we think ahead. We are forward thinkers. . . . Cause people was like, "Aww, they getting them TV's and ain't no power!" ' Well, it ain't no power today. You know. . . . It ain't no power today.

As with the jokes discussed before, Thompson rouses laughter and lessons concerning empathy, the limits of respectability, and the imperative of "real" Blackness. Namely, Thompson's sardonic quip normalizes and even moralizes "stealing" amid the hunger, financial strain, and compounded chaos of natural disaster (i.e., federal government inefficacy). He also generously collapses Black Katrina survivors within a collective "we," effectively linking their fates with those of his Black audience. The way he gestures away from respectability toward empathy still cracks me up, saving a part of my fractured soul. Thompson remixes Black-White racial difference, a canonical trope in Black humor that exaggerates and essentializes the way Black and White folks differ and frequently stages Black or underdog one-upmanship by any means possible as a path to victory and redemption. While "Whites" are admittedly absented from explicit comparison here, they no doubt linger in the backdrop as [mainstream] "media," inspiring this counternarrative to the representational hazard of the "Black looter." He begins this joke by slamming his loyalty cards on the table (i.e., "They was tryna say we was lootin" . . .) before offering a cheeky gloss that stresses yet another "truth" at the generalized expense of "White folks" (i.e., "'Cause White folks like to use code words for stealing"). Here, Thompson's use of "stealing" works double-time by acknowledging the cost-free scavenging of Black Katrina survivors as "stealing" indeed, as well as inferentially highlighting how White Katrina survivors who were engaged in the same practice got graciously and differentially tagged as "finders." The rest of Thompson's quip normalizes and rationalizes the behavior of Black Katrina survivors who nabbed what they felt they needed in the absence of governmental aid. Further, as he animates them, he enacts a translation that doesn't mince words or is not duplicitous or insincere in describing what they essentially did. His "we"-drenched joke basically says, "Kindly ignore what you've heard about so-called Black looters. Not only do they and other Black folks do what they must do in dire circumstances, they/we are also forward-thinking and enterprising, as opposed to exploitative, idiotic, immoral or otherwise shady thinkers." Notably, Thompson's comedic revision of the "Black looter [not finder]" script does not rely on respectability to redeem Black Katrina survivors as empathetic; rather, in order to coalesce those who, say, nabbed TVs and tennis shoes instead of Pampers and baby food, he seems to eschew respectability altogether—or at the very least cheekily rebrand it, thus holding Black Katrina victims and his Black (live) audience firmly in heart and hand.[29]

Thompson also excavates a new riff from what is actually an old comedic play in the African American comedic archive. In August 1965, following the Watts Riots, late comic-activist Dick Gregory quipped on national television: "I just got back from Los Angeles, Vietnam. I saw a Negro carrying a couch. I asked him, 'Are you a looter?' He said, 'No, I'm a furniture salesman.'" Notice, first, a similarity: as with Thompson's sly wit, Gregory's joke acknowledges the questionable survival tactics of some Blacks during the riots and alludes to Black looters' capacity for strategy and industrious (e.g., long-term thinking). Notice, as well, a discrepancy: whereas Thompson harnesses empathetic recognition to redemptively recast Black looters in Katrina as industrious and worthy of empathy—respect even—Gregory's joke lands a bit harder; perhaps because he's on national TV during another tumultuous time, Gregory expertly calibrates his humor such that it's hard(er) for audiences to tell whether he is being cynical or celebratory of the looter's retort. Herein lies his genius in affording multiple a- and b-side reads for an audience that encompasses mainstream America (i.e., Whites) and another constituency—Black folks—capable of hearing this joke a different way.[30] Both Gregory and Thompson likewise play in a similar field of re-writing morality scripts for Black folks strained by poverty, limited economic opportunities, natural disaster, and the government's passive indifference to their plight. Said another way, Gregory endows the Black looter of the 1960s with speculative trickster voice and acuity, while Thompson boldfaces the looter's trickster acuity and long-rage thinking via his winking comedic sensibility. Further, Gregory affords room for both respectful regard and critique—perhaps utterly necessary to grease the reception of his racial satire in the '60s—for the Black male looter (or hustler). Thompson, however, disavows respectability and even in-group critique to instead suggest a counternarrative that asks, rhetorically of course, "What do you mean by calling them/us insipid "looters"?! We are resilient and industrious!"

Having spent some time unpacking how comics' jokes center empathy and lovability, let's return to the question of audience. By audience, I mean to include readers like you who may wonder why Black audiences laugh with equal fervor at jokes that both love and lampoon looters (think of Wells's and Hughley's questioning of Katrina survivors who nabbed TVs instead of, say, Pampers), and jokes (like Thompson's) that seem to thumb their nose at respectability-steeped caveats and, instead, trump the underdog. I think the answer rests in each joke's comedic affordances: ultimately, both comedic perspectives reconcile Blacks as empathetic subjects versus "looters," a damning designee that nulls their citizenship and associated entitlements by rooting them out of house and home (the nation) because of their perceived disrespectful behavior. Additionally, both comedic stances coalesce bids to authenticity—as in, this is what "real" Black folks do when faced with tragedy and no aid—sometimes with caveated bids to respectability (e.g., "the niggah with the fishing pole should be shot in the neck") and other times by denouncing descriptions of Black Katrina victims as reckless "looters" via unapologetic bids to authenticity; the unapologetic bids salute Blacks' supposed penchant for "making do" and "doing what one must do," thus saving them from the storm's representational traps and snares. Whether routed through respectability or disavowing it altogether, both appeals thus "work" as retorts, caveats, and counternarratives to popular and political discourses that pathologize and abnegate Black folks' humanity in troubled times. Both bestow empathy to Black storm survivors at a time when it was sorely lacking, aggravating their premature and quite public death.

There's more on the b-side—the extra-situational factors—stuff just out of the frame of the audible (i.e., what we can hear) —that Thompson's joke, in particular, suggests. For me, his joke seems to answer a tacit question at the heart of comics' calibrated empathy and bids to sincerity and realness (e.g., racial authenticity): namely, what does it matter when even so-called good behavior doesn't make a bit of difference in Blacks' fates? What are Black Americans to do if and, increasingly, when empathy alone does not save them/us? Then, perhaps, it doesn't matter what we/they do, nor should we/they act like it should. And maybe, as Thompson's joke and some young #BlackLivesMatter activists suggest to me: fuck respectability altogether, and instead mine the b-side of "a" real Black to unearth Black ingenuity and resilience.

"Failed" Katrina Humor: Bracketing Empathy and Salvaging Bids to "a" Real

Black comics won laughter by nodding toward respectability and damning it altogether, but few comics of any race managed to coax laughter from Katrina humor devoid of empathy. Black audiences, in particular, weren't having it, and overwhelmingly chided comics of all races whom they felt dolled it out too conservatively. Take DeRay Davis, the hilarious and intrepid host of the Hollywood Improv's *Mo' Better Monday Show* (since rebranded as MonDeRays); when he criticized storm victims for remaining in NOLA despite last-minute evacuation orders, his audience bristled aloud—likely because flood waters still clogged the arteries of New Orleans's streets. Ever audacious, Davis redeemed the joke by appealing to bids to authenticity or, more precisely, "keeping it real."

Similarly, Paula Bel, a bodacious White comedienne who frequently rips in Black rooms and clubs, earned audible groans when she questioned, preemptively I think, the sincerity of Black audience members' rage during her sets at The Comedy Store's second-year anniversary "Crack 'Em Up Thursday" Show and The Laugh Factory's *Chocolate Sundaes* [sic] Show." She started her set this way: "We don't give a fuck!" Almost immediately, a Black man sitting next to me leaned over and said, "It ain't right" and recommended that the red (i.e., "finish your set") light be turned on for her. Fearless, Bel continued:

> Fuck those people. You were born in a swamp, and you can't fuckin swim. [*feigns sympathy toward audience members who didn't laugh*] Oh I'm sorry. Do you have family over there? And you're here yucking it up while your family floats on a lawn chair—fuck you!

Unlike the prior jokes, Bel then softens her disciplining of both Katrina victims and audience members who might understandably have problems with her humor. Her caustic delivery, part and parcel of her shtick (and at times belied by her self-conscious and self-deprecating smile) don't do her any favors in this regard, but her empathizing personal testimony about a near-death experience at the end of her joke does. Hear her:

> People say, "I can't believe this is America!" I live in a bigoted racist America. What the fuck was so shocking about Black people crying for help?! And why is it that the poorest folks in America are always the largest? We see some 600-pound mother-fucker waiting to be picked up by a picnic basket. You been snacking on Zataran's all year. . . . I'm 39 years old. I'm almost 40 years old! I got hit head on at Fountain Avenue. I was near dead. But just as I was going down, I felt something hot nearby. I know where I'm going. . . . I know it's a little harsh . . . but yeah, you're gonna die bitch . . . I'm Paula Bel. Goodnight.

Humor scholars affirm what many of us already know and feel: if they want to win audience laughter and comic loyalty, comics should avoid kicking folks when they're down. (At least not the "empathetic" ones).[31] When and if they do purposely flaunt societal expectations regarding the proper care and comedic treatment of folks in duress (i.e., ignore respectability decrees and their disciplining imperatives on Black bodies), comics risk getting booed and, nowadays, "canceled." To mitigate against these risks, comics like Bel (and Davis earlier) brashly appeal to "realness" to coax laughter from reluctant audiences. Bel, in particular, calibrates her audacity by questioning the sincerity of her primarily Black audience's presumed empathy—that is, their willingness to "hold as if one's own" versus "yuk it up as their relatives float in the water."[32] Bel also preserves her comedic authority throughout her set via bold unapologetic posturing—a brave thing in this crowd, eventually earning a spattering of laughter and applause. She gets by, I believe, on the strength of her fiery resolve and sincerity, both of which signal something "real" or "authentic"; her veiled story about a near-death experience also functions as an endearing personal testimony that further validates her "right to speak" candidly.[33] When she figuratively delivers herself, and maybe even audience members who laughed at her jokes—again, it's deliciously hard to tell—to a future hell, she harnesses the subversive power of innuendo alongside the transgressive intensity of the expletives "fuck" and "bitch" to convey her angry cynicism about Katrina's equally hellish reveals concerning race and class.[34] Along the way, she even risks chiding "the victim" by conjuring an overweight Katrina victim whose "snacking on Zataran's all year" and inability to swim required air rescue by the blessed US Coast Guard.[35] Through it all, Black audiences get a sense from Bel's dark humor that, contrary to her belligerent demeanor, she cares deeply about the world and maybe even the folks she seemingly condemns; moreover, her final remarks winkingly chide audience members, implying that those who laughed at her jokes may be just as guilty as she for telling them—coaxing their laughter yet again.

Davis and Bel weren't the only comics whose daring jokes about Katrina aroused explicit back talk given a presumed lack of empathy toward Katrina victims and/or a controversial marshaling of racial authenticity. Carlos Mencia managed to draw fire from Black audiences and comics alike during his former Comedy Central show, *Mind of Mencia*, which aired between 2005 and 2008; in 2006 (Hurricane Katrina struck in 2005), he posed the rhetorical and admittedly "tough" question, "Why are we re-building New Orleans?! . . . Whose idea was this, Aqua Man?!," as a setup for a succession of jokes that tough-lovingly chided Black New Orleanians for daring to want to rebuild their city and preserve their culture. Mencia said he had no problem with "New Orleanites'" desire to preserve their culture (even though he mocked it via caricature) but suggested that they "move [their culture] like 200 feet away from [hits his head with microphone and strikes his signature pose suggestive of—and mocking—an intellectual disability] waterrrrr!!" [*predominantly Latino/Chicano TV audience claps*].

Mencia's joke was bold on numerous fronts, especially considering atrocious conditions in New Orleans's predominantly Black and poor Ninth Ward then (and now), as well as the show's ensuing music video parody of Kanye West's (2005) hit, "Gold Digger" (ft. Jamie Foxx) that was re-titled "Kanye West is a Crazy Ni**a." Mencia's spoof featured him, two unnamed Black female dancers (one plus-sized, one petite), and the ever-intrepid Black comic Arie Spears. (Neither Mencia nor Spears, who frequently parodies rap quite well, had a problem articulating "nigga" during the video.) Most folks in Mencia's viewing audience probably knew that, a year earlier, West famously stunned telethon viewers (and co-presenter Mike Myers) with his unscripted complaint: "George Bush doesn't care about Black people," which Alex Thomas revamped for comedic effect as "George Bush don't give a fuck about niggahs." (Here again, the n-word carries the sting of racial castigation but washes it clean via Thomas's and [Rod Man] Thompson's empathetic stance toward the "niggahs" in question.) However, Mencia's spoof in no way celebrates West's intrepid remarks about the hurricane during that 2005 telethon; instead, Mencia lampooned West for being cocky, whiny, entitled, and racially inauthentic, even suggesting, at one point, that then-president George Bush was more "hood" than West since he had "Condoleezza [Rice]," among other put-downs impugning West's 'hood' credentials or racial "realness." Note, too, how Mencia marshals trite notions of racial authenticity, specifically those that wed "real Blackness" with stereotypical allusions to "the hood" to stoke the occasional "ha" of incongruity: West, a Black rapper, becomes racially "inauthentic" in comparison to President Bush if even at the controversial expense of then-secretary of state Rice, who is rendered the president's "Black ho."

By all palpable (i.e., televised) signs, Mencia's humorous appeals seemed to hit their mark, but his ensuing jokes during this episode ultimately earned him public reproof.[36] Mencia said, "Black people, you're fuckin' funny. . . . [Y]ou will get on a bus to go to Million Man March, but you won't get on a bus to get away from [*hits microphone on his head to further underscore the foolish and questionable nature of Black Katrina victims who remained in NOLA*][37] Katrina! That's funny to me. That's hilarious.," Then he chastised White folks for not laughing at the joke or ethnic humor more broadly (and in a manner similar to Bel's chastising of Black audience members who silently disliked her opening line, "We don't give a fuck!"). Mencia then zeroed in on the elephants in the room:

> Black people are pissed. I don't know if you know this. Did you know that Black people were pissed cause they said that [*animates tough-sounding Black male voice*] "Yey-hey-hey! If you're gonna rebuild New Orleans [*pats chest*], we wanna have a part in rebuilding it!" [*cynically*] "Uh . . . [*points toward a Black audience member*] No. [*audience laughter*] I love you Black people, but you cannot help in the rebuilding of New Orleans. You cannot have anything to do with rebuilding the city. Two reasons: Detroit. Oakland. [*audience laughter*] We gave them two chances and both times—dunh dunh duuhhh [*strikes his canonical intellectually challenged pose*]—you screwed it up. Sorry, but you can't have it this time." [*audience applause; caricaturing imaginary intellectually challenged Black Katrina survivor*] "We wanna rebuild New Orleans!" "Shut up! No, you don't! Just be quiet, let the 'beaners' do it, and enjoy that plasma that you [*gestures quote marks*] 'rescued' during Katrina." [*audience laughter and applause*]

Mencia appeared to win applause from his predominantly Latino/Chicano audience for this stretch of his set too. Notice how he exploits the "looter" trope to juxtapose so-called "beaners" with Blacks in America. He also demonstrates how the "looting" charge leveled by the media against some Black Katrina survivors (which he, himself, preemptively questioned) can be dangerously generalized to all Black survivors and residents, deeming them unempathetic and even, ironically, insincere in their bids to return to and help rebuild the Big Easy. (One can likewise better appreciate Thompson's joke highlighting the forethought of a Black looter nabbing a TV; in many ways, it's a preemptive counternarrative to Mencia's damning quips and characterizations.) Mencia is a comedian but not a fool; sensing the risky nature of his jokes, he then waxed unapologetic, issuing three signature words and further exposition:

> I said it. [*audience laughter*] "Beaners" are the ones that are going to New Orleans now. Ye(hh)a(hh):::h. Cause Black people are like, "We wanna rebuild." [*cynically*] Do you really want to rebuild Bro'? N::o. You want to design. That's what you should've said. We want to design this city. Black people don't want to [*gestures quote marks*] "build" it. I'm not tryna saying Black people are lazy or anything. All I'm saying is, you and I, right now, let's go to Home Depot, see how many Black people we find in the front. [*audience laughter*] That's all I'm saying. That's all I'm saying. That's all I'm saying. That's all I'm saying. [*audience laughter and applause*]

Then, by way of a cloaked caveat, he offered this:

> But by the way. I don't blame you bro. I don't blame you. If my people had been enslaved for 400 years, I'd take a little time off after that shit too. And you know a lot of people say that, "Man, Black people are lazy." No they're not; 400 years of working every single day for free. That is a lot of accrued vacation time. We never gave them a mule and 40 acres. And the United States of America, though we apologized to Japanese people for putting them in an internment camp for a few years, we never said I'm sorry to Black people. So, I say you get to get the day off until 2012. That's when it (is)/(ends). Until 2012—Black people, look at me: Until 2012, just run free and go, "Carlos said it!" Just run free. Just go. But but wait. After 2012, you gotta work, bitch. After that, that's when it's like, gotta go cha-ching. Go to Home Depot, whatever you need to do. But they, you guys aren't doin' it. The "beaners" are.

I want to again appreciate Mencia's comedic stylings and affective labor even as I discuss what many perceived to be his most critical omission: empathy and sincerity—that affective tone and stance that subtexted much of the Katrina humor I observed, even among Black and Latino comics who told jokes quite similar to Mencia's.[38] To start, Mencia's use of "beaners," a racial slur for Latino immigrants, is tactical, much like Katt Williams's marshaling of "niggas" and "rednecks" during Comic Relief 2006 to lovingly chide (poor) Black and White Katrina victims for their post-storm fates. Mencia marks his alignment with "beaners" through his in-group use of the term while also assuming and brokering a comradery with the "Black people" he also lovingly chides. He does this in a manner similar to comics discussed earlier, namely, Thea Vidale (i.e., "White people, I love you dearly. I do. But Osama bin Laden—he ain't mad at us, he mad at y'all") and Katt Williams (i.e., "White people, we love you. Black people love you White people . . ."), by first confessing his love for Black people and then delivering "hard truths," leavened by a dash of historical knowledge of past American atrocities (i.e., Japanese American internment during World War II) and a rebuttal of a central stereotype underlying anti-Blackness (i.e., "And you know a lot of people say that, 'Man, Black people are lazy.' No, they're not. 400 years of working every single day for free. That is a lot of accrued vacation time. We never gave them a mule and 40 acres.") Despite his artful labor, Mencia's joke nonetheless managed to offend Black New Orleanians, many of whom have been dispersed like "refugees" and, unlike the Mexican immigrant population (which Mencia exaggeratingly concedes, has grown by "300%" but actually grew by 40% in the year following Hurricane Katrina), might never be able to return to their hometowns again.[39] There's more: Mencia's joke acknowledges but ultimately trivializes slavery's enduring impact on the lives of African Americans as well as the multiple socioeconomic, political, and historical factors contributing to the decline (or gentrification, in the case of Oakland, California, where I grew up) and the slow revitalization of US cities like Detroit, Michigan. Worst, his joke suggests that Black Americans do not want to work when, in fact, many evacuees clearly did and still do, and would help rebuild NOLA if merely afforded an opportunity.

When read against jokes by Davis and Bel, the two comics discussed earlier, we see a common theme. In targeting storm victims, empathy sits precariously in their critiques of them, almost like a caveat; this is why they audaciously appeal to hard truth and racial authenticity, with mixed success, in order to redeem themselves and their jokes. Their experiences, or, rather, audiences' responses, remind us of the fraught dance that is standup comedy: both comics and audiences must agree to the twirl, and audiences, in particular, always have the right to opt out.[40] They—Bel, Davis, and Mencia—also remind us about the work of joke-telling, especially when they implicate living breathing subjects who are widely perceived to be marginalized or vulnerable; audiences bristling against jokes that berate or lampoon Black Katrina victims likewise prove that some jokes "work" whereas others may be perceived as divisive, due to an insufficient degree of expected empathy and/or limitations on comics' presumed "right to speak." Their mixed comedic fates remind us, too, of how audiences determine (with audible consequence—that is, laughter or worst, silence or "un-laughter") whether comics' valiant attempts to make difficult subjects funny will pass muster.

It bears noting that several Black comics also celebrated the venerated work ethic of "Mexicans" in and around the time of Hurricane Katrina. Cedric the Entertainer remarked on his short-lived variety TV show on FOX, *Cedric the Entertainer Presents*,

A lot of folk are tryna say Black folks and Latinas are the same. I dunno. 'Cause if you think about slavery, . . . Latinos work too hard. Master would be like, "Go pick that cotton." [*caricaturing an enslaved Latino*] "We already have." [*impersonating White master*] "Knit that sweater." [*impersonating enslaved Latino*] "Maria, show him the sweater." They'd mess it up for us. We're supposed to be out singing and praying. Can't we pray sometimes? Can't we sing a spiritual or something?[41]

Similarly, Sheryl Underwood remarked during the Bay Area Black Comedy Competition: "Black people don't sleep on the Mexicans. They could've rebuilt New Orleans in two days." Then, as if astute to media reports of escalating tensions between Blacks and Latinos/Chicanos—a scapegoating strategy that divides and conquers versus unifies—she added, "And Black people, we can't hate on them either." Resonant riffs flowed from comic Lil G, who quipped, "Jesus is Latino!," and Brandon Bowlin, who praised Mexicans' work ethic and added, "Us (i.e., Blacks) and Latinos together, the world is brown." More recently, during his 2017 Netflix Special, "Dave Chappelle: Equanimity and The Bird Revelation," Chappelle affirmed the subtext of the aforementioned jokes and Ian Edwards's 9/11 joke about the "Arab being the new 'nigger'":

America has a racial hot seat. I think we can all agree that that's the truth. And we can also agree that that hot seat is traditionally occupied by African Americans in general. African American men in particular. Although I concede that, in recent years, that seat has been occupied by . . . Mexicans. And I dare say Arabs. And we, the Black Americans, would like to thank you both for your sacrifice in the struggle. [*Audience roars*] We needed a goddamn break. We all go through something but at least I can leave my backpack some place. If you Arab and forget your backpack, you got about twenty minutes before they send that robot to blow your shit up. "You can kiss all that engineering homework goodbye Fuhaad." [He adds that the ones who have it the worst, though, are fat Black people being slain by salt.]

Suffice it to say, Chappelle's got empathy to give, even as a Black assailed subject ever cognizant that Black folks need a reprieve as the perpetual always-and-already "niggahs" discussed in 9/11 humor. So, too, did comic and frequent Comedy Union host Rodney Perry, who told me during a phone interview that he'd found Mencia's joke and even its concession about slavery to be particularly offensive since it unfairly equates the experiences and expectations of Black Americans with that of undocumented Mexican day laborers or recent Mexican immigrants. Worst, he felt that these kinds of sentiments create and then pit marginalized groups deemed by Whites (and often other racial and ethnic minorities) as "model minorities" against Black Americans who are contrastingly deemed "lazy," or otherwise unempathetic.[42] Rodney's concern, which I heard from other Black comedians like Brandon Bowlin, D. C. Curry, and Dannon Green, was this: What do jokes that ceremoniously pit Mexican immigrants against Black Americans do for people's perceptions of African Americans? Perry funneled his query to the stage at The Comedy Union in October 2006 even though he worried that his joke was derivative of a joke Chris Rock once told:[43]

> And we got to support the other minorities Black folks. See they be tryna divide and conquer us. Getting us all against the Mexicans. . . . Man support the Mexicans! [*polling audience*] Any Mexicans? [*to rest of audience*] Man, next time you see some Mexicans—niggah join 'em! . . . The Mexicans starting to march! Only problem I got with the way that we have been characterized with Mexicans is people'll say, "Mexicans, you know they doing all the work . . ." Like Black folk don't work. . . . Get the fuck out of here! We work! Niggah we worked 200 years! Niggah we worked! We put our time in! It's just they fucking turn you understand me? . . . It's the Mexicans' turn to work. . . . When they get through working, it's some Filipinos waiting to take they goddamn place.

Perry's joke is a shrewd retort to Mencia and others who would prematurely if not preemptively declare exile as, in fact, "good" for so-called Black "refugees" in order to accommodate a Mexican workforce who will accept less pay and no benefits, and risk racial profiling or, worse, forced exile themselves if deemed "undocumented" under Trump's restrictive immigration policies. Perry told me he felt obligated to say it because he felt Mencia's joke unfairly equates the experiences and expectations of Blacks with those of undocumented Mexican workers. His joke primarily concerns the political stakes of representation, specifically those who would deem Blacks "looters," "refugees," or in other ways ill-suited for employment and, further, not eligible even as US citizens. These concerns likewise bespeak the stakes of representation that undergird respectability politics, or bids to "good" behavior with the oft-futile hope that it might save our lives.

The following joke told in August 2002 by Evan Lionel during the live-taping of his "Too Real for Ya'll" show (now a CD) at The Comedy Union, also preempts the subtext of Mencia's humor:

Ya'll know they [Mexicans] be having jobs! . . . I love Mexican people. When I moved to L.A., all my neighbors were Mexican. . . . And they be they self. That's what I like about ya'll. Ya'll be yourself. Ya'll believe in family and ya'll [*predominantly Black audience*] should give it up for that. [*audience applauds*] Everybody can live at they house!! [*audience laughs*] . . . And they work! You ever see 'em?—And that's why I can't stand a motherfuckah that don't work 'cause I been working since I was 11. I can't stand a lazy motherfuckah who don't wanna get up and work! I been living on my own since I was 19; [at] 18 years old, I done had my own place. I respect ya'll "Hector" and "Juan" 'cause ya'll work. They be on the corner with fruit. It be 185 degrees! They don't wanna be there! But they don't give a fuck about what you think. They be like, "Fruit. Tamales. I got it all! . . . Roses, what you need?!"

Empathy for Mexican Americans and "undocumented" Mexican laborers in the United States remains a formidable through-line in Perry and Lionel's jokes. This empathy is cued "sincerely," much like Mencia's "I love you Black people BUT," showing again how sincerity can be leveraged to deliver tough lessons about personal and collective responsibility and accountability. But there's something else in Perry's joke, as well as jokes by few other African American comics, that is worth noting: an astute awareness of how these jokes participate in dividing racialized groups who sometimes compete, as Black and Mexicans do in New Orleans, for scarce resources and empathy as if their lives literally depend on it. They often do.

I and another comic I know and love, Brandon Bowlin, have since occupied many hours of each other's time discussing that what ails New Orleans, specifically its Ninth Ward, is not merely racist practices at play pre- and post-Hurricane Katrina, including cronyism, disaster capitalism, gentrification, and other policies that make it virtually impossible for poor African Americans to return to New Orleans and that put other African American homeowners who are unable to return at risk for losing their homes under the cloak of "imminent domain" and state seizure.[44] I knew his perspectives on these matters informed his onstage quips about Hurricane Katrina at Mixed Nuts Comedy Club and The Comedy Union, including this wry admission: "I'm sad about the folks down in New Orleans . . . but they can't stay at my house. They can't stay at my house," followed by a self-conscious laugh. We in his predominantly Black audience knew what he meant without him having to spell it out, especially given sensationalized reports at the time of Katrina evacuees exploiting the graciousness of residents in other cities who accommodated them.

Late one night as I stood outside talking to him in front of the former Mixed Nuts Comedy Club, he was approached by a Black man who said he was in

L.A. having fled Hurricane Katrina and, more recently, Hurricane Rita. It was clear from his inebriated affect that things remained uncertain in his life. It was also clear to him that Brandon's b-side chide didn't preclude love or empathy since he'd approached him post-show looking to connect in some way. As they chatted soulfully, I quietly backed out of the conversation and headed for home surer of something I hadn't sensed before—even though comics had hipped me to it when I'd first written about 9/11 humor back in 2002. It's this: some of the things comics say onstage are "real" comedically but not "real" in a generalizable way, as comics' impassioned caveats to my 9/11 piece showed me. This felt-epiphany got me thinking not merely about authenticity and how comics and audiences police the boundaries of acceptable humor that hinges on it, but also how they marshal sincerity, authenticity, and empathy to pull certain jokes off, solidify communal belonging and dis-belonging, and mark their and others' visibility or invisibility. This literal encounter between a comedian and a Hurricane Katrina survivor thus helped me better appreciate humor's many risks, including when laughter, or bids to it, seem to come at the "wrong place and time" or otherwise hit their mark with discriminating and feeling audiences. Important work happens in these fraught encounters; comics and audiences draw lines between what are acceptable or unacceptable jokes about Katrina that are contingent on comics' artful appeals and strategic enactments of empathy, sincerity, and authenticity; in doing so, they transform what might simply be understood as subjective affects—empathy, sincerity, and authenticity, into moral stances and political practice.

Summary (Or I Can't Believe I'm Here Now)

This chapter took the longest to write because it meant revisiting the angst-riddled humor that rattled hearts and sobered minds in a moment when anti-Blackness, xenophobia, sexism, and other diminishing discourses continuously cloud our skies and dull our horizons. For a moment, a long one actually, extending from 2005 on further to 2008 and longer still to 2019, I could see but not quite parlay how comics were marshaling sincerity and bids to authenticity to coax deep empathy for Black and other Katrina victims; I was stuck in my own despair crying for the first time aloud for a racism that wasn't broadcast for all the world to see. In this space of mourning and grief, I couldn't harness their resolve because the global spectacle of state-sanctioned Black death given what President Barack Obama called "passive indifference" overwhelmed me. So, too, did the senseless murder of Joe McKnight, a former USC football player and student of mine who was gunned down in New

Orleans, his birthplace, by a White man in a fit of road rage; this man who first shot McKnight from his car, and later stood over him as he lay dying and apologizing on the ground and shot him again *before* witnesses, was released hours afterward.[45] I couldn't write because I was watching my students grow increasingly numb from the cumulative narrative suggested by racial profiling pre- and post-9/11, state-sanctioned violence against unarmed Black persons in the intervening years, and, more recently, the 2016 election of US president Donald Trump; much like the despairing tale encapsulated in Chatman's and Wells's riffs, some of them took the election in relative stride as an apt chaser to Hurricane Katrina, if not #Black Lives Matter. (So, too, did comics Chris Rock and Dave Chappelle whose Blackness and star-power spoke volumes in a *Saturday Night Live* (*SNL*) sketch in which White liberals at an election-results viewing party slowly come undone while Rock and Chappelle remain nonplused; the joke, they suggest via their deadpanned response, is that Black folks were neither shocked nor felled by Trump's election win. Further, the contrast posed by their White liberal friends, whose optimism gives way to utter shock and awe as the poll results roll in, offers an honest and hilarious-but-for-its-incongruity window into how race shapes different ways of seeing and being in America.

Over time, however, writing this chapter as sincerely as I could became cathartic versus muddied by my own emotional turmoil and distress. Inspired by the visions and freedoms articulated in Afro-pessimism and affect studies, I stopped merely analyzing the way comics like Wells and Thompson literally "laugh to keep from crying" via their appeals to "a" real Black—which is to say, Black authenticity and sincerity. I didn't just chart how counternarratives flip damning scripts about Black lawlessness and so-natural-as-to-be-normalized fugitivity such that they spoke truth to power and fiercely held onto Black and other Hurricane Katrin a victims in their frank and utter abandonment. I started to feel them deep in my heart and let them teach and heal me in the present. I remembered, too, that many comics were beset with personal issues that asked more of them than their fledgling careers could provide during Hurricane Katrina; still, while momentarily felled by grief (as I was frequently during this research), they took their grievances to the stage to shout: They/we are not what they say we are! We are a resilient people and will survive even this! I see and hold onto you. I heard them in my own way as saying, effectively: So, you want to know, per W. E. B. Du Bois, "How does it feel to be a problem?" Let me *ha* tell *ha* you *har har* what that *haa haaaa* is like to have to be deemed "good" first in order to have your humanity count. Let me laugh at you and me while doing so and undermine the whole affair. Let me see, too, if, over time, I can get you to laugh with me, not just *at* me, about our shared suspension in the trick bag of race such that we all can be made whole. Because laughter may be the one thing that can set us free and hopefully not set us up. Once I was able to make this transition (or translation), laughter never felt so good, so collectivizing, so necessary! And I began to write again with an even fiercer commitment to "keeping real."[46] I began to write with a fuller understanding of what it means to fight for legibility from a place of vulnerability as if your very life depended on being seen as "empathetic," while knowing it very well does.

Hurricane Katrina clarified the stakes of race and representation, race and empathy, and Black folks' inescapable intersubjectivity or linked fates in times of tragedy and calm. Jokes screamed like fierce echoes of Du Boisian double consciousness stripped of respectability's politeness and stoked in naked rage. The aforementioned complexities often give rise to stances around authenticity, my unforsaken cry in this book, provoking counternarratives that resound as authenticity scripts, and even presume them, too. That's the tension or intricacy I hope to lay bare as I home in on moments wherein I realized, once again, how laughter can serve to hold and care for colored folks.

As major media outlets indicted Black Katrina victims as lawless looters, several Black comics revised these damning descriptions by celebrating Black Katrina victims as "real" Blacks (and sometimes beloved "niggahs") who were as industrious as they were resilient, and whose "eyes were watching God' instead of the weather channel or Mayor Nagin's much-belated evacuation before Hurricane Katrina struck. (A few even condemned looters who stole, say, TVs and fishing poles, but didn't throw them in the hurricane's murky waters to drown in an unrespectable and proverbial death. Their jokes made play of "tough love," the kind that bristles and chastens but ultimately never casts loved ones aside.) In these and other ways, comics presumed their own and Black Katrina victims' humanity and linked fates and beckoned their predominantly Black and other times, diverse audiences to do the same.

Their palpable rage bespoke despair on the a-side, and "we gon' make it" hope on the b-side. Black comics and audiences held their sisters and brothers by speaking to and through media representations of Black Hurricane survivors as merely looters and, at worst, refugees on the cusp of seemingly state-sanctioned—and to many, orchestrated—exile. Their capacity to collectively hold Black and other storm survivors empathetically, whether through "tough love" and disciplining shade, or counternarratives that rebranded their industrious survival skills as both "authentic" and celebratory, teaching us once more how comedy can literally and figuratively save.

3

On Michael Richards, Racial Authenticity, and the "N-word"

SHUT UP! Fifty years ago, we'd have you upside-down with a fucking fork up your ass! . . .

YOU CAN TALK! YOU CAN TALK! YOU CAN TALK! You're brave now motherfuckah!

Throw his ass out. He's a NIGGER! He's a NIGGER!"

Michael Richards (aka "[Cosmo] Kramer" from NBC's *Seinfeld*)

In 2006, Michael Richards, best known for playing "Kramer" on the American sitcom *Seinfeld*, caught flack after a cell phone recording of him lambasting four Black males at The Laugh Factory went viral. As the excerpt above attests, this was not any ordinary tongue-lashing; Richards rained White supremacist fire down on these men to shame and silence them but ended up killing his set and the show instead. In response, Jamie Masada, The Laugh Factory's owner, invited Richards to apologize during a subsequent set at the club and then banned him altogether when he refused; surprisingly, Masada also banned all comics from using the n-word onstage, catching Black comics affected by the ban in yet another storm wherein language, namely, the n-word, proved to be a high-stakes affair.

In this chapter, I aim to say something new about Richards's rant and the temporary n-word ban it instigated with a caveat most comics treat as fact: while there's admittedly nothing new under the sun, there are, blessedly, new ways of making something understood.[1] As such, I won't be homing in on, say, how Richards's rant exposed his once-hidden racist ideations and what this says, if anything at all, about "racism in all of us." Nor will I be chasing evidence of sincerity in his Black and celebrity-backed apologies after his racist rant was exposed. I also won't belabor how social media abets the success and shaming of many a comic—not just Richards—in the contemporary moment. (I will say more about this, though, in Chapter 4 concerning Kevin Hart; I'll

To Be Real. Lanita Jacobs, Oxford University Press. © Oxford University Press 2023.
DOI: 10.1093/oso/9780190870096.003.0004

make a case for him as a modern-day trickster whose "success" hinges on his most-calibrated sincerity, racial authenticity, and, for a powerful contingency [e.g., fans, Hollywood execs, critics on social media], public apology.)

Instead, I take cues primarily from Black comics and their extended tribe (e.g., Black comedy club owners, waitresses, show promoters, Black fans), many of whom could care less if Richards's onstage remarks qualified him as a racist or if his subsequent public apologies were "sincere." This, they suggested, was none of their business or even their chief concern. Instead, they dared anyone who *really* cared about Black standup comedy to "keep it real" by telling the truth and shaming the proverbial "devil" (i.e., Richards) and "keep real *Black*" by affirming Black comics' right to marshal the n-word to comedic effect.

I'd be lying if I didn't admit that their appeals to "real talk" and "real Blackness" hit me dead in the chest, challenging me to have more than just scholarly curiosity about the "why" of racial authenticity and own my stance as a native scholar with skin in the game. This meant appreciating this book's conceptual abides (i.e., racial authenticity chiefly, but also its frequent bedfellows: sincerity and truth)—not just in academia's pre-delimited and forever-bracketed terms—but, rather, as cultural values, if not communal imperatives. It meant *feeling some kind of way*, again, as an African American researcher by purposely wedding my curiosity about the "why" of racial authenticity with a bolder stance on its bearings on Black folks' cries for respect, recognition, and freedom.

In this and other ways, the controversy surrounding Richards got me closer to answering the "why" of racial authenticity via what I've been calling "a" real Black.[2] I'll explain how and why in three parts: first, I'll revisit Richards's rant with aid of a transcript to better deconstruct this comedic breakdown and offer insights into humor's incessant promise and occasional demise [Part I]. (This analytical "first take" inflects my footing in both linguistic anthropology and humor studies.) Then, in Part II, I'll discuss Black comics' and their extended tribe's diverse responses to the controversy so that readers can feel their fire and appreciate how they ignited what seemed a movement-like moment in L.A.'s Black comedy scene. During this movement-like moment, they seemed to care less about Hollywood's recuperative machinations and more about the real imperative of self-governance and communal accountability. Throughout this telling, I'll offer my own take-aways as a native ethnographer coming full circle: whereas I began this research as a righteous cynic of racial authenticity, I was beginning to see comics' appeals to "a" real Black in a new and even teachable light; this light shone as brightly as righteous calls to anti-essentialism (e.g., *Let's STOP generalizing ALL Black folk as xyz!*) because it didn't stand in opposition to it. In many ways, it recalled that comforting dream I had years back about two houses ("Authenticity" and "Sincerity") oozing laughter on a shared foundation; somehow, the fact that laughter rose from both houses calmed a stifling fear that I was inadvertently playing to racial essentialism while convincing myself that I wasn't! The dream, backed now by the light of epiphany, made way for a b-side or a flip-side interpretation of "the" real Black; I call this "a" real Black in praise of that which is decidedly Black about Blackness and, in the unapologetic parlance of African American Vernacular English, ain't never wrong! (Consider this then less a riff *against* racial sincerity as much as a kindred pursuit to understand why "realness" constantly surfaces as both a racial and cultural imperative in Black folks' humor and everyday lives. If you must, consider my focus on "a" real Black even (ha!) as *racial sincerity's* third undisciplined cousin for I am saying the same thing, more or less, in a different way given my concerted, if not dogged emphasis on racial authenticity; this emphasis makes a whole heap of difference in where one lands when faced with the task of reconciling many Black folks' investment in "a" real Black against the anthropological imperatives to decry antiquated biological and essentialist fallacies of race. As such, I ask readers to stay curious: leave open the possibility that this focus might also turn up a more sustainable and, for many, sustaining read of the "why" of racial authenticity; stay hopeful that this analytical pursuit of "a" real Black might settle up with and/or (softly) against the pre-delimited and hyper-disciplined way we tend to study and understand "real" Blackness. Back now to Richards.

Part I: Unpacking Richards's (Recorded) Rant

Readers might well wonder what happened at The Laugh Factory the day Michael Richards went off onstage. Some news reports suggest that Richards was in the middle of an experimental set when an ethnically diverse group of about twenty partygoers entered the club mid-show, situated themselves in the balcony, and began to order drinks. According to Kyle Doss and Frank McBride, two Black men in this group whom Richards later singled out, Richards had actually made derisive remarks about their ethnically mixed group, remarks that were not recorded. During an on-camera interview with former *Today* show host Matt Lauer, they allege that Richards remarked, "All the stupid . . . Blacks and Mexicans are here" when their group of about fifteen to twenty, which included Whites, Asians, and Blacks, entered the club. This bothered one (unnamed) member of their party, who, once seated, said, "Hey, you're not funny." When Doss repeated it from the balcony, telling Richards, "Hey, my friend doesn't think you're funny," Richards reportedly looked up at him from the stage, flipped him off, and said, "Fuck you nigger."

What Happened Next?

Doss and McBride said they and other audience members sat stunned, but one of their Black male friends, Patrick McLucas, looked first at McBride before walking over to Doss as if to say, "Whoa, we got to do something about this." Richards allegedly issued additional unrecorded boasts about being rich enough to "buy them" and "put them in jail," and, "When I wake up, I'll still be rich, but you'll still be a nigger." When Doss and McBride's party made moves to leave the club, Richards intensified his excoriation. I've transcribed this recorded portion of their exchange and need to concede a few things before I get there: first, like all transcripts of naturally occurring talk and interaction,[3] mine is admittedly partial and selective since portions of Richards's rant were removed from the public posting, making it hard to isolate who is speaking when. I likewise identify speakers as well as I can after carefully reviewing TMZ's grainy camera phone footage, alongside relevant interviews, news stories, and podcasts.[4] Second, I deploy a transcript not to provide textual "proof" of Richards's "inner-racism" (again, not even my goal) but instead to reveal something in Richards's rant that most comics and only a few journalists managed to catch: sure-fire evidence of Richards's improvisational skills as a comic, to say nothing of the work that audiences do to stay with a comic up until that "alas" point, where, for myriad (e.g., personal, moral) reasons, they simply can't. In my mind, this transcript of the TMZ footage marks the beginning of an "alas" point, signaled by Richards's explicit silencer, "Shut up!" followed by a litany of racist put-downs. While it seems that Richards seeks to destroy a heckler with words, his racist vitriol transforms his exchange with select audience members into something way more punishing and complicated than the usual heckler assault.

A Question of a Heckler Assault Gone Bad?

The heat in this exchange practically leaps off the page. But was this descent to an "alas" point merely a case of a heckler retort gone *very* wrong as many folks, including a few comics, thought at the time? My answer: not quite or more precisely, not even, especially if one trusts and empathizes with Doss's and

Transcript Michael Richards's Rant

Michael Richards:	[*yelling, enraged*] SHUT UP! Fifty years ago, we'd have you upside-down with a fucking fork up your ass! [*Some audience members laugh, and a few applaud*]
Black Male in Balcony:	That was uncalled for. That wasn't called for.
Michael Richards:	[*shouting*] YOU CAN TALK! YOU CAN TALK! YOU CAN TALK! You're brave now motherfucker! [*points to the balcony*] Throw his ass out. He's a nigger. He's a NIGGER!
Female in Audience:	[*shocked*] Oh my God. [*several audience members say "Oooh"*]
Michael Richards:	He's a NIGGER! [*continues pointing to balcony*] A nigger! Look! There's a nigger! [*mimes the audience*] "Oooh! Ooh!" [*Moderates tone; assumes the voice of an instigator as he scans the audience accusingly*] All right, you see? This shocks you. [*male in audience begins to laugh giddily*] It shocks you to see what's buried beneath [you/your] stupid motherfuckahs?
Black Male in Balcony:	That was uncalled for.
Michael Richards:	What "was uncalled for"? It's uncalled for you to interrupt my ass, you cheap motherfuckAHS!
Female in Audience:	[*incredulously*] Oh my goodness.
Michael Richards:	[*looking up at balcony*] You guys have been talkin' and talkin' and talkin'!
Black Male in Balcony:	[*inaudible*]
Michael Richards:	[*mimics "hecklers" as male audience member laughs*] "I don't know. I don't know. I don't know!" [*several audience members laugh*]
Female in Audience:	[*jovially*] This guy's going nuts. [*audience members begin leaving*]
Michael Richards:	[*soothing voice, as if to audience*] What's the matter? Is this too much for you people to handle? [*abrupt cut of cell phone footage*]
Michael Richards:	[*audience laughter*] . . . They are going to arrest me for calling a Black man a neegga? [*audience laughter*] [*One Black male audience member targeted by Richards comes down from the balcony to speak directly to Richards; he stands just behind the row of seats near the stage*]
Male in Audience:	I don't arrest shit! . . . really fuck you up next time! [*cross-talk among offended parties*]
Michael Richards:	Wait a minute; where's he going?
Black Male in Audience:	That was uncalled for you fucking cracker-ass motherfucker! You call me a nigger—
Michael Richards:	[*mockingly*] "Cracker-ass?" You calling me "cracker-ass," nigga?!! [*female audience member laughs*]
Black Male in Audience:	[*now on first floor talking to Richards*] ... [*Inaudible*] Fucking White boy! [*mimics Richards using new words*] ["I'm a bad White boy!"]
Michael Richards:	Are you threatening me?
Black Male in Audience:	We'll see what's up!

Transcript Continued

Michael Richards:	[*talking into the microphone while pacing the stage*] Oh, it's a big threat. That's how you get back at "The Man."
Black Male in Audience	[*growing angrier*] THAT WAS REAL UNCALLED FOR!
Michael Richards:	Wait a minute. He's not going is he?
Male in Audience:	[*shouting*] YOU'RE JUST NOT FUNNY! That's why you're a reject—never had no shows, never had no movies! *Seinfeld*, that's it!
Michael Richards:	[*feigns petulance*] Oh, I guess you got me there. You're absolutely right. I'm just a wash up.
Black Male in Audience:	THAT WAS UNCALLED FOR!
Michael Richards:	Gotta stand on the stage. [*Richards mumbles to himself as more audience members leave*] Ah, she's/they're leaving. [*assumes audience's voice*] "That's it. We've had it. We've had it."
Black Male in Audience:	If anybody [*inaudible*] you "nigger"! That's un-fucking called for!
Another Black Male:	[*agrees*] That ain't necessary.
Black Male in Audience:	That ain't necessary!
Michael Richards:	Well, you interrupted me, pal. That's what happens when you interrupt the White man . . .
Black Male In Audience:	Uncalled for. That was uncalled for!
Michael Richards:	[*Talking as if to himself*] You see? You see, there's still those words [*looks at microphone*], those words, those words. [*Richards drops microphone and leaves stage*]
Audience Members:	[*A few audience members sit, some leave, one audience member says, "Money back"; a female audience member sadly observes, "Everyone's leaving?" to which a Black male responds, "Out of respect; I mean, he did lash . . ."*]
Frazer Smith (comic host):	[*takes the stage*] Don't know what to say guys, uh—Sorry about that.

McBride's revelation that Richards dissed them and their group for no other reason than their entry into the club during his set. (This is not an uncommon occurrence at The Laugh Factory, nor is it something veteran comics are unaccustomed to handling.) To them, Richards's unrecorded burn (i.e., "All the stupid blacks and Mexicans are here") blatantly ignored the actual diversity of their group and, given his use of "stupid," nixed his right to annihilate them as though they were hecklers.

Many readers might also wonder about Doss's seeming "bad behavior"? Could his angry retorts have contributed to and even escalated Richards's verbal assault? Here, I think it's important to note that while Doss admittedly fired back, diplomatically at first, followed by other audience members who called Richards "cracker ass" and "White boy"—insults McBride says neither he nor Doss made (and the grainy footage supports this), the moralistic adage that "two wrongs don't make a right" doesn't necessarily apply or "absolve" Richards (or condemn Doss) for several reasons: first, comedy routinely flouts moral expectations and, in fact, even moralizes "wrong" so long as it's deemed funny. Second, Richards's outburst belied what one might expect from stage-worn comics who must regularly confront and deflate hecklers, ideally in ways that don't end a show.[5]

Indeed, Richards's set-and-show-ending fate certainly seems to provide strong evidence that Richards instigated what humor scholar Michael Billig (2005) calls "un-laughter," or "a display of not laughing when laughter might otherwise be expected, hoped for, or demanded (192)." Billig argues that in more severe cases of "un-laughter," audiences can not only withhold laughter but question whether performances of humor even qualify as jokes at all through gasps, murmurs, and other outcries. Smith (2009) adds that *un-laughter* can mark more than a comedian's spectacular failure. Note Richards's outburst (e.g., "SHUT UP! Fifty years ago, we'd have you upside-down with a fucking fork up your ass!"; "YOU CAN TALK! YOU CAN TALK! YOU CAN TALK! You're brave now motherfucker! [*points to the balcony*] Throw his ass out, he's a nigger. He's a NIGGER! He's a NIGGER!") and one audience member's angry retort ("YOU'RE JUST NOT FUNNY! That's why you're a reject—never had no shoes, never had no movies! Seinfeld, that's it!"). These show that instances of *un-laughter* can be exploited by joke instigators (e.g., comics) and audience members alike to highlight supposed differences between them (e.g., naming who presumably "belongs" or does not), thus intensifying exclusionary social boundaries. There are, of course, multiple shouting matches between Richards and audience members before their arrival at a mutual and non-retractable "alas" point.

Namely, Richards's efforts to put Doss and his party in their proverbial place and thus regain control of the stage rely on racist ideology and onstage bullying; the latter, onstage bullying, is seldom a problem for comics when they need to lyrically spank would-be hecklers. In fact, disciplining hecklers, sometimes by whatever means possible, is widely presumed to be comics' responsibility to "rep" and protect their literal and figurative set (i.e., their routines and their profession), as well as to shelter paying audience members who want to see comics (and not fellow audience members) steal the show. However, comics' deployment of White supremacist ideology when doing so is a bit more hazardous since White supremacy—to say nothing of racism, its over-arching doctrine—is real and stalwart about its fallacious hierarchies and vile dictates. Had Richards opted for a gentler tool from racism's (and standup comedy's!) wheelhouse—racial stereotype—and played around the edges of its capacity to subversively riff on a figment of a truth, he might have placated and even amused his audience and central targets (i.e., Doss and his crew).[6]

Did Laughter Come at the "Wrong" Place?

That said, there's more to this story than meets the eye, starting even with the aforementioned conjecture about un-laughter. Anyone who closely mines the transcript or TMZ's grainy cell phone footage will catch what many comics discerned with their proverbial "third eye": laughter, even if seemingly ill-placed, actually punctuates Richards's set, though it's hard to say from whom or to ascertain whether the laughter is cynical, mocking, incredulous, nervous, or corroborating. More specifically, at least a few audience members laugh throughout his set, including after his most racist remarks, thus enacting what humor scholars appreciate as laughter's incessant ambiguity: we can't always know for sure whether these audience members are laughing *at* his audacity (i.e., mockingly), in agreement with him (i.e., corroborating), and/ or because they're "lifted" (e.g., drunk or high)—if not some combination of all three or more.[7] This uncertainty didn't stop me (or, apparently, Richards) from wondering why audience members were laughing. Were they corroborating his racist remarks outright, laughing at the spectacle of his "coming undone," or using laughter to slyly endorse his racist chides like a wink? And this too: while I may be unable to delineate a firm answer to the "why" of laughter in this case, I can harness insights from humor studies and linguistic anthropology to decode the discursive and grammatical "conditions of possibility and impossibility" that may have abetted laughter, un-*laughter*, and an unmitigated "alas point" of no return.

Toward that end, I've bolded moments in the above transcript wherein laughter seems to come at the wrong place, understanding full well that the notion of a "wrong place" is a subjective matter. Who's to even say what's the "wrong" place or not, right? Especially when laughter itself is difficult to unpack definitively since it's hard to get in someone's head and heart, so to speak, and figure out why they're laughing at any given time. I pitch the question of laughter coming at the "wrong" place nonetheless if only to suggest another related question: what does one need to presume of oneself and/or others to tell and/or laugh at a particular joke? This complicated question moves us, productively I think, beyond merely morally laden considerations of "right" or "wrong" and fault versus innocence toward an appreciation of all the complicated stuff that makes laughter possible for each of us. Please know that this is different from pitching Richards's racist outburst as an invitation to explore the "racism that presumably lives in all of us." Please know, too, that addressing when and especially why we laugh at racial humor—or racism cloaked as humor—is as difficult a task as deciphering what, beyond what we can see and/or hear on TMZ's grainy footage, motivated Richards's racist assault and ideations? We may not be able to generate an answer to the "why" behind his racist outburst or some audience members' steady laughter in response, but we can excavate the exchange as best we can toward additional take-aways like the following.

Even if one labels this exchange "a heckler assault gone wrong" or opts for a more audience-facing descriptor (i.e., the dreaded "alas" point well beyond *un-laughter* to a mutual place of no return), we'd do well to appreciate that Richards doesn't go down without an improvisational fight. Contrary to those who saw the TMZ footage and declared Richards's set and career a wrap (i.e., finished) after he shouted, "SHUT UP! Fifty years ago, we'd have you upside-down with a fucking fork up your ass!," I demur. For me, this is where things get especially interesting, almost as interesting as when comics take the stage, grab the mic, and introduce themselves to their audience. (I say again: I love the space between their initial greeting and the audience's response! I especially love the sound of the microphone's hum; it's that barely audible space between words and laughter, betwixt a comic's invitation and an audience's we-making acceptance via applause or other agreement expletives (e.g., laughter, shoutouts), that reminds me that just about anything can happen.) Granted, winning laughter after a racist outburst like Richards's would be a longshot akin to a basketball player trying to land a last-minute shot in fourth overtime for the win. But hey, as on the court, it is on the stage: anything can happen. Most important, anything was *still* possible at this point in Richards's set. Richards and a few others knew this too.

Recuperating Racism via Mad Improv

As a few comics and journalists pointed out, Richards steps up to center court post-violation, as it were, and aims for a winning shot in overtime. (If you're still fuzzy on why Richards is "in trouble," consider, again, Richards's first recorded verbal assault, "SHUT UP! Fifty years ago, we'd have you upside-down with a fucking fork up your ass!" and what came next. This is just the beginning of Richards's heckler assault, but it costs him points, so to speak, since his chides come across as a gross mishandling of a heckler [i.e., Doss] who is a modest one at best, and relies on math (or historical accounting) that is not only ahistorical but worrisome. Richards's ongoing taunts—he screams, "YOU CAN TALK! YOU CAN TALK! YOU CAN TALK! You're a brave mother-fucker!," before calling Doss a "nigger" ["Throw his ass out. He's a nigger. He's a NIGGER! He's a NIGGER!"] and then asking his audience to literally regard him as such ["A nigger! Look! There's a nigger!"]—don't do him any favors on-stage either since most of his audience bristles audibly and only a few laugh. Thus, while Richards arguably "wins" by momentarily stunning and silencing Doss, he "loses" ground [or "points" in keeping with the game metaphor] by stunning and silencing the audience too. They likewise hear Doss when he responds loudly so as to be heard this time, "That was uncalled for." When heard against Richards's loud racist vitriol, Doss's response sounds wise and apt. Suffice it to say, *this* violation gets Richards in trouble onstage and forces him to deploy his gift of *mad* improv to regain the floor.[8]

Richards's attempted heckler-take-down, however racist, specious, and/or petty we deem it to be, likewise constitutes his first attempt to slide into a safe zone of comedic redemption.[9] His second attempt, I argue, involves trying to flip his racist insults into fodder for a teachable set. I want to replay that record analogy I used in Chapter 2 and offer a "b-side read" that speculates on the many possible stories playing on the flip side of his set. In pursuit of this b-side read, I don my linguistic anthropology cap and use a transcript of Richards's recorded set as a text (or "data") that I return to again and again.[10] I want readers to better see Richards doing language in all its myriad forms to shapeshift in real time from a racist comic to a comic who merely plays around in racism's wheelhouse.

I'll begin by homing in on Richards's linguistic and discursive work, par-ticularly his alternating pronunciation of the expletive "motherfucker" in the aforementioned rant. Here's a quick replay: Richards screams at Doss, "YOU CAN TALK! YOU CAN TALK! YOU CAN TALK! You're a brave mother-fucker," before indiscriminately hurling the n-word at Doss. When Doss replies, "That was uncalled for," Richards mocks him by way of mime by saying, "What 'wasn't called for'? It's uncalled for you to interrupt my ass, you cheap motherfuckAHS!" Note that in his second marshaling of the expletive, "motherfucker," Richards deploys a significant feature of African American Vernacular English (AAVE) phonology known to linguists as "r-lessness" or post-vocalic r deletion or vocalization; in particular, he pronounces "moth-erfucker" by omitting the "r" or phonetically reducing the –er suffice to "ah" (i.e., "motherfuckAHS").[11] He also folds in and castigates other members of Doss's party through his use of the plural suffix. With consequence, too.

Richards's oscillating pronunciation of "motherfucker" arguably works double-time insofar as (a) his curse helps him slay the heckler he sees in Doss even as it (b) simultaneously marks his "hipness" and subversive wordplay. That's because saying "motherfucker" versus "motherfuckAH[S]" is semantically loaded in everyday discourse. Both iterations of the expletive can be leveled as insults, but the latter, "motherfuckAH[S]" (Richards's emphasis) gestures toward expressive Black language; which is to say, it/he sounds "Black." Richards's racist mimicry thus acts as a distancing maneuver wherein his cross (or phonetic and prosodic codeswitch) into African American Vernacular English acts as a double-cross: essentially, he appropriates and mocks Black speech styles as both laughable and racially inferior even as he slyly hips us to his improvisational dexterity and even, perhaps, his codeswitching capacities in American Mainstream English and AAVE phonology. He likewise disses them using phraseology from their "own" presupposed linguistic arsenal, effecting a double-diss.

This b-side read applies to his oscillating pronunciation of "nigger" as well since Richards alternates between a clear enunciation of the "n-word" in a couple of his earlier chides (i.e., "Throw his ass out. He's a nigger. He's a NIGGER! He's a NIGGER! [points] A nigger! Look! There's a nigger!") to a hyper- or gross mis-articulation of this same slur a bit later in his set (i.e., "The are going to arrest me for calling a Black man a nigga."). Given the explosive repercussions that fall on non-Blacks who use the term derisively (if not one audience member's fiery retort to Richards: "I don't 'arrest' shit . . . really fuck you up next time!"), it's not hard to imagine that Richards's r-less pronunciation of "nigger" is both dramatic and recuperative, judiciously attentive, if you recall, to Chris Spencer's strict caution about the n-word to non-minorities: "Avoid the –er [suffix] if you want to avoid the E.R. [Emergency Room]!" Richards, arguably, attends to this caution; his r-less enunciation of "nigga" is not only emphasized, but awkwardly pronounced as "knee-ga." This audible bracketing or marked pronunciation of "motherfuckAHS" seems to parody as if by intention Black male speakers and himself at the same time, thus diffusing and minimalizing his responsibility for his expressed racism. By playing with AAVE phonology to play at Black speech and hence one-up Doss and other Black men in his party, Richards can effect a comedic play of disavowal, one that slyly displaces accountability for his anger and racism onto another allegedly "guilty" party: Doss and his (Black) friends who are the targets of Richards racist putdowns.

Let's move past Richards's use of AAVE phonology and prosody (how he speaks) for just a moment to appreciate the grammatical and gestural weight of his denotational choices (what he's saying with continued focus on how) because they also service his attempt to transmute his patently racist set to a teachable one with he, himself, in redemptive tow. (Stay with me; I'll need to revisit portions of Richards's racist vitriol, sometimes again and again, to unpack it.) Recall that Richards first calls Doss a "nigger"—about three times in fact—before acting, I believe, as if he is literally acting via a switch from highly direct(ed) speech (i.e., "A nigger!") to an audience-facing directive (i.e., "Look! There's a nigger!"). Even on paper, his shift from a racist declarative to a racist directive, accompanied all the while by wild pointing gestures, seems carnivalesque; one might even deem it "jest-icular" caricature recalling racist and queer freak shows of days old.[12] This caricature of a played-out caricature, a meta-caricature if you will, again suggests a subtext of concerted play that makes sense on a comedy stage. My b-side response to this, then, is curiosity: namely, could Richards's pivot from a litany of racist declaratives ("He's a nigger! He's a NIGGER! He's a NIGGER!") to the directive ("Look! There's a nigger!") performatively riff on the well-known antics of Richards's more popular and ever gesticulating and pantomiming character, "Kramer" [from *Seinfeld*]? If so, Richards may be gesturing, both literally and figuratively, toward a self-directed mockery insofar as he "plays" himself in the loaded and Urban Dictionary sense of the term toward a soft disavowal of his racist chides. Which is to say, he literally plays himself playing Kramer even as he betrays the sincerity of his very performance, casting dubious shade on the whole racist charade.

Yet another b-side read or flat-out suspicion I have concerns the eerie similarity between Richards's call-out, "A nigger! Look! There's a nigger!," to ridicule Doss and Frantz Fanon, a renown Martiniquais psychiatrist and philosopher. Richards' call-out, "A nigger! Look! There's a nigger!," was designed to belittle Doss; Frantz's traumatic memory was of a White child who, upon seeing Frantz on a train platform in Paris, cried these equally objectivitying words: "Look! A Negro!" So, I wonder, could Richards be unwittingly and uncannily miming this little boy, too, effecting a masterful meta-nod to Fanon's indictment of the dehumanizing effects of colonization on the colonized racialized subject if not the colonizers themselves? Granted, the timespan, context, and interlocutors are different in this case, and the child (who might otherwise be presumed "innocent" given his age and childish naivete)[13] deploys what many consider a more acceptable albeit dated word to refer to Fanon's Blackness (as opposed to his status as a Martiniquais citizen, a man, etc.). But for Fanon, the child's cry was akin to saying, "Dirty nigger!," especially when the child fearfully added, "Maman, look, a Negro; I'm scared!" This experience was one of many that forced Fanon to try to reconcile his humanity, his being-hereness, his very psychic and corporeal embodiment with the publicly made spectacle he represented in that White child's mind. Thus, it might well be argued that both the child and Richards stage a spectacle of fixing Black men in terms their Black male taunters deem damning and damnable. Whereas Doss refuses laughter by repeatedly telling Richards, "That was uncalled for," Fanon resists and then succumbs to laughter's biting relief. When the child singled him out, Fanon first says, "I wanted to kill myself laughing, but laughter had become out of the question" and later, adds, "I wanted quite simply to be a man among men. I would have liked to enter our world young and sleek, a world we could build together." Later, though, he managed to deliver a caustic retort to the mother's attempted repair; for example, when she reportedly sought to comfort and reprove her son by saying, "Look how handsome the Negro is," Fanon publicly shamed her with this cutting rebuttal: "Kiss the handsome Negro's ass, madame!" Reflecting on the shame that "flooded her face"—a tangible sign of his "win"—Fanon notes, "At last I was free from my humiliation. At the same time, I accomplished two things: I identified my enemies, and I made a scene. A grand slam. Now one would be able to laugh" (Fanon 1967, 114). In their own ways then, both Fanon and Doss echo the tenor of James Baldwin's retort to some of the oldest lies told about race and Black men: "I Am Not Your Negro/Nigger!"[14] Whereas Fanon deploys biting humor, Doss refuses laughter altogether to both decry and bespeak their humanity as men who are racially marginalized.

Let me not neglect Richards's comedic excess in my attempt to see Doss, whom Fanon and Baldwin in many ways anticipate in their writings. If Richards was, in fact, nodding to Fanon, I say again: what a masterful trickster play—a true turn-on-a-dime execution! If only his anger hadn't betrayed his sincerity by casting a negative pall on the whole comedic charade. (Notice the irony of what I just said: if only his anger didn't nix the "truth" or "sincerity" of his comedy; ha! It's funny how comedy, a literal play for humor and laughter, also relies on the notions driving this book: sincerity and authenticity, for real.) Better yet, dig Brandon Bowlin, a comic I've followed closely since 2001 and love like "a brother from another mother"; while impersonating "Kramer," Richards's endearingly neurotic character on *Seinfeld*, he quipped, "So you want me to be racist. I'll show you racist!" before reiterating a few of Richards's choice offerings in comical fashion. Brandon's point is that "Kramer's" unpredictable demeanor and friendly disposition could have provided the necessary cloak for Richards's racism and maybe even charmed the audience to process and accept it as mere humor versus a racist and racism-abetting riff.

These b-side speculations and conjectures aside, I want to further mine Richards's language to posit another potential means through which he rebrands his racist humor as teachable: namely, he relies on the boundary-making and quiet nation-building magic afforded by pronominals. Said another way, he uses pronouns in interesting ways to mark and make what Elijah Anderson calls "imagined communities"; that is, an "us/we" and sometimes a first-person directed "you" [often] in stark opposition to "Others" codified as a "they/them" in nation-making and nationhood. Recall, for example, that when Richards becomes enraged after his set is interrupted, he signals an unseen and presumed constituency with a shout (i.e., "SHUT UP! Fifty years ago, we'd have you upside-down with a fucking fork up your ass!"); the "we" he references clearly does not include Doss or people who look like him since Richards's "we" was capable—just "fifty years ago" he says—of stringing up an outspoken Black man and violently raping him. Despite its historical inaccuracy, this veiled reference to the enslavement, rape, and lynching of Africans in America is violently clear and even occasions laughter and a smattering of enthusiastic applause. It is also consistent with other White supremacist comments Richards allegedly said about Whites like himself being situated at the top of a racial hierarchy while Blacks like Doss and his diverse peers are consigned to the bottom. It's striking then that as Richards's racist set loses momentum and he provokes more grumbles from the crowd than laughter and applause, he invokes a different "we." Specifically, he laments, as if miming disgruntled audience members this time, "That's it. We've had it." His observations come near the end of his stage time and bespeak, almost empathetically, what many audience members were proclaiming with their feet by walking out. Richards's oscillating "we's" likewise service his shift from a seemingly staunch racist and instigator (e.g., "Look! There's a nigger!") to a comic who is merely reporting on the room's affective state via an empathetic—and potentially empathizing—parody.

Doing Racism or (Just) Curating Racism?

This point relates to yet another discursive strategy that services Richards's efforts to transmute his racist outburst into a collective and teachable moment: multi-voice (e.g., first-, second-, and third-person) curation. If the act of curation, executed using an array of seemingly objective and objectifying pronouns—and Richards exploits them all—enables a curator to stand slightly apart from their expositional target so as to unpack or contextualize it, then it might well be argued that Richards's slip-then-slide into curatorial "voice" seeks to distance him from his highly intentional and directed racist vitriol toward that of a racial-envelope-pushing comic who is tragically misunderstood versus unconvincing and/or unfunny. To see how this works, return with me to the exact point in the grainy TMZ footage or transcript wherein he shouts while gesturing wildly toward Doss's party in the balcony:

"A nigger! Look! There's a nigger! [*mimes the audience*] 'Ooooh! Ooh!' [*moderates tone; shifts to the voice of an instigator as he scans the audience accusingly*] Alright, you see? This shocks you? [*male in audience begins to laugh giddily*][15] It shocks you to see what's buried beneath [you/your] stupid motherfuckahs!"

Here, Richards morphs from a comic to a meta-commentator and a skilled one to boot! Check out his execution (and forbear a few reiterations necessary to wage this and other analytical double-takes): first, he serves the would-be heckler with a sure silencer by calling him a "nigger" while asking the audience (who can't help but go along given the imperative encoded in the deictic, "Look," and his accompanying pointing gesture) to fix their gaze on Doss; then, in the next breath, he adopts a damning curatorial voice that is, incidentally, no longer directed at an invisible and commiserating "we" but rather, a condemnable and visible "you" that sweeps his entire listening audience into a collective damnable fold; then, when he lobs the insult, "you stupid motherfuckahs!," he fixes his accusatory gaze on the entire audience as if to target *them* for public reproof. Maybe, I wonder in b-side curiosity, he does this because he is shocked that his shockingly racist remarks managed to earn some laughter in the first place?[16] Or maybe, just maybe, he pursues something universal and universalizing in this stretch of his set—toward redemption even?

Consider again that moments prior, he winkingly exploited one of AAVE's most-recognizable phonological features, r-lessness, to deride Doss and his friends ("What 'was uncalled for'? It's uncalled for you to interrupt my ass, you cheap motherfuckAHS!"); later, though, he uses this same linguistic feature to indict the whole crowd ("Alright, you see? This shocks you. It shocks you to see what's buried beneath [you/your] stupid motherfuckahs?!"). To cheekily and most ironically paraphrase one of Oprah Winfrey's generous refrains, "Everybody gets to [be a motherfuckA::::H]" at this point in Richards's (now) all-audience-encompassing set, his verbal sleight of hand flips the racist tenor he'd previously assigned to "motherfuckAH" when disparaging Doss and other Black men in his party; he marshals it now as an equal-opportunity slur to indict the entire audience and seems to deliver a moral punch to anyone who has deigned to laugh at his set thus far. In particular, his chide and query—"Alright, you see? This shocks you. It shocks you to see what's buried beneath [you/your] stupid motherfuckahs?!"—evinces this turn so deftly that

one almost needs to slow it down, transcribe it, and cull insights from linguistic anthropology so as to appreciate how this statement, this indictment,
simultaneously functions as a direct and ambiguous curation that displaces
the insult and error of his own unabashedly racist remarks to the audience,
especially those who bore witness and maybe even laughed in response. In
the midst of this, he also seems to disavow any racist intentionality on his
part by slyly suggesting, by way of inference and, again, displacement, that
his set heretofore is/was merely an "act" or set, or, perhaps best, a "set-up" to
those who need to be shocked by what is presumably "buried beneath" their
psyches.[17]

Richards adopts this safe distancing stance later in his set too; that is, when
the initial trickles of laughter he receives get drowned out by the audience's
gasps of shock and horror. Only this time, he oscillates between targeting a
distant guilty party of "you's" ("What's the matter? Is this too much for you
people to handle?") to a decidedly empathic "we" whom he quotes sympa-
thetically by way of imaginative ventriloquism ("Gotta stand on the stage.
[*mumbles to himself as he audibly notices audience members leave*] 'That's it.
We've had it. We've had it"). In that first utterance, his use of "you people"
works over time as a homogenizing and scare-quote worthy signifier that
winkingly sweeps his entire audience into a stigmatized "ya'll can't take *this
joke*" collective. In his subsequent utterance, he doesn't indict his audience
via a patronizing play on "you people" [who are incapable of taking a layered
joke]; instead, he's at a different place now, likely just shy of his own "alas"
point of no return. He marks it by assuming the voice of his fatigued audience
who, by this time, have decided to leave the club en masse ("That's it. We've
had it. We've had it"); it must be noted, too, that this collective, generic, and
maybe even all-encompassing "we" stands in stark contrast to the veiled "we"
he deployed in his earlier White supremacist rant (i.e., "SHUT UP! Fifty years
ago, we'd have you upside-down with a fucking fork up your ass!").

In sum, although Richards ultimately fails to salvage his set, he does manage
to curate his and his audience members' collective arrival to, it turns out, an
unmitigated "alas" point—which is to say, his curation attempts are not cura-
tive; they do not imbue him with the necessary authority and objective exper-
tise he desires and rallies for—even if only in his mind. Whereas his audience
explicitly enacts their arrival at this "alas point" through a series of murmurs,
hisses, and eventually a mass walkout, Richards manifests his own "alas point"
by visibly evacuating his set discursively, affectively (e.g., emotionally), and
physically (e.g., dropping the mic and exiting the stage). But not, I humbly
submit, before another grand gesture epitomizing Richards's fortitude as a
comic. Just before Frazer Smith, the comic host that night, takes the stage and

apologizes to the crowd, Richards makes one final effort to redeem his set via these final words: "You see? You see, there's still those words, those words, those words," before dropping the mic loose-handedly and going offstage.[18] That curatorial comment incidentally mirrors the "teachable-moment" cadence of several of his prior accusatory and lamentive quips. If read in isolation and succession versus sandwiched, as they are, betwixt and between his more incendiary insults and retorts, these cumulative quips, which I hope we can now appreciate as much more than just "quips," read like benchmarks of a morality tale:

- "Alright, you see? This shocks you? It shocks you to see what's buried underneath you stupid motherfuckers?" (Again, this rhetorical question, aptly coupled with an implied answer and laden with judgment, evinces a curatorial and accusatory cadence that suggests Richards's whole racist act was but a teachable provocation to racial tolerance and mutual respect.)
- "What's the matter? Is this too much for you people to handle?" (These questions, arguably a retrospective curation, also service an attempt to rebrand this set as a teachable provocation.)
- "They are going to arrest me for calling a Black man a nigga" (Two things seem to be happening at once here: first, in this literal projection and lamentation, Richards curates his projected fate and inserts the specter of unfairness; his cynical cadence seems to suggest that he is or will be treated unfairly for his "act"; second, Richards implies, via this radical turn toward empathetic recognition, an acute awareness of both his racist faux pas and Doss's humanity as a "Black man" while abnegating it and seeking to exonerate himself at the same time.)
- "Gotta stand on the stage. . . . 'That's it. That's it. We've had it.'" (This curation offers a literal play-by-play of his set in real time! Having nearly arrived at his own "alas point," he laments the fact that he must remain onstage (for his own safety, it turns out) and verbally sympathizes with and ventriloquizes the sentiments of his disgruntled audience. In doing so, he sounds as though he's literally looking at himself from outside himself; his animated surreal-ity thus evinces the literal sounding out of the internal ramblings of a brilliantly erratic comic [think "Kramer" anyone?]—one who, again, mustn't be taken too seriously.)
- "You see? You see. There's still those words, those words, those words." (Richards's final comment before his literal mic drop and exit harken back to his initial attempts to curate and rebrand his racist humor as a teachable provocation [see first bullet point above]. It seems then that he

holds fiercely to his own b-sided play of his set despite the fact that his audience is clearly not buying it or has otherwise "alas(ed)" out.)

Richards's discursive maneuverings throughout his stage time likewise reveal way more than his capacity for ingenuity and resilience onstage; he also exemplifies, in this more thematic read of his set, comics' capacity to practice and even condone discriminatory beliefs and practices while cloaking them under laughter's shady umbrella.[19] Humor thus becomes a way to practice racism as leisurely sport, replete in Richards's case with borrowings from African American linguistic (e.g., AAVE) and discursive styles and maybe even uncanny riffs on revolutionary African diasporan scholars like Franz Fanon.[20]

Before concluding Part I, I feel compelled to consider a somewhat similar read of Richards's devolving set from his very own pal and colleague, the late and beautiful comedian Norm McDonald. He, as well as Jerry Seinfeld, have both said on air that they do not feel Richards is racist. McDonald went so far as to point to Richards's set as proof, citing his incredibly crazy and loud-voiced racism (as opposed to quieter [e.g., whispered] or veiled racism one might expect from modern-day racists). McDonald's read stands to expand the interpretations offered heretofore: namely, he suggests that Richards's comedy, which sounds oh so racist on its surface, is actually an exaggerated performance, which is to say "fake": a caricature of White unbridled racism.

For some readers (and me, too), digesting McDonald's read that Richards was just playing racist in order to check a specious heckler and save his dying set may nonetheless be hard to stomach for obvious reasons, including the "proof" afforded by the damning cell phone footage; the precision of Richards's racist targeting of Doss (who, again, is Black); Richards's own acknowledgment and regret about his inner-demons during a series of awkward public apologies (apologies neither Doss nor McBride initially accepted since they deemed them insincere public spectacles for TV versus addressed to them personally); his failure to sign a release for The Laugh Factory, which taped the night of his set (although this did not stop the cell phone footage from getting out), and, most important for me, his sheer capacity as a self-admitted "White man" in full possession of the privileges and historical contingencies Whiteness affords to pull these racist insults off. As Rodney Perry told a crowd at The Laugh Factory's *Chocolate Sundaes* show shortly after Richards's set went viral, "The reason why [Richards's words] were so hurtful is that we ain't got no comparable words. "Cracker" [one of the racial slurs that Black males leveled back at Richards] ain't shit."[21]

I take time to seriously consider McDonald's perspective because it is nuanced and comic-facing; which is to say, he, too, appreciates Richards's parodic stylings and strategic plays likely given his own years wielding mics on treacherous comedy club stages. (Given his expressed confidence in Richards's unintentional and performative albeit regretful racism, he may also be familiar with the more silent ways in which White racism is whispered on public stages and/or in plain sight.) Still, while I appreciate McDonald's read and can certainly entertain the notion, I can't, as Smokey Robinson and The Miracles crooned back in 1967, "second that emotion." At least not without remembering how Blackface minstrelsy—or, in Richards's case, "Black"-voiced mimicry—affords Whites who purposefully don Black-sounding masks the guise and, apparently, the gall to say just about anything and then disavow it by displacing wildly errant behavior or so-called "truth-speak" onto Black subjugated subjects and anti-Black stereotypes whose very existence makes such an oppressive play even possible. Which is to say, they can act like racists but then lie about not doing so because they were "just pretending" or, worst, miming their targets to expose *their* presupposed hypocrisy or culpability.[22] Thus, whether one views his performance as "real" or "fake," and whether one views his racist insults and retorts as "right" or even "fair game" (since he viewed Doss as a heckler) doesn't kill the truth that racism *is* often as racism *does*. This is true regardless of whether the speaker did not intend to enact racism or simply had a "bad moment, set, day, etc."

In riffing on McDonald's read in this way, I risk sounding like a hypocrite. Specifically, in weighing in on the racist nature of Richards's performance, I seem to have contradicted my professed dis-interest in whether his behavior onstage qualifies him as a racist. I don't think saying his behavior is racist is a contradiction, though. (I reiterate: my professed disinterest in whether Richards is, in fact, racist or simply "did" a racist thing remains less central to the story I'm trying to tell, and something I think Richards would do best to interrogate). For me to argue otherwise, even as a self-admitted comedy fan and scholar, would likewise be irresponsible and unaccountable. I'd have to exaggerate comedy's literal make-shiftiness and reify its artistic spontaneity so as to blanket the sins comics sometimes commit on a public stage in the very name of comedy.[23] I'd have to ignore the ways explicit enactments of racism even by "good" Whites who don't make a practice of doling out racism with a "j/k" (just kidding) chaser can also play in its reductive and violent fields, reducing others and themselves at the same time much like early nineteenth-century White minstrel performers donning literal and figurative Blackface did.

Yet another reason I might sound hypocritical is because my own ventured read of Richards's comedic stylings could, in fact, provide "proof" of McDonald's read. For example, I argue that Richards both cloaks and fuels his racist verbal assault by skillfully borrowing aspects of African American Vernacular English, namely, phonetics and what some consider to be in-group slang (e.g., switching from "motherfucker" to r-less "motherfuckAH[S]") and shifting from "nigger" to r-less "nigga" [pronounced "knee-ga"]; additionally, he shields his assault by using discursive styles prevalent in Black humor and folklore (e.g., signifyin'; riffing, perhaps, on Fanon's pained recollection of a child seeing him and saying, "Look! A Negro!"), to both cloak and fuel his racist verbal assault. Moreover, I just suggested out of my own writerly mouth (!) that Richards strategically maneuvers language and discursive styles to "shapeshift in real-time from a racist comic to a comic who merely plays around in racism's wheelhouse." If all of this is true and quotable, then maybe Richards was *indeed* playing racist. Readers may well wonder, how do I reconcile my and McDonald's near similar reads?

I'll answer that fair question another way because the last thing I want to do is belabor what I believe is a tangential discussion of whether Richards's racism is "real" versus "fake" (i.e., performed). Quite frankly, that, too, is beyond what I am after in this book and is perhaps soul searching that Richards would again do best. Instead, what I'm after, besides a serious consideration of all that encompasses Black comics' unapologetic and occasionally fierce articulations of "a" real Black, is also what I believe Richards, Doss, and the broader audience were after: a chance to be recognized, whether as a comic or audience member, via humor that coaxes empathy for our collective similarities and individual differences—which is to say, our mutuality.

A Failed Groove on a Comedy Stage

It's in this spirit, that I ask you, Dear Reader, to extend your curiosity a bit further, beyond Richards's comedic stylings to what, in his own words, "lies just beneath" this highly charged exchange. If we do this together, I on the page and you in your heart and mind, we can get at something way deeper than, say, Richards's inability to recuperate his racist chides via "mad improv" and audience's right, privilege, and power to withhold laughter and, thus, end a show.[24] We get tragic evidence of comedy's blessed and incessant invitation to laugh, play, and dance with laughter and its cathartic release. Yes, *dance!* Especially since standup comedy, under fire, can suddenly become a comedian's battleground in ways that recall the intensity and coordinated synchronicity—in essence, the dance—of basketball players rallying for the win in overtime. And especially since standup comedy, at its heart, is a concerted invitation to play with humor toward laughter, itself an expression of mutuality and empathetic recognition. We can hear it in audience's laughter as well as their hisses and boo's, applause and agreement expletives (e.g., "Yes!," "Tell it!," "Finally!") alongside silence otherwise known as "hearing" or deep listening. To most comics, this is the central payoff, the thing that matters most. Richards's set should thus be understood with far greater nuance than a "spectacular fail," "heckler assault gone wrong," or a racist screed cloaked in humorous play. No, the story of Richards's set is fundamentally about a failed or unrequited groove between a comic and the audience: granted, unlike basketball players on a team, comics are individuals who appear solely responsible for their "wins" or "losses" onstage. But the truth in all cases is that comics, like dancers and ballers, play an intersubjective game since they invite their audiences to literally play, imagine, and dance with them. The cumulative series of malevolent plays recounted above reveals what happens when the dance goes unrequited or a ball pass is dropped; neither Richards noror Doss, nor the audience manage to dance together via an exchange of words and laughter.

In saying this, I wish in no way to fetishize laughter; having interviewed comics and otherwise learned of their many diverse motivations, I know that individual comics are after way more than audience's laughter. Some want empathy, love, acceptance, clout, and fame; and others use the stage to work out and through a host of ego-drenched issues irrespective of how their audience responds. (Heck, some comics even poke at their audience as if they're trying to provoke a battle they know they'll surely win!) I also know full well (and will discuss later in this book's Conclusion) how jovial laughter can evince racism, sexism, or other kinds of violence; I know, too, that when humor is executed with expert cunning, racism can hide in plain sight behind well-told jokes and even convince those who are the literal and figurative butt of the joke to—"oh . . . *damn*"—laugh at themselves alongside others.)

Accordingly, my greatest take away from this b-side read of Richards's rant likewise concerns matters of mutuality and possibility. We must never forget that Richards and Doss fail to reach a shared groove because Richards and Doss disagree over the right-ness of Doss's reported critique of Richards (i.e., Hey, my friend doesn't think you're funny.) In Richards's mind, this reported critique qualifies Doss as a "heckler," maybe even a petty feckless one who instigates bullshit while hiding safely behind their friends' backs. He likewise treats him like one via racist defamation in order to regain the proverbial floor.

And what of Doss, who is more than just a racialized target and "victim" here? If one pays as close attention to Doss as I have to Richards, they'll notice that Doss's angry retorts scream so loudly that they mask his underlying hurt and drown out his diplomatic labor in this exchange. In fact, Doss initially pursues empathy and understanding from Richards despite his confusion over Richards's highly directed and public racist chides. That is, until Doss reaches an "alas" point of his own wherein his corrective and lamenting refrain (i.e., "That was [REAL] uncalled for")—he actually repeats this about nine or ten times—crescendos into what is essentially a rhetorical question: "If anybody [*inaudible*] you 'nigger'! That's un-fucking called for!" (Again, his precise words are hard to decipher from the cell phone footage, but he seems to direct it at fellow audience members). Doss eventually finds resonance when another deep voiced and Black-sounding male hears his lament as an invitation for empathy and, blessedly, provides it by calmly intoning, "It ain't necessary." Doss shouts this man's words aloud, as if to the audience, and then calms down, reminding me, much like Hurricane Katrina humor, of the redemptive power of empathy in racially tumultuous encounters. Meanwhile, Richards oscillates from a comic doing—no, wait, improvising racism; that is, up until the point where he tries to pass himself off as a self-appointed excavator of the ugly racism that presumably lives in all of us. But neither Doss, the broader audience, and maybe even Richards, himself, believes it.[25] They eventually reach an "alas" point with Richards orchestrating and curating all the while.

There's but one more thing I'd like to flag about this exchange, and it's a quieter conversation that takes place between disgruntled audience members as the room clears. Although this barely audible conversation did not garner as much attention as Richards's rant, it underscores how sincerity and empathy—terms that keep popping up in this study—bespeak laughter's fraught stakes and possibilities. It also highlights the intra-audience dynamics that are always at work when a comic takes the stage and socializes their audience into a collective "you" or even a "we."[26] The dialogue involves what sounds like a White female who laments the audience's rapid departure (and effective end of the show) and a Black man who patiently explains the potential reasons why. Essentially, they tally up the social costs of laughter and un-laughter while embodying them all the while in their different reads of the situation. Much like the first call back I heard from a Black female audience member in response to Ian Edwards's 9/11 joke back in 2001, this dialogue between audience members reaffirms that comedy is always a conversation between a comic and their audiences. This too: audiences *matter*. Without them, there would be no live comedy show, and without their laughter, there would be no proof of a joke's "success." I and fellow humor scholars rely on this shared faith even though we remain ever-curious about all that laughter says and doesn't say in live standup comedy shows.[27] This quieter conversation near the show's end should also remind us that comedy begins and ends with the prospect of a vocal, discriminating audience whose muffled debriefings in this case offer teachable meta-dialogues—talk about talk—about comedy's stakes and consequences. Essentially, their dialogue acts as a teachable coda that reminds us of comics' ever-fleeting power whenever jokes hit their mark or, like Richards, happen to fall flat in the worst way, triggering audience's power; that is, their *un-laughter*, mass walkouts, ticket refund requests, and demands for formal apology and legal redress.[28]

Part II: Black Comics and Their Tribe "Arrest" Sense of the Richards's Controversy

I turn my attention now to Black comics and their extended tribe (e.g., comedy club staff, owners, promoters, and fans) who wrestled with their own and others' conflicting truths about whether or not Richards was racist, his apologies sincere, and The Laugh Factory's n-word ban "fair." In doing so, they once again brought notions of "real" Blackness center stage with the stakes of sincerity and empathy in steady tow. The initial hook of my book—the "why" of racial authenticity—got richer as a result. Blessedly, my writerly voice and stance did too. I'll say a bit more about this before discussing their attempts to, per Richards, "arrest" sense from this controversy.

Thus far in my fieldwork, I had focused almost relentlessly on comics' appeals to authenticity in order to unpack the "why" of real Blackness. Along the way, I realized what my colleague John Jackson Jr. had already learned in his ethnographic study of Black Harlemites and discussed in his book, *Real Black: Adventures in Racial Sincerity*: sincerity often undergirded Black folks' appeals to "real Blackness"—so much so that Jackson coined the term "racial sincerity" in deference to race's inherent performativity and folks' subjective assessments of others' artful or successful execution of "real" Blackness;[29] Jackson was after something else too, via his conceptual innovation and analytical intervention, and that was to elide the essentialist trappings and seductions of "real Blackness." Still, even he couldn't completely ignore and hence, dismiss Black folks' insistence, some might even say stubborn conviction, that "real" Blackness mattered as a cultural value, ethos, if not an imperative at times. Nor could I dismiss Blackness as a cultural imperative, especially given Black comics' consummate appeals to notions of real Blackness in highly charged moments (e.g., September 11, Hurricane Katrina, Michael Richards's racist outburst), as well as when things were calm and still.[30]

By remaining curious about the "why" of real Blackness and steadily chasing comics' emergent riffs on the subject and the back stories behind them, I came to better understand authenticity and sincerity's intersubjective dance, or the fact that they often relied on each other—danced together so to speak—since comics' appeals to racial authenticity simultaneously relied on their own or others' perceived sincerity. And much like their jokes about "real" Black folks' penchant for resilience and industriousness during Hurricane Katrina, the jokes comics told about "real" Black folks or Richards's "fake" sincerity are both linked to the pursuit of empathy, a felt mutuality, or the prospect of being unconditionally seen and respected. As in the Chapter 2 concerning Hurricane Katrina humor, this understanding of empathy's indelible link to bids to real Blackness would emerge as one of my greatest discoveries and lessons. I thus held fast to what this epiphany *could* mean for my and others' understandings of race and notions of "real Blackness"; in this way I found that while the rush to redress antiquated notions of race is righteous, it sometimes means that race + authenticity gets a bad rap. Rather than deliver yet another academic treatise against racial authenticity as always and already tethered to racial identity politics ("Booooo"), I began to appreciate how *some* appeals to racial authenticity also constitute calls to life-saving and communally sustaining mutuality. Black comics' capacity for empathy, which I turn to next, had a lot to do with that.

Weighing Comedic Sincerity and Calibrating Empathy

Much like their astute colleague Norm McDonald, many Black comics "saw" and "felt" Richards as a comic, even while they deemed his behavior deplorable. In backstage conversations and onstage sets, several comics identified what many fans and lay folk could not see: Richards was trying to be funny while and/or after being unmistakably racist. A few hard-hitting comics like Jamie Foxx and the late veteran comic Paul Mooney were especially kind during on-camera interviews. Foxx, in particular, initially criticized Richards's racist rant during a press conference but he also admitted that he did not want to kick the man while he was down. During an interview shortly after Richards's tirade went public, Mooney also stated this:[31]

I have known Michael Richards for something like twenty years. We're friends. But I heard about the tape, and I said, "That doesn't sound like a comic routine. That sounds like a breakdown." Then I saw the tape and I had an out-of-body experience. It was so ugly, so horrible. I hadn't heard (the n-word) like this—from someone I knew. Suddenly, I was directly connected. I was able to look at it not just through my eyes but through the eyes of the world. I had always thought it was

endearing. It's NOT. It's not an equal opportunity word. I don't want everyone running around saying it.[32]

Mooney's comments are a gracious concession given his own liberal if not
infamous use of the n-word throughout his comedic career, as well as the
notable difference in his complex wielding of the term: namely, Mooney's deployment of "nigga" was often "er"–less (i.e., not "nigger") and less of a racial
slur as much as an in-group, class-demarcated, and not entirely unproblematic signifier that was never solely tethered to race (e.g., one didn't need to be
Black to get called a "nigga" by Mooney!).[33]

Other comics, including Brandon Bowlin, the late Patrice O'Neal, and Dave
Chappelle, empathized with Richards's onstage predicament of having to slay a
heckler but didn't stop short of heckling the sincerity of Richards's subsequent
apologies. Chappelle joked at The Laugh Factory in 2010 that Richards's rant
made him realize he must be "only 20% Black and 80% comedian"; although
he was furious at first, he could also commiserate with Richards and assumed
he must have "been having a bad set." He added cheekily, "Hang in there
Kramer! Don't let 'em break you Kramer!" before his signature microphone-
knee-slapping laugh break. "You know he was thinking, 'I'll get 'em the next
show!' . . . There won't be a next show." O'Neal also roundly rejected the sincerity of Richards's public apologies and threw shade on the n-word ban, but
he, like Foxx and Mooney, was initially reluctant—publicly at least—to write
Richards off as a racist.[34] Why? O'Neal, and other comics I'll discuss soon,
could see Richards attempting humor, even if in rage; he also understood how
audience members can say things that trigger comics' fierce reprisal and likewise wondered aloud what the audience member (e.g., Doss) may have said
off-camera to enrage Richards so.

Brandon Bowlin especially understood Richards's breakdown, which he
felt was stoked by both Richards's well-established fame and the capacity of
folks adept at social media and branding to make or break said fame. When
considering how Richards might have felt after his improvisational set fal-
tered before a crowd of phone-wielding "fans," Bowlin surmised: "He choked.
I've done it. Every comic's done it." Brandon then shared a story about having
fumed about the Holocaust onstage some years ago in a manner he now finds
utterly disrespectful. While playing to a mixed crowd, he'd quipped that he
was "tired of hearing about the Holocaust." "What about the Armenian genocide?" he asked indignantly. "What about slavery in America?!" In a bid toward humor, he added a comment that has derailed comic/actress Roseanne
Barr's career much like Richards's n-word-laced tirade did his:[35] "I'm tired of
hearing about Jew cookies." Ever the humble ethnographer, I asked, "And you

don't think there was a difference between your attempt to relativize histor-ical genocides and atrocities and Richards's racist rant?" Patiently, Brandon replied, "Lanita, sure yes. But anytime you say `Jew cookies' . . . that's just not cool."[36] I nodded and asked what happened next. "Tension."

Comedic Retorts and Bids to "A" Real Black

A palpable tension permeated The Laugh Factory stage on *Chocolate Sundaes* when, two weeks after Richards's outburst, the show's long-time host Chris Spencer and producer, Leland "Pookey" Wigington Jr., attempted to address the situation.[37] Pookey, in addition to producing one of Los Angeles's most popular Black standup comedy shows, is also an established businessman; he told the predominantly African American crowd that Richards's words "don't matter to us. He'll go on. Our concern is how The Laugh Factory handled the situation." Ultimately, he and Chris felt that Jamie Masada was sincere in answering a pivotal question: Why was Richards able to come back and perform following his racist rant? Masada told them that the only reason Richards was allowed back was to apologize in the presence of a CNN camera. (Masada's astute fear was that African Americans would never believe Richards had apologized if it was not on record.) However, when Richards did not apologize during his in-itial moments on the stage, Masada gave him the light and decided that Richards was no longer welcome at the club. Chris and Pookey followed this explanation with an unprecedented Q&A session. I had never seen this room, let alone any comedy club, in such a serious state. (Hurricane Katrina was sobering, perhaps rightly so given the death toll and blatant abandonment of US citizens on American soil—on TV no less. Still, this was something altogether startling for one of L.A.'s premiere and most lively comedy shows.) A Black male guest seated near the stage diffused the tension by shouting, "It's all good!" Pookey replied, "That's what I'm talking about. Let's have some fun." Then the 8:00 PM show began.

In short order, Chris and Pookey revealed a series of comedic sketches and retorts steeped in notions of Black authenticity and truth; namely, they invoked the prospect of racism and the high probability of a different out-come had Richards lost it during, say, The Laugh Factory's "Black" night, *Chocolate Sundaes*. During one set, Chris told the crowd, "This is what would've happened if Richards had said that during *Chocolate Sundaes*," and then pointed stage left. The audience saw two feet dangling from the club's bal-cony, a dummy stand-in for Richards and a vivid redux of the lynching images most audience members might be accustomed to featuring dead Black bodies dangling from trees in the aftermath of racial violence. During *Chocolate Sundae*'s second 10:00 PM show, Chris doubled down on this riff, enlisting the only White comic who played that night, "R.T." Acting quite like "Kramer," R.T. moved around erratically and repeated some of Richards's remarks word for word: "Fifty years ago we'd have you upside down with a fucking fork up your ass. . . . He's a nig-." Just as R.T. began to enunciate the n-word, he is cut down by the sound of gunshots and ends up on the floor. Notably, the ethnically mixed crowd assembled that night applauded and laughed at this violent and clearly staged display. Later, R.T. had his own joke to tell about the Richards event, one reminiscent of Ray Chatman's joke about the devastation he felt when he learned that the Washington, DC, snipers back in 2002 were Black: "Tension. Can you feel it? Richards set white people back 100 years with that shit."[38] I wondered if this joke rang true in a personal way for R.T. Backstage, among the comics, I noticed R.T. milling about, shut out of several private conversations among African American comics concerning Richards, race, and comedy.

Similar riffs echoed in other Los Angeles comedy clubs. Pierre Edwards, a comic who occasionally hosted The Comedy Store's *Phat Tuesday* Show, said in the week following Richards's rant: "If some _real_ niggahs has been there, they would've had the whole club rearranged." Katt Williams joked similarly, saying, "That was some gangsta shit. He [Richards] said it right in front of niggahs. He couldn't have done it _tonight_. He would've been like [*impersonates Richards*] 'Nigger—fifty years ago—[*imitates Richards getting knocked to the ground and then getting up in a daze*] Seinfeld? Where's Seinfeld?'" Williams added, "Now he's got to be on the lookout for _real_ niggahs who'll hit him and tell him, 'That was because fifty years ago, you put a fork up my ass.'"

Other comics "kept real" about their reasons for discouraging the use of the "n-word" by White folks, including comics, and, in doing so, underscore how appeals to racial authenticity and speaking truth to (White) power act as cultural "clap back" imperatives in Black standup comedy. Chris Spencer, whom you may recall cautioned White folks to "avoid the –er (suffix) if [they] want to avoid the E.R. (emergency room)," revised this joke in the wake of the Richards controversy by telling his *Chocolate Sundaes* audience, "Many whites want to know why they can't use the 'n-word.' Because, you already had your chance and fucked it up."[39] Dannon Green's lament at The Laugh Factory's *Chocolate Sundaes* show seemed to corroborate the subtext of Spencer's joke: "That Richards thing made me mad! . . . But that's just how it is in life"—while ABC news cameras were filming. (News reporters showed up to witness the aftermath of Richards's viral set and the institution of the club's n-word ban.) The only part of Green's joke that aired on the news later that night, was his lament ("That Richards thing made me mad!"), not his weary rejoinder ("But that's just how it is in life.") ABC news cameras also missed David Arnold's set later on in the show wherein he chide-quipped: "Give it up for R.T. [the White comic who lent his comedic talents and White skin to several violent sketches castigating Richards]. . . . Yeah, white people know how to do damage control. [*Imitates news reporter*] 'The niggahs are still laughing after the travesty.' Like we're not going to come—or be sad because you said 'nigger?' Y'all say it every day behind closed doors. . . . They got cameras out. I been coming here for years and cameras ain't never been here." Then he added, "I feel kind of sorry for the niggah [Richards]."[40]

In these meta-commentaries and quips about the n-word, Black comics marshal notions of "real" Blackness toward two ends: they critique Richards on the one hand while troubling the rush toward censorship on the other—with nary a hint of contradiction. Note, for example, how Black comics' deft deployment of the n-word to rebuke Richards's racist remarks and subsequent apologies simultaneously preserves their freedom to use the n-word while they are doing so. Note, too, how the n-word signals race (i.e., Black folks) and implies that "real" Blackness mandates a swift repudiation, even if violent, of comics who practice racism as leisurely sport. This nod to "real Blackness" is similar to 9/11 jokes asserting that "real" Black folks would inevitably sneer if/when faced with a terrorist wielding only a boxcutter; it also slaps back at comedy that flagrantly trades racist barbs as comedic sucker punches—where "sucker punch" is the operative word. Black comics' appeals to "real" Blackness are thus less about identity politics or restrictive gatekeeping and more about effectively serving racists with swift punitive verbal and physical assault. Surprisingly, such appeals to "a" real Black can also contain empathy. Consider again David Arnold's use of "niggah" to reference Richards in his rejoinder, "I feel kind of sorry for the niggah." David's marshaling of the word "niggah" imbues the racial signifier with a more capacious signaling quite different from Richards's use of it as a racial slur; much like Chris Rock's tough-loving and castigating use of "niggah" to distinguish trifling African Americans (i.e., "niggahs") from hard-working ones (i.e., "Black people") in his (1996) chart-topping HBO special, *Bring the Pain*, Dave's reference to Richards might begrudgingly bestow him speculative (i.e., side-eye) membership in standup comedy's hard-won tribe.

Toward the Imperative of a "Real" Black

Still, comics' fiery retorts and especially their caveated empathy for Richards, to say nothing of the complex reasons informing them, failed to appease some members of the Black comics' extended tribe, including "Andrea," a Black woman who worked at The Comedy Union, the Black-owned club I religiously frequented. She surprised me by crouching down beside me as I took notes in the shadows of The Laugh Factory and huffed: "I can't believe we're (Black folks) sitting here after that! If a Black comic had said something about a Jew, this place would be turned out! They (Pookey and Chris) are doing this to preserve their night. Because it's 'The Laugh Factory.' This is their meal ticket!"[41] I quietly thanked Andrea for sharing her thoughts and then watched show host Chris Spencer anew as he warmed up the crowd. His very presence onstage was politicized, explicitly so as a response to Richards's disrespect of African Americans and the club's questionable decision to allow Richards to return. But, I wondered, was Chris's performance equivalent to "Condi" telling America that Hurricane Katrina was not about race and class—a stance she later publicly regretted?[42] Or, was this Chris, having already voiced his opinion on Richards and having few expectations about race and fairness in his field, doing what makes him feel alive?

Andrea was not alone in her critique. In fact, there were communal deliberations about the Richards debacle prior to Chris and Pookey's onstage discussion. In a flurry of emails, phone calls, letters that circulated at the time concerning how Black people should respond to Richards's rant, opinions varied. Some people argued that his behavior should not be construed as the solo action of a disturbed White celebrity but rather as a poignant reminder of Black people's enduring struggle against racism and White supremacy in the United States. Other stewards of Black standup comedy (e.g., fans, waitresses) framed the controversy as a civil rights issue, calling for the end of "niggah nights" or ethnically oriented shows in mainstream clubs so that people of color could monitor White comics. (The thinking here was that Richards would not have said what he said had comics of color been present that day. But Paul Rodriguez, Sinbad, and other venerated comics of color were, indeed, present during the night of Richards's controversial set.)

Enss Mitchell, who owns The Comedy Union and has run it stalwartly through thick-and-thin over the last two decades, wanted way more from Black comics than bristles of discontent, calibrated loyalty to Richards, and not-so-veiled threats akin to "this is what would've happened if *real* Blacks had been in the room when Richards waxed racist." Enss advocated a boycott of The Laugh Factory by Black comics and audiences and suggested that the *Chocolate Sundaes* show's producer and host move their highly successful Sunday night show to his club in a stance of racial solidarity. He explained why when he and I met late one night as The Comedy Union's popular Saturday night show ended.

After waving his staff off repeatedly, he showed me an email that comedienne/actress Adriane Kelly had circulated calling for a boycott of The Laugh Factory. Her email was powerful not simply because of her direct prose but also because she attached two images of Black men hanging from trees. Many of us have seen these photos. They are iconic of African Americans' not so recent history of brutalization via state-sanctioned lynchings. I could see the rage of this history reflected in Enss's eyes when he said, "I'm not a shuffling and jiving kind of niggah." In our conversation, as well as in interviews with news reporters, Enss made sure to note that the injustice occurred not merely at the level of Richards's remarks but also at the level of management. "There is no way he [Richards] should've been able to continue his tirade. The owner or manager should have cut his microphone immediately for the sake of the audience and . . . business." And he cemented this point with me in whispered intensity that night, saying: "I mean, could you imagine Martin Lawrence . . . joking about Jews . . . in concentration camps?" He took it further, "in trains . . . being gassed?" Enss concluded, "He would never work in this town again, let alone be invited on any stage to perform!"

My and Enss's improvisational back and forth picked up where Andrea's whispered allegation left off. Much like a wildly popular joke premise (e.g., "The Arab is the new 'nigger'") which can occur at the same time to different comics, our riff also proved resonant among comics themselves. When I chatted with comic/author Darryl Littleton and comic "Tony Tone" about the Richards fiasco in The Laugh Factory's balcony during a *Chocolate Sundaes* late-night show, they doubled down on the premise like real comics do. Darryl told Tony Tone: "If I had said [*mimics Richards when he pointed out the Black men in the balcony*] 'He's a Jew! He's a Jew!' [*hits an invisible microphone quizzically; soon realizes that the sound has been cut*], I would have been escorted out of the club, arrested for disturbing the peace, my books would've been pulled from the shelf, and I would've been beat up three times on my way to the jailhouse." Tony Tone agreed, though neither he nor Darryl could agree on whether he (Darryl) would then be out of work indefinitely or just consigned to selling encyclopedias door to door.

Like and unlike Richards, we may have all just been riffing on Frantz Fanon (the late Martinique philosopher I invoked earlier given my suspicion that Richards *may* have unwittingly borrowed his words to unrealized comedic effect). When Fanon bemoaned his perverse hypervisibility to the

White child who regarded him with fear and loathing (i.e., "Look! A Negro!," "Maman, I'm scared"), he actually invoked the marginalization of White Jews, saying: "Granted, the Jews are harassed. . . . They are hunted down, exterminated, cremated. . . . The Jew is disliked from the moment he is tracked down. But in my case, everything takes on a new guise. I am given no chance. I am overdetermined from without. I am the slave not of the 'idea' that others have of me but of my own appearance." This, he argued, is unlike the dilemma facing (White) Jews who, like White Italians and other US immigrants, have managed to overcome staunch racial and religious discrimination and violence and secure unmarked "White" citizenship in the United States insofar as "one has only not to be a nigger" and Jews "can sometimes go unnoticed."[43] (This is also why Richard Pryor once quipped that Vietnamese children adopted by Americans during the Vietnam War (aka "American War" according to Vietnamese) got socialized into American identity by learning how to say "nigger" repeatedly in rapid fashion. Scholars of Jewish and Italian identity substantiate the premise of this joke be detailing how Jews and other ethnically White (and non-White!) immigrants ostensibly "became White"—or jockeyed for legible American citizenship and state protection—by consciously and concertedly differentiating themselves from African Americans.[44]

In his book, *Look, A White!*, George Yancy (2012) offers another poignant through-line connecting Fanon's experience and the aforementioned speculative riffs by Andrea, Darryl and Tony Tone, and Enss and me. Recall that Fanon was rendered both legible and illegible when a White child saw him and was frightened by his black skin. Recall, too, that rather than being chastised, the child was comforted by his mother who tried to point out how "attractive" Fanon was, a gesture Fanon tough-laughingly refuted. What, pray tell, is Yancy after then by essentially challenging his readers to singularly call out White folks, and what on earth might it have to do with the foreboding speculations recounted earlier by Andrea, Enss, and Darryl and Tony Tone concerning Black comics' no-win capacity to essentially shout, "Look! A Jew!"?

Yancy conscientiously asks his White college students (and White readers) to shout on a daily basis, "Look, a White!" when moving through a world wherein Whiteness remains an unmarked and privileged category. Why? By consciously marking and mapping the workings of White privilege and White supremacy in "the everyday," White citizens can essentially "flip the script" on the lies of White normativity and color blindness; these lies, Yancy reasons, often compel non-critical Whites to unconsciously read Whiteness in opposition to Blackness instead of seeing Whiteness from the perspective of Black people. Herein lies one of Yancy's key interventions: he's asking White folks to view the world *from the perspective of Black people and people of color* almost like a mirror. "The mirror," Yancy assures, "will tell the truth," as in "No, damn it! Snow White is not the 'fairest of them all.' She is precisely the problem!" Here, Yancy is not serving notice on White femininity or Eurocentric presumptions of White-as-beautiful per say as much as indicting how Whites like the ones Fanon encountered in a Paris train platform routinely miss how their ways of "seeing" Black folks always and already implicate themselves.

Further, by asking White folks to critically shout, "Look, a White!," Yancy is invested in complicating White identity versus fixing it according to racist myths and legends. This, he concedes, would risk reinscribing racial essentialism (or generalized and objectifying notions of "real" Whiteness) versus actively bringing Whiteness into the foreground such that "Whiteness as a site of privilege and power is named and identified" and Whiteness is further understood as a "set of social practices that render White people complicit in larger social practices of White racism" (Yancey 2012, 12). He adds: "It is about turning our bodies (and our attentions) in the direction of White discourse and White social performances that attempt to pass themselves off as racially neutral, and it is about finding the courage to say, 'Look, a White!' [. . . in a way] that militates against its reduction to identifying singular, individual, intentional acts of racism only" (12–13), and further, "does not open the door to facile claims about symmetrically hurtful racial stereotypes, 'reverse discrimination,' and the rhetoric of a so-called color-blind perpetrator perspective." To Yancy, such rhetorical moves are "sites of obfuscation" [and] "forms of 'mystificatory digression from the clearly *a*symmetrical and enduring system of White power itself'" (13).

This, I'd argue, is what Darryl and Tony Tone are after as well in their rhetorical riff session; like Andrea and Enss (with my assist), they are trying to shine a critical light on the unfairness underlying Richards's capacity to wax racist on a comedy stage in the first place, let alone be allowed to perform again as a pretense for offering a public apology as penance for his publicized sin and to restore honor to the comedy stage. They are also underscoring the crazy-making notion that Richards's racist faux pas served to "make policy," namely, the short-lived n-word ban. And they are suggesting, rightly so I believe, that had Richards essentially shouted, "Look, a Jew!" (something neither Darryl or Tony Tone articulate explicitly in the manner of Fanon's report and Richards's potential post-millennial riff), all professional bets in Hollywood would be canceled for the comic in question—likely without the institution of policies that directly or indirectly indict Jewish comics skilled in the practice of self-parody.

In their rhetorical comic-sparring session, Darryl and Tony Tone also do much more than nod back to Fanon (and Andrea and Enss) by bearing witness to the differential stakes facing White and Black comics playing in standup comedy's risky fields, especially where race and racism are concerned.[45] They also animate one of the many underlying provocations for Black comics' appeals to "real" Blackness and truth. The "why" of truth-telling—a kind that exposes hidden privileges and decries White supremacy and racist denials + lies—emerges here as a *cultural imperative* in an unfair world and comedy industry that asks Black comics to stretch to play and then punishes them indiscriminately for the sins of select members (e.g., Richards) of their tribe. The "why" of real Blackness also emerges as an imperative when and if Black folks need to deploy humor and humorous speculation to speak truth to power and otherwise tell the truth about race, collective identity, and responsibility to each other, regardless of the outcome or vast differences of opinion.

This imperative necessarily implicates and disciplines me as well. When I shared an early draft of this chapter with Brandon Bowlin about six years ago (it's taken that long to figure out this story), I had used the word "weary" to describe my and comics' stance on the work of talking about race. In my mind, the work was tough for comics like Dannon Green (who lamented, "That Richards thing made me mad! But that's just how it is in life") because he and many other Black comics have had to vet their responses to the Richards video through a series of preliminary questions in order to even authenticate their "right to speak": How does one talk about Richards's behavior while maintaining a sense of personal and communal integrity and tribe loyalty? Further, how does one speak out in ways that recognize Richards's humanity and vulnerability without missing a chance to problematize his behavior and even name it as hurtful? Additionally, many of the comics I followed worked especially hard to hone their comedic voices in pursuit of mainstream legibility (e.g., the sitcom or *HBO* or *Netflix* special!); sometimes, their affective, ideological, and even linguistic labor imposes a catch-22 by alienating them from their Black core constituencies while, ironically, consigning them to the oft-ghettoized but lucrative niche of "Black comedy." All of this, I'd reasoned in my heart, was wearying for Black comics attempting to engage the Michael Richards affair, let alone endure the many ways that Whites fail time and time again to see their own relative privilege.[46]

In short order, I received a cautionary email from Brandon that rekindled memories of the consequential feedback I received from several comics after sharing drafts of my 9/11 humor chapter years back. This is what he told me:

Context is the grail here . . . for me and you! The Jew Cookie statement, I think, should be buttressed by my comment about them being burned after they died as opposed to being thrown overboard alive in the middle passage as ballast. Both are horrific ends and I honored none of the dead by my insensitive comment. . . . Is it our job to be sensitive? . . . That's my point. I said that and had to recognize whatever the lesson. It didn't warrant an abrupt apology from all Black to Jews and all Jews to Black or a behavior forum for the races involved. Despite your weariness of the subject, I would caution you to be brave AND thoughtful. These are choppy, deep, and long and soon to be well remembered torrential words we are all adding to the conversation.

I still hear Brandon loud and clear. He was telling me many things, not the least of which is that what he tells me in private as a friend requires sufficient context when aired publicly, lest the nuances and implications of his story (and my own!) be lost.[47]

As I processed the implications of Brandon's note for my own public and scholarly musings, the stories surrounding Richards's racist outburst steadily grew and complicated this very telling.[48] The Laugh Factory continued to host press conferences and impromptu protests about the realities of racism and other –isms in "urban" and mainstream comedy. Late comic/author Dick Gregory, whose autobiography is titled *Nigger,* went public about his opposition to the recent crackdown on the n-word.

Other comics consciously and conscientiously used the n-word onstage after the short-lived ban to throw explicit and copious shade on the whole affair—even as The Laugh Factory's owner Jamie Masada joined Oprah Winfrey, the Reverend Jesse Jackson, and other influential Black folks in calling for Black folks to stop using the n-word. Damon Wayans essentially said "naw" when he used the n-word repeatedly on The Laugh Factory stage after the controversy, dropping dollar bills with every iteration. And well before the Richards's controversy drew conspicuous attention to n-word usage in L.A.'s comedy's scene, Eddie Griffin promised to keep using the n-word in his sets because that's how "they [White people] see us." (Only, Griffin's use inflects the abundant nuances of Black comics' marshaling of this highly charged term.) It was as if Black comics took the whole notion of n-word censorship as a literal joke and provocation. For these and other comics of all hues, The Laugh Factory's short-lived "no n-word or face fine" policy felt like an overcorrection, a punishing one that instigated outright mockery since it conflated Richards's actions with the ever-complex uses of the n-word among African American comics.[49]

I draw optimism from Brandon's poignant cautions about context while reflecting on past jokes he now regrets having told. I am also inspired by comics like Rodney Perry and then *Chocolate Sundaes* host Chris Spencer, each of whom managed to excavate a newfound resolve from the Richards's affair. Before performing at The Laugh Factory's *Chocolate Sundaes* Show, Rodney told me that while he "understood where Richards was. Not where he went. He was drowning . . ." he saw little merit in the club's short-lived n-word ban. As he explained, "I don't buy into the belief that my use of the word in any way condones Richards's use . . . but I do feel it gets used too much as a filler. I just want to work on myself." Working on himself meant minimizing his own use of the n-word and recalibrating one of his race-facing jokes, which he performed that very night.

Rodney told the crowd, "I've been working on my inner-racism. . . . We've all got some," before launching into his physically animated routine wherein Rodney, angry from incessant racial violence against him and other Black folks, pretends to tackle unsuspecting elderly White folks, hold them down, and berate them through gritted teeth as follows: "This is for [slain civil rights leader] Medgar Evans bitch. . . . This is for Martin Luther King [Jr.] bitch. . . . Remember the water hose?! . . . . Remember the water hose?!" (Rodney typically uses the stool or the microphone holder as a stand-in for his unsuspecting White victims and wins howls of laughter as he flies through the air with them in hand.)

Rodney felt that this joke had a special resonance and urgency in the wake of the Michael Richards flack. "I knew my set was going to mean something to somebody," he said. He vowed to keep telling it while minimizing his use of the n-word despite a few enduring fears. Rodney's joke, it turns out, has come under fire—twice, in fact. First, from a White gentleman who created a Myspace page for the sole purpose of telling Rodney that he'd found this joke to be ignorant since Whites like him had also fought in the civil rights movement. I still wonder if that critic was so offended by Rodney's words (e.g., "bitch") and enactments of physical violence that he missed the aspect of play in the telling, as well as the concession that Rodney makes every time he tells the joke (i.e., "I'm working on my own inner-racism")?[50] Rodney's concession gives *me* gracious pause since his joke bears out the differences between historical and structurally entrenched racism and prejudice and bias but graciously democratizes the social justice work facing us all. The second time Rodney's joke came under fire was after his televised performance on HBO's *Def Comedy Jam.* This time, the offended party was not a White person but his biological sister; she called to tell him she didn't like the joke and wanted him to consider dropping it from his routine. When he asked her why, she expressed fear that he would get hurt for telling it, thus highlighting the literal and figurative life-or-death stakes Black comics are perceived to face for deigning to joke not only about race, but about White folks, Jews inclusive, in a "White" industry.[51]

I mention Chris Spencer too as a source of inspiration in this telling. Before he and "Pookey" (*Chocolate Sundaes'* producer) convened their first show under The Laugh Factory's new no n-word, policy, I called Chris, the show's then long-standing host, to see if he planned to avoid using the n-word. He replied, "Just for the night. I will treat it as a T.V. set [set for T.V.] where I can't say it anyway." But he was also thinking well beyond the club's policy, adding, "It's also time for me to separate myself from the pack. When I watch myself on TV, [I see] that me and too much foul language don't match. I still won't be afraid to use it, but only where it counts (e.g., for emphasis or in character). . . . It's time to treat my career with a business mind. . . . I'm going to be a student of myself and . . . watch and study the DVD's you've given me and tape every performance. I have the ability to be the next NIGGA!" Ever the comic performer and writer, Chris breathed second wind into his career shortly thereafter, landing a series of writing, acting, and producing gigs on TV and film.

In their own distinct ways then, they (Brandon Bowlin, Rodney Perry, Chris Spencer, and so many others)[52] each remind me that while issues of race pose challenges and dilemmas that can make us weary and even break our hearts, they also present opportunities to reflect and grow. I take heart in their efforts because the work is hard, especially where race and representation are concerned, and the vulnerability we all feel, especially those of us who are Black, endures. It's hard, too, when Black comics and Black folks run up against repeated failures of the state or even club policy to protect their lives, interests, and capacities to be free. They learn that racism is not merely the malicious treatment of one marginalized group by a more powerful group on the basis of assumed racial superiority; it also entails a withholding of empathy, such as when Black storm victims were deemed "looters" versus "finders" and "refugees" versus "citizens" during Hurricane Katrina. This withholding, comics teach us, can make already vulnerable groups feel dehumanized. It is also why Doss and many Black comics felt dehumanized not only when Richards blew his lid but also when he was allowed back to perform again for the benefit of making an apology while Black comics (and all non-Black comics), in turn, were banned from using the n-word onstage.[53]

Conclusion

In this chapter, I've considered the stakes of Richards's rant and subsequent apologies for Black comics who were arguably most affected by the club's n-word ban if not also symbolically targeted by Richards's racist condemnation. Strikingly, while much of the media expressed outrage at Richards's revealed racism to stage debates around the use and censure of the n-word, comics articulated another story more befitting their lived realities. For them, this controversy concerned far more than a famous White comic coming undone, exposing his inner racism and "White rage" in the process; Richards's "break-down" exposed the risks of comedy's liberal mandate on free speech. The idea that Richards's breach subjected his sincerity to question made sense, but Black comics found it ironic, crazy even, that their freedom of speech ended up standing trial, with the n-word being indicted as merely a racial slur in need of exorcising.

Not surprisingly, Black comics, whom we have already seen marshal "nigga/h" in myriad ways, scoffed at the n-word ban via jokes and sketches that eviscerated Richards and affirmed their "freedom of speech" while not entirely disavowing Richards's right to it as well; in doing so, they punted other responses proffered by the media, including charges of hypocrisy, to instead center themselves as bona fide members of both a comedic and Black tribe. Some Black comics, with calibrated empathy and grace, also called Richards out for his presumed insincerity during onstage sets and subsequent televised apologies; others spared no punches as they invoked convictions around "real Blackness" or "real niggas" to indict not only Richards but also racist and inequitable practices in their industry.[54] As they issued their own call-backs, their ever-attentive and disciplining constituency (e.g., Black fans, club owners) weighed in as well with riffs of their own and calls for "real" accountability to a Black collective.

Their soulful reckonings stuck with me. As Black comics asserted their creative agency and "right to speak" around matters of race while deftly marshaling the n-word, they hipped me once again to the contextual provocations subtexting bids to "a" real Black. They also re-wrote the n-word debate in their own terms, culling insights from their racial and professional realities as if their careers, if not their and other Black folks' very lives, relied on their capacity to be funny, sincere (e.g., really mean what you say), "real," and unapologetic about what I call "a" real Black.

Kevin Hart, who I discuss in the next chapter, knows something about this.

4

"It's About to Get Real"

Kevin Hart as a Modern-Day Trickster

Kevin Hart fans around the globe might easily recall his star-affirming role in Hyundai's (2016) Super Bowl commercial, "First Date." Going overboard to convince his teen daughter's courter to keep his hands to himself, Hart's antics belie the insecure father he frequently makes himself out to be on-stage. Scrutinizing his daughter's way-too-cavalier date, Hart "kindly" offers him keys to his brand new car. As soon as they leave, Hart trails them using Hyundai's "car finder" app, allowing him to intimidate the fella without his daughter's knowledge. His scare tactics, fittingly backed by Queen's '80s hit, "Another One Bites the Dust," hit their mark. At the movies, the suitor decides against the old reach around when he catches Hart glaring at him from three rows back. Later, he rejects a hug from Hart's daughter after winning her a stuffed carnival toy because he spots Hart's' disapproving face nestled among the plush prizes. His sexual advances are thwarted a final time at a scenic over-look when he notices Hart dangling from a shark-emblazoned helicopter shouting, "You messin' with the wrong Daddy!" Aptly shaken from having "bit the dust," the young man promptly returns Hart's daughter and car, and with greater deference this time around. Yet Hart can't resist a final bit of fun, so he activates his car alarm just as the dejected lad walks by, startling him yet again. Hart stages one more whimsical play at the commercial's end: after asking his daughter oh-so-innocently about her date, he turns to the camera to flash a mischievous smile.

When I first saw this commercial and homed in on Hart's winking smile, I thought: Kevin is a bona fide trickster who has been winking at us for quite some time now. When I pitched this idea to my African American Humor and Culture class, however, my students looked at me sideways, as if saying, "Hmmm?" While in this prized TV-spot Hart certainly plays the trickster—one who represents nearly all fathers in their willingness to protect their girls at all costs—they weren't entirely convinced that his multi-million-dollar-grossing standup comedy albums, TV and movie roles, and "HartBeat"

To Be Real. Lanita Jacobs, Oxford University Press. © Oxford University Press 2023.
DOI: 10.1093/oso/9780190870096.003.0005

production deals satisfied the requirements for a "trickster"—especially a Black one.[1]

To them, tricksters included "Brer Rabbit" (also known as Bruh, Br'er, or Bre'r Rabbit), a canonical figure in the African American folklore and slave humor we'd read.[2] Intensely human, which is to say fallible, and allegorical of Blacks' position in a racist social order, Brer Rabbit routinely uses his wits to outpace bigger opponents and stay alive. In one of many interpretations of Brer Rabbit tales recorded by folklorist Joel Chandler Harris,[3] Brer Rabbit's pride gets the best of him in a confrontation with Brer Fox. Infuriated, Brer Fox threatens to kill Brer Rabbit in various ways (e.g., cook, hang, drown), but none of these murderous ends scares Brer Rabbit as much as the briar patch: "Do what you want but please don't throw me in that briar patch!" he pleads. When Brer Fox does precisely that, he soon realizes he's been tricked, as Brer Rabbit dashes away boasting, "I was born and bred in a briar patch! Born and bred in a briar patch!"

Enslaved African Americans and their descendants readily identified with Brer Rabbit. While he was not always "right" or "good" (his pride sometimes felled him), he often survived and outwitted his physically superior and scary foes. Williams (1995) adds that while Brer Rabbit did not have, say, the turtle's protective shell, a bumblebee's sting, or an eagle's sharp beak and claws, his big floppy ears allowed him to hear widely and thus discern how to succeed in iffy situations. When Black folks told trickster tales involving Brer Rabbit and other cunning animal and human figures,[4] they were not just aiming to entertain; rather, they used the cloak of Brer Rabbit tales to protest their subjugation, affirm their moral superiority over racist Whites, and, ultimately, laugh at and through their pain.

Besides "Brer Rabbit," my students identified two Black humorists we studied whom they felt more deserving than Hart of the "trickster" title: famed vaudevillian Bert Williams, and one of America's first cross-over Black comics, Jackie "Moms" Mabley. Williams was a preeminent entertainer in the early 1900s whose expressive nuance, mime capabilities, and impeccable timing enabled him to eventually shed the burnt cork (i.e., Blackface) and racist crud that Blackface minstrelsy required. Described by fellow vaudevillian W. C. Fields as "the funniest man I ever saw—and the saddest man I ever knew," Williams was the top-grossing Black performer of his time.[5] His popularity and talent eventually exceeded Blackface minstrelsy, enabling him to articulate for racially mixed audiences the nuances of Black vulnerability and joyful abandon despite it.

Like Williams, Mabley was also cloaked, but instead of burnt cork, she donned a "granny" persona of her own design. Onstage, Mabley wore a house dress and a colorful floppy hat, and she spoke in a raspy southern accent; this guise strategically masked her queer identity offstage and enabled her to joke freely about raunchy and politically subversive matters.[6] "Moms" fame on the Black "chitlin' circuit"[7] eventually earned her TV and movie roles. "Moms" became a mother to "*all* of God's chillun'" with a quip as rich as, if not richer than, Brer Rabbit's boast: "No *damn* MAMMY. 'Moms.' I don't know nothin' 'bout no log cabin; I ain't never seen no log cabin. . . . Split level in the suburbs *baby*!"

Set against the cunning of Brer Rabbit, Williams, and Mabley, Hart's status as a trickster elicited an informed cynicism from my students, which made me pensive. Was my framing of Hart as a "trickster" mere wishful thinking—a hopeful ideation born of an eight-year ethnographic study of Black comics in L.A. and beyond? Or were my students' expectations of Hart too high to appreciate what he must do to ignore his many critics[8] and blast through Hollywood's racially stratified star-scape to cement himself as a globally recognized brand? Most important, what else could I say about Hart's self-deprecating pose, Hollywood's demands of Black funny men, and core Black audience expectations to show that Hart's status as a trickster was conceivable?

I titled this chapter "It's about to get real" as a callback to Hart. It riffs on one of his frequent rejoinders onstage but also means to say something critical about what global stardom and Black audiences, in particular, require of him: that is, that Hart remain both racially authentic (i.e., "really Black" or, at least, Black "enough") and sincere (i.e., earnest or truthful). Arguably, Hart "stays winning" because he conveys sincerity and *keys* a recognizable, even if calibrated, Blackness. His ability to convey both racial authenticity and sincerity guarantees his spot in the Black standup game, and on top of the comedy game writ large—albeit, I argue—in trickster pose.

Staking this claim about Hart's sincere, yet trickster pose requires some care, as I'm dabbling in subjective matters of race, namely, Blackness. Race is, admittedly, a social construction and, thus, hard to pin down—especially in the realm of comedic performance. I'd do best to ask, then: how does Kevin Hart *do* being "Black" such that he might be deemed a trickster? (The scare quotes and italicized "do" are meant to stress Black performativity over essentialist claims about Hart and/or notions of Blackness, masculinity, sexuality, etc.). In tracing some notion of "real" Blackness, discerning readers might wonder how I square up with African Americans' inherent diversity; since, for example, many hail from various African diasporic places, class locations, ideological viewpoints, and the like, as did Bert Williams.[9] Others, like "Moms" Mabley, and arguably Hart, essentially "quare" heteronormative assumptions of "real" Black women and men.[10] (I consciously use E. Patrick

Johnson's [2001] concept, "quare" versus "queer" for reasons I'll soon explain.) I hear all of this loud and clear; in fact, I've rehearsed these and other complexities for quite some time, yet only to feel that my endless rehearsals leave something important unsaid.

As Darnell Hunt (2005) unapologetically asserts, "Blackness remains," and it does so "in a time when the U.S. population is diversifying at a dizzying rate, when popular accounts of race present it as an anachronistic concern, when color-blind ideology shapes much of our public policy, and when affirmation of cultural hybridity and multiple subjectivities is all the rage" (1). Additionally, Blackness, however subjectively assessed, artfully performed, and/or delicately calibrated, *materially matters* for those who are Black.[11] As such, Blackness is worth fighting over, laughing about, and articulating sans apology, lest it be appropriated, co-opted, diluted, or otherwise misunderstood. Having observed Black comedians in and beyond Los Angeles for eight years (and anxiously pondered what I'd learned for another six), I realized that I couldn't discuss Hart or Black standup comedy as if measures of racial authenticity, as opposed to matters of sincerity [i.e., earnestness] and even "racial sincerity,"[12] are not paramount. Cultural/communal imperatives around "keeping real [Black]" and true (i.e., sincere/earnest) undoubtedly inform Hart's ability to stay famous and bear on any claims of him as a "trickster."

Hart's legibility as a trickster might in fact remain unfathomable until we concede that there is something decidedly "Black" about Blackness, and then gingerly excavate his standup comedy for cultural and discursive signs of Blackness and trickster tales and guises. By "signs of Blackness," I mean such markers as his fluency in African American English, "Black" aesthetics,[13] racial experiences, and communal ideologies/stances thought core to African American culture. I also mean the ways Hart's incessant self-deprecation (onstage at least) enables critiques of White apathy and privilege; decidedly ingroup deployments of the n-word; and generous aid to other Black comics looking to get some Hollywood "shine." I turn to these excavating tasks now and aim, per Hart's gender-policing uncle, to "say it with my chest"; that is, boldly, yet with healthy regard for how emasculating tropes of Black men both precede and color Hart's legibility as a Black comedic trickster.

If, like "Brer Rabbit," tricksters use their wits to survive in hostile and unequal terrains; and if, like Williams and Mabley, tricksters "wear the mask" *precisely in order to* speak truth to power, then we must concede: Hart is not a trickster just because he broke through Hollywood's glass ceiling as a Black man. No; according to my students' studied conjectures, more is required of a trickster than this stupendous feat. Chiefly, a trickster must be able to discern how to win in a decidedly unequal game. My students' standards were even higher for a Black comedic trickster: much like the proverbial "spook who sat by the door," the trickster's job is to incessantly and shrewdly observe, if only to rise up and shout: "Black lives matter!"; "The n-word ain't for everybody!"; "Racism and homophobia kill"; or something akin.

Hart's standup belied many of my students' expectations; they wondered, for example, if he was even "wearing the mask" that African American poet Paul Laurence Dunbar waxed poetic about in 1896,[14] or strategically posted at the [closed] door of opportunity. Admittedly, Hart has routinely downplayed his role as a politically attuned "comic spokesman" (Mintz 1985), instead stressing his artistic license as an entertainer who, at his best, not only makes audiences laugh but understand (Hart 2017).[15] His comedic repertoire also grapples, in the main, with existential and, hence, "universal" questions: what kind of man am I/can I be? Notably, Hart does not always center race in his onstage deliberations (what kind of *Black* man am I/can I be?)—at least not explicitly—because Blackness is *always* and *already* an integral part of his intersectional identity. Hart is a dark-skinned, at times anxiously straight, attractive Black male. At 5"4', he is also relatively short. "Sometimes, I've got to convince people I'm grown," he likewise laments in his monumental DVD, *I'm a Grown Little Man* (2009).[16] This "little man" theme saturates his comedy repertoire like a high-gloss shellac, coating every quip he makes about family, relationships, the gender-divide, [Hart's] crazy real-life experiences, and fame. Consider, for example, a sampling of Hart laments excerpted from his comedic archive, in which self-deprecation is a clear through-line and shtick:

"I really want to be a tougher guy. Seen so many things; seen too much."[17] "I wish I could be a thug. I just don't have it in me. Don't do good with thug shit." Hart can't "do" rappers either. As he explains, "My voice is too small." When he shares his impersonation of rappers—"Pee-yoom everybody gon' die!"—he sounds more like a pubescent Michael Jackson.[18]

Hart won't fight for his woman or boys if the situation calls for it either; he carries a whistle in case such an occasion arises. "Why the hell would I walk into that ass-whooping?!" he asks rhetorically. If a fight seems imminent, Hart admits he'll be the first to exclaim, "Let's go! These niggas are real! . . . I might look like a fighter but I'm not."

If hypersexuality is an admittedly fraught barometer of "authentic" Black hyper masculinity,[19] then Hart falters here too. In one of his jokes, he admits to having been sexually overwhelmed by a woman who took *his* clothes off—such that he needed a safe word: "I wanna go home! I don't like it! Pineapple!"[20] During his equally fraught entrée to the dating scene after his marriage failed, he describes how he managed to catch the attention of two women while driving a truck but lost it when he jumped out to engage them. "Oh my god! He doesn't have any knees!,"[21] one of them exclaimed before driving away. Hart's dismount from the truck was further compromised by a fall and a head bump. Hart also quips about his own unintended "gay" moments, including stories involving riding shotgun on a horse with a male instructor and accepting a blown kiss from a man: "If a guy blows you a kiss and you catch it, does that make you gay?"

Hart's comedic repertoire is replete with stories of so-called unmanly acts, like pooping his pants while getting mugged and then telling the thief about it because he's "honest."[22] Hart also variously cries real tears onstage when thanking his audience for his success, and feigned tears when re-enacting his emotional response to quarrels with his mom, ex-wife, and dialogues with cops summoned to his home to handle domestic spats. Not surprisingly, he's also had to shore up his masculinity despite his status as "father" and successful "breadwinner"; his five-year-old daughter reportedly called him a "punk midget bitch" in a spat about juice. Hart also says he watched his son get beat up (as is the sad custom among men in his family) on the playground while throwing imaginary webs a la Spiderman. When Hart later asks his son what happened, his son explains that his web was "turned off" during the fight.[23]

Corralling his diverse audience's judgments and coaxing their laughter through rhetorical reprimands that invite laughter and pause before particularly sensitive reveals ("Don't make me laugh"; "I'ma stop talking 'cause I can tell ya'll judging"), Hart finesses such humble guises through unabashed heteronormative stances. Hart may be small but he's a "man's man" too. He encourages men in his audience to get loud with their women to show them their love and chides men who cower: "Fag. Get some balls!"[24] Hart's explanation for his behavior is not so much an apology as a concession: "[I'm] not homophobic but if I can prevent it, I will."[25] For instance, perturbed by his son's first unintentional "gay moment" at the birthday party where he was "freaked" by another little boy, he says, "The black in me came out." Before he knew it, he said, "Hey! Stop, that's gay!" before knocking both boys to the ground. Similarly, when his daughter ended up on the line while he (Kevin) was having phone sex with her mother, his first wife, he shouted, "No! That's gay!"[26]

Are these seemingly apolitical, self-deprecating, and, at times, homophobic jokes the ramblings of a trickster? Potentially, if and only if one grants Hart the creative agency to marshal tropes to essentially "quare" himself. I explicitly employ Patrick E. Johnson's concept "quare" to accentuate how issues of race, gender, and class, corporeality, and [the] discursive—which is to say Hart's Black male body and words—collectively inform his legibility as a trickster, imbuing his comedic choices with representational stakes (e.g., is Hart's comedy mere "buffoonery" that reinforces racist stereotypes of the past?) and symbolic weight (e.g., is Hart's comedy a "positive" or regressive representation of Black folk and Black humor?).[27]

Consider again my students' initial skepticism of Hart as a trickster. Given the regressive and buffoonish tropes rampant in Blackfaced minstrelsy[28] and their enduring consequences for the way Black folks and Black humorists are viewed today, many felt Hart's physical humor and consummate self-deprecating stance skirt too close to the racial shenanigans of past and contemporary representations of Black funny men. Even worse for some was the suspicion that Hart's quare pose sought to placate and appease Hollywood gatekeepers who'd prefer to see Black men emasculated and, in fact, reward them for assuming this and other queer poses on stage and screen. Other students could not see Hart on his own terms; that is, as an other-worldly comic who doesn't allow himself "to be pigeonholed," "loves representing [his] race at the highest level," and believes, "if you can laugh together, you can live together,"[29] and instead compared him to other touted Black comics.

Hart indexes these representational politics with trickster acuity when he publicly vowed to never wear a dress. (Despite his promise, Hart later donned a dress during a 2013 *Saturday Night Live* sketch and then told critics he did so purely to be funny.) Dave Chappelle, whom Hart respects both for what he has "said yes and no to," has explicitly critiqued the demasculinization of Black comics in Hollywood through roles that require them to wear dresses. Similarly, several comics featured in the (2010) film, *Why We Laugh: Black Comedians on Black Comedy*, celebrated pioneering Black comics like Flip Wilson and Richard Pryor for wearing dresses so that future Black male comics wouldn't have to. In a heteronormative and perhaps "post-racial" world, sure, man + dress spells incongruity and, hence, laughter, but not just because the equation subverts normative gender roles. Given prevailing tropes and representations of Black men as comedic subjects (e.g., "sambos," "coons," "laughing darkies"), on the one hand, and hypermasculine and hypersexual threats, on the other, *Black* man + dress is perhaps more complicated and even dangerous.[30] To several of the Black male comics featured in *Why We Laugh*, the dress and other forms of drag represent a literal un-manning, with palpable consequences for the way they and other Black males are viewed today.

Ironically, though, Black comics who resist the literal and proverbial "dress" as a matter of principle also must calibrate their performances against charges of homophobia, lest they be censored, blackballed, or otherwise taken to consequential task. Black comics confront a catch-22 when they critique Black male comics wearing dresses, as Chappelle, Chris Rock, and Eddie Griffin have done, by referencing the need to defend their masculinity as Black men. If they do so, they can be charged as homophobic. Johnson (2003), who gingerly calls out Black male comic and literary icons whose homophobic humor denies obvious homosocial yearnings, gives me pause before condemning Chappelle et al. and Hart as merely homophobic. While a "queer" analysis might celebrate the ways Hart's comedy unsettles tropes of the Black hypermasculine and hypersexual male subject and critique him for his more regressive homophobic humor, a "quare" reading makes room for the possibility that Hart's seemingly contradictory yet vacillating heteronormative stances and outright homophobia *are the very means* by which he calibrates his comic persona and navigates the racial and sexual politics of the entertainment industry.

Hart has seemed to try to mitigate against the charge of homophobia in several ways, including his considerably "queer" humor in his sets and his roles in movies like *Get Hard* (2015) with comic Will Ferrell, *Ride Along* (2014) with rapper/actor Ice Cube as the "straight" man and would-be father-in-law, and, more recently, *Central Intelligence* (2016) with similarly but atypically queered actor/semi-retired professional wrestler Dwayne "The Rock" Johnson. Hart's final joke about a misadventurous horse-riding lesson in *Let Me Explain* (2013) is another case in point: When Hart's horse goes buck wild, he's saved by his male horse instructor and ends up clinging to his instructor while riding shotgun. Hart's re-enactment of their bumpy ride, which looks a lot like sex, climaxes when the instructor turns around and tells Hart, "Let's ri:::de!" Hart's willingness to play the inept and quare foil here and elsewhere in his standup harnesses physicality and ever-jocular self-effacement toward strategic ends: he appeals to heteronormativity but subverts it too. Ultimately, Hart shouldn't simply be dismissed as homophobic or celebrated as queer but rather understood in a longer history of contradictory representations of Black masculinity (i.e., the catch-22s: hypermasculinity and emasculated; queer and homophobic and woefully heteronormative) in the entertainment industry.[31]

Still, while I think it is important to identify Hart as a trickster by recognizing the many ways he strategically "quares" himself and keeps "racially and culturally real," naming him as such could also be risky. Exposing Hart's trickster pose bares a strategy that is best enacted undercover, especially given the many hurdles Black comics must circumvent and the discursive choices they employ to make their humor palatable to vast audiences (Jacobs-Huey 2003, 2011). Hart said in a *Playboy* interview, "I'm not a political guy. I don't really deal with Democrats or Republicans. I don't find that funny. . . . And I don't talk about the gay community, be it male or female. No thank you! It's such a sensitive subject. I've seen comics get into serious trouble by joking about gay people. It's too dangerous. Whatever you say, any joke you make about the gay community, it's going to be misconstrued. It's not worth it." Unpacking Hart's potential trickster pose is thus akin to exposing folks' hiding spots in a game of hide-and-seek when they're trying to win just like everybody else. So why do it?

I'll tell you why.

Kevin Hart is one of many comics who steadily remind me that Black standup comedy "keeps it real" by throwing constant shade on fixed notions of "the real," whether concerning race or other matters, even as it takes notions of "a" real [Black] quite seriously. In doing so, he helps me say what I've been needing to say about race and authenticity and stake a claim on notions of "a" real Black. I realized I couldn't even wage this argument without settling up, firmly and unapologetically, with what is arguably "Black" and "quare" about Hart's trickster pose. Many of the Black comics I interviewed in and beyond Los Angeles from 2001 to 2008 would argue that Hart's status as Black sufficiently qualifies him as a trickster. Black folks routinely "wear the mask" in order to negotiate expectations and representations of themselves and Black folks more broadly. To them, Hart *necessarily* acts as a trickster, as Black comics chasing Hollywood dreams must, by exploiting a persona both available and true to him, massaging it to comedic flourish, and capitalizing on it in shockingly fool-proof ways. It remains a successful strategy because, within all his self-deprecating stories, quare poses, and jokes about his difficult childhood and failed marriage, he establishes his racial "authenticity" in ways that resonate with Black audiences while welcoming mainstream and diverse global audiences to get in on the joke.

Arguably, one of the "Blackest" if not triumphant things Hart does in and through his standup is demonstrate his allegiance to communal values of reciprocity, humility, and racial uplift via a "he ain't heavy; he's my brother" entrepreneurial sensibility that takes others along with him in his Hollywood ascent. Demonstrating an allegiance that mitigates against charges of communal abandonment and further secures his "trickster" pose, Hart leaves no one behind, not the "thugs" or hyper-expressive nonsensical rappers; the "buff for no reason," "unproductive," loud, and potentially queer weight lifters he sometimes castigates;[32] the "Plastic Cup Boys," Hart's close-knit team of Black male cohorts with whom he shares stage time, includes in DVD sketches, and formally "presents" (along with other male and female comics) on his *Comedy Central* show (i.e., *Kevin Hart Presents 'Hart of the City'*); the loyal Black male comedians who stood by him when his stage moniker as an amateur comic was "Lil Kevin the Bastard"; his hometown of Philadelphia, Pennsylvania where he filmed his break-through comedy special, *Live Comedy at the Laff House* (2006); and not even his potentially embarrassing and oft-disappointing family members.

Hart's inclusive approach is evident, too, in his small-voiced performance of a hyper-"thug," which queers him (insofar as it marks his distance from a so-called real hypermasculine and stereotypical thug) and also normalizes him (by showing him capable of performing his gender a-normativity and comparative "respectability") without completely abnegating thugs or erasing his points of convergence with them, especially when he quickly adds that he has "real thugs" in his family. Similarly, while he admits that "Rappers make me laugh though" and mimes them as comedic threats at best, he calls out real rappers who attend his shows by name, enlists them to soundtrack his live comedy shows and DVDS, and subjugates himself in comparison to them—thus making room for a critique that they might laugh at too.

Hart's communal approach also mitigated against the kinds of critiques leveled at comedian Chris Rock after his infamous distinction between "Black folks" and "niggas" in *Bring the Pain* (1996). Contrary to Rock's castigation of "niggas" in mixed company (insofar as his star-factor all but guaranteed a bigger, non-Black viewing audience), Hart holds on to the so-called niggas he lovingly chides, and even expands our understanding of what "nigga" signifies. One of his many oft-quoted jokes is a lament and cloaked request to a friend to cover for him as he tries to lie to his former wife about his sexual escapades. When the friend misses their pre-agreed signal and basically gives him away during a speakerphone chat in the presence of his ex, Hart intones, "Help me. Help me. NIGGAH?! Help me."[33] Yet, lest any (i.e., non-Black) audience members think they can adopt this lament as a personal slogan or sharable quip, Hart tells additional jokes that serve to police the indiscriminate use of the n-word. One involves a revised "Duck-Duck-Goose" game that becomes "Duck-Duck-Nigga" at his daughter's birthday party. Hart tells his audience that the lone White kid at the party knew well enough not to join in this game—"'Nope. Nope. I'm not gonna run.'" Hart's emphasis on the highly charged term "nigga" is especially circumscribed in both its targets: Hart's "sincere" appeal is directed to another Black man in the first instance and presumably to Black kids in the second; additionally, Hart's use of "niggah" is decidedly in-group in both instances, marking its nuanced deployment before a diverse global audience. Hart's usage of this controversial multi-valenced signifier is thus disciplined and disciplining.[34]

Finally, despite their sometimes traumatic influence in his life, Hart's family members are never cast aside in his sets (well, save for a cousin who tries to steal the show at his mother's funeral).[35] Hart's father is among them; he was a drug addict and a "step" father, because his mother kicked him out of the house and would only let him come up to the second "step" of their home when visiting. His father called Hart a "bitch" when he cried at his mother's funeral; threw Hart in a pool when he was a child, even though he couldn't swim (and didn't jump in to save him); and showed up at his childhood spelling bee in revealing sweatpants. Still, Hart wraps up his family sagas with redeeming and endearing comments like: "That's my pop though. . . . I love my dad because of the way he is. I can be a bitch because of the way I was raised"[36] and "I am just like my father. If it wasn't for him, I wouldn't be the man I am today. I love him to death. Difference is, I don't do drugs and I know how to control my temper."[37]

Hart also expresses considerable love for his uncle, a recently released inmate, who, when greeted, told Hart, "Say it with your chest lil ass niggah!"[38] Hart doesn't leave his family members who are "thugs" sitting in the critiques he makes about them; he redeems and commemorates them in and through these jokes. Hart exploits his uncle's hypermasculine pose and verbiage for contrastive comedic effect, but he also empathizes him through a subsequent story set at his mother's funeral,[39] wherein he delivers what Hart calls a "thug speech to cancer." "Kevin, whoever did this is gon' die tonight! I'm about to peel this motherfuckah's muffin cap black blue." Hart replies warily, "I can't. You go tell cancer by yourself."

Similarly, Hart's first marriage, which ended in divorce, and his second enduring "through the fire" marriage have begotten extensive and sometimes binary and sexist discussions of the gender-divide, but they nonetheless remain redeeming testaments of Black love in all its fraught enactments; it is in this way that his aesthetics, sensibilities, speech, and rhythm also *key* a recognizable Blackness that shores up his communal standing precisely as his global stardom rises. Hart establishes a "right to speak" through stories of suffering that authenticate his firsthand experience with racial challenges and experiences, thereby attending to the racial matters and cultural and class-rooted experiences shared by the working-class African Americans who comprise his core audience. Hart's short stature and early exposure to a drug-addicted father cultivated both his enduring fears and steady resolve to be safe and secure. Hart's reverence for his mother recalls, for this writer, a heart-tweaking poem by a poet of the same name.[40]

Hart also keys Blackness and secures his racial affinities through veiled critiques of White presumption and privilege, an ultimate trickster move.

For instance, he quips about "a rich White guy laugh" (i.e., a laugh following an awful joke that is, incidentally, funnier than said joke), which when he impersonates it, demonstrates that his "laugh to clap" ratio—something you often see in Black laughter—is "off." Most folks in Hart's audience laugh during Hart's exaggerated performance of what is truly one of the quirkiest laughs yet. A smaller constituency hip to Hart's embedded critique laugh a bit earlier, too; that is, when Hart tells us what the White rich guy said before he told and then laughed at his own awful joke: "Ummm, so you're a comic right? Okay, . . . alright, alright, alright, okay, listen: I gotta joke for you. You can keep it if you want. I don't mind." Here, Hart's sly joke affords an opportunity to laugh at multiple places, even as it enables him to laugh outwardly at a rich White guy presumptuous enough to "offer" a successful comedian a bad joke.

Hart's communal loyalty was also called into question back in 2010, just as his star was rising, because of his resolution on Twitter of what sometimes passes as a pssshaww-worthy and strictly inside-joke—which is *not* to say outside the bounds of in-group critique, especially considering Hart's fame. As Bambi Haggins (2007) notes in her discussion of Whoopi Goldberg as a "cross-over diva," this is an especially dangerous thing for Black comics, especially famous ones, because they stand to lose Black audience's respect and support. Hart's tweeted remarks[41] under question wreaked of colorism, the preference for light skin over dark skin. Still, he initially refused to apologize for them, citing his artistic license as a comic.[42] Later, though, Hart staged a reparative sketch (in the style of *Dead Presidents* meets *Reservoir Dogs*) featuring the Plastic Cup Boys and a cameo appearance by Academy Award–winning actress Taraji Henson. In one party scene celebrating Hart's comedic success, he runs afoul of several Black women who've read his tweets. One of them, a light-skinned woman, asks him, "Is it true you don't fuck with dark skinned girls no more?!" Her question sparks an onslaught of audible grimaces and scowls from her "sisters," one of whom intones, "You darker than me niggah!" Before Hart can bristle, various members of his Plastic Cup Boys team chide him: "Niggah, you asked for that. That's the price of fame!"; "Jackass over here gets mad cuz he can't compare to Eddie Murphy!"; "Don't nobody wanna hear that shit!"; "Kevin over here mad cuz *Soul Plane* bombed;" "That's the price of fame. You asked for this."

Talk about a "trickster" move.[43] Not unlike Black entertainers before him, this scripted sketch centers Black folks as the source of Hart's authenticity and accountability, here via the Plastic Cup Boys' brotherly comradery and their and Black women's successive shaming.[44] Hart continues the work of "keeping real" and being responsive to core Black audiences in his global comedy tour, "What Now?," which was filmed and released in 2016 as a comedy documentary. I attended Hart's show when the tour stopped in Los Angeles, California, in 2015; one of his jokes about being cash-strapped hit home for me. Whereas Hart's newfound "baller" buddies in the entertainment industry had money to rent out Disneyland for their child's birthday party, Hart still had to move money from his savings to his checking account to handle big expenses. As he explained, "Yeah, I got the money but see, I have a checking and a savings, and I have to pull money out of my savings into my checking to clear." I'd used the same explanation when trying to compel a former friend to pay their half of concert tickets I'd purchased.

Hart's jokes in the film are equally endearing and authenticating. Hart's dad reappears in his set, less as a tragic and comedic foil who is graciously pardoned by his son; instead, Hart and his dad become bona fide partners in the crime of woeful paternity. When things go bump in the night—or Hart's daughter (Heaven) startles him, Kevin abandons his whole family and hightails it out of the house to his car (scaling staircases with one leap and baring all like his father once did during his childhood spelling bee).[45] Once there, Hart discovers his dad already seated in the backseat asking, "Did you hear that shit? . . . we gotta get the fuck out of here!" Hart's paternal shortcomings are thus redeemed as a humorous "like father like son" tribute and testament, one that trickles down to Hart's own dealings with his (then) seven-year-old son, Hendrix. Hendrix and his dad *both* fear the Batman ceiling decoy in Hendrix's room which, in Hart's mind, seems poised to rape when the lights are off. As in past performances, Hart's final joke of the night daringly flirts with homophobia while securing his [Hart's] ever-fraught heteronormativity; essentially, he says, "Suck my dick!" to pretentious and lamentably queer-acting men whose Starbucks coffee requests involve vanilla, foam, soy or almond milk, and other spices and specifications.

Hart also, if not increasingly, hints at his trickster acuity. For example, he congratulates himself for only telling one "small guy joke," outing and perhaps problematizing it as shtick. Before lamenting his son for acting "White-Black," Hart also affirms his own "edge" by saying, "I'm not a thug. I'm not a killer. But I got some edge. You need edge to survive in this life"; further, when he re-enacts how he and his, say, edgier friends reminisce about growing up (and losing buddies to violence) in Philadelphia's inner city, Hart reminds audiences of his humble upbringing and enduring fellowship with [Black] folks who "knew him when."[46] Moreover, Hart marshals steady support from Black women, a supportive and, at times, disciplining constituency, via a joke that is not only *about* them but *just for* them. Namely, Hart quips that Black women don't suffer bullshit long; to cement his point, he performs their (again, alleged) "don't believe shit face" (i.e., hyper-cynicism) and sets it against a rejoinder, "Oh re:::ally?" that they and only they have license to repeat throughout his set. In essence, "sisters" get their own call-back in a diverse packed stadium! Black women are likewise authenticated as "truth-discerners," if not sources of Hart's racial authenticity and communal groundedness.[47]

Hart's trickster acuity is also evident in his most recent work, including his apology and personal accountability-facing "Irresponsibility Tour" during 2017–2018.[48] During his sixth comedy tour traversing the United States and parts of Europe, Hart publicly admits to private indiscretions that derailed his first marriage and threatened his second; he also asserts his own personal boundaries by simultaneously reminding his audience that what happened between him and his first wife is essentially *their* business. In this way, Hart seems to take responsibility for his private actions rather than merely apologize for them. Hart's (2020) *Netflix* series, *Don't F**k This Up*, gestures toward Hart's desire to literally "own" his personal accountability versus be cajoled or pressured into a merely apologetic stance as a Black entertainer. In particular, the series homes in on Hart's twin refusals to the Oscars committee before he was slated to host this fame-cementing affair.[49] It bears noting that Hart accomplishes way more in *Don't F**k This Up* than another installment of what his dear friend, Dave Chappelle, jokingly and ostensibly described as an apology tour. Instead, Hart's *Netflix* series puts the Oscars committee's imperative of apology in direct conversation if not confrontation with his stalwart refusal to issue what would essentially be a second if not third apology. What emerges from this representational tension is an empathetic tribute to Hart's excessive work ethic and enduring and mutual loyalty to his crew, the Plastic Cup Boys—with a twist: Hart's work ethic as a globally recognized celebrity may enable him to, say, charter private jets, buy luxury designer shirts for his crew to wear onstage (and mint vintage cars for their enduring loyalty), and easily gift $20,000 to his never-abandoned father; even still, the series suggests, Hart's celebrity cannot save him from the need to contend with past sins resurrected on a public stage right before his sure bid to host the Oscars. This subtle lamentation subtexts the symbolic weight of Hart's refusals as a bona fide Black comic celebrity star who deigns to tell Hollywood's gatekeepers essentially, "No thank you; I won't apologize yet again for things I've already apologized for. I'm a grown ass man. You can keep [your] Oscars." Hart also devotes screen time to apologize to White members of his creative team who expressed their lingering hurt over his past homophobic quips. This carefully calibrated series likewise helps viewers appreciate Hart's refusals and demarcated apologies as part and parcel of the incessant "work" he must do as a world-renowned African American comic to unapologetically secure his and others' (e.g., Tiffany Haddish) star power and creative freedom.

Hart's most recent *Netflix* special, *Zero *ucks Given* [2021], though, is a cheeky addendum to *Don't F**k This Up*.[50] Whereas his preceding *Netflix* special toed the line between personal accountability to himself and intimate and trusted parties, this one doubles down on the trickster acuity of his expressed sincerity and fidelity to "a" real Black. Here, "a" real Black hinges on sincerity insofar as it entails speaking one's truth, especially in one's own home (where Kevin taped *this* special) and essentially saying, "No" without the polite "thanks" to critics and entreaties to apologize yet again. Let's look a bit closer at how he does this and why.

Hart begins his set with a few admissions that sound self-deprecatory on their surface: "I don't like people anymore. . . . You won. You beat me up. You guys have fucked up the game." Here, Hart indicts the way fame and the pursuit of it—not just by comics but fans and lay persons now too—abet surveillance (e.g., "You guys are Feds for free . . . bunch of walking fuckin' snitches"), repeat calls for apology, and make "cancel" threats amid all that life delivers up for straight married men and fathers over forty. Hart also hints by way of a brick pizza oven story how his celebrity and its affordances are not the same as, say, Jerry Seinfeld's. According to Hart, the reason he gets asked to be a "greeter" as opposed to a bona fide performer at his kid's school fair is in some ways similar to why the same contractor who built his and Jerry Seinfeld's home neglected to offer him (Hart) an outdoor brick pizza oven though they did this for Jerry: "Not once did they ask if I wanted an outdoor pizza oven! This is racism at the highest level. . . . You know what I'm talkin' about! Black Lives Matter!," Hart quips.[51]

Make no mistake though: Hart's anger and allegations of racism in *this* case are strictly tongue in cheek. For one, his Black friends do nothing to scaffold his anger as either "righteous" or shared; in fact, they could care less that he installed a pizza oven like Seinfeld's or would like to be known for something other than fame such as road biking, boxing, or, well, brick oven pizza.[52] Furthermore, Hart *still* can't evade the trappings of homoerotic jesting at his own behest. His final joke, onstage at least, is yet another set-ending nod to queer humor: while reflecting on his recovery from a car crash in 2019, Hart lets his audience in on something a sixty-year-old male nurse named José told him while cleaning him up: "This is my first famous ass." Hart, though, is not yet done playing with his virtual audience. After this homoeroticizing quip and right before the credits roll, Hart inserts a dream sequence featuring him and his wife, Eniko Parrish (now Eniko Hart), in their marital bed. Perturbed, Hart rehearses several controversial quips from his set, recasting them as nightmarish scenes. In essence, he nullifies a few of his most audacious jokes by deeming them outlandish; in doing so, he bestows himself an "out" should critics come for him.

Hart's trickster acuity here winkingly affords the "ha" and more meditative "ah" of live, recorded standup humor in a world increasingly policed by "cancel culture." Consider, for example, how "cancel culture" polices sincerity, mandating it via censure, shaming, bullying, and coordinated rebuke. Consider, too, that perpetrators of cancel culture (or callout culture) don't always welcome a dialogue with or from their target, especially if the target-to-be-canceled has routinely abdicated personal accountability. What then, one might ask, does a Black modern-day trickster do with all of these complexities, to say nothing of the ginormous work of taking personal accountability in fame-drenched adulthood? Well, according to Hart, they might elect to "come in hot"—that is, boldly on controversial matters like race, sex, and gender before cheekily disavowing their quips and barbs as comedic charade.

Don't sleep, Dear Reader. I believe Hart is after waaaay more than mere laughs in that dream sequence finale with his wife, who has, it turns out, routinely cautioned him not to become bitter. Hart aims to tame cancel culture itself, or the very culture that reputedly "came for him" and presumably other comics when their chips were down (or up). To do so, he oozes sincerity as an enactment of racial authenticity or what I call "a" real Black toward a more sustaining win: Hart fastidiously calibrates his sincerity and racial authenticity to ensure his enduring right to joke freely. *This* feat, to use Hart's words, is a "big motherfuckin' deal."[53]

Still, how long can Hart remain "real" and accessible to core Black folks who may not share his fame-based experiences and shifting worldviews? Could Hart be a modern-day trickster who performs Black feisty femininity without drag, invokes his dad's dick as a gesture of homosociality (if not a sly and self-aggrandizing projection), and practices self-deprecation as a measure of his manhood and a gateway to power, prestige, and possibility? Further, are Hart's incessant performances of Black women in his life regressive, insofar as they invoke the trope of the neck-rolling hyper-sassy Black Sapphire? Or does Hart "trick" that trope to new and redemptive heights following examples set by Mabley and a select few Black male comics?[54] Could not his very discussion (and impersonations) of fraught Black male and female subjects, family members, Black experience, and worldviews—his and others'—on the world stage be the ultimate proof of his trickster win? Especially in *this* brave new world?

Again, *potentially*. Tricksters don't always let us in on their sly maneuverings, but a small few, and maybe even Hart himself, have the audacity to look back at cynics through the TV screen with a gaze that seems to ask—rhetorically of course—"Wait, are *you* done deliberating? Are (.) You (.) Done?" before gracing us with a smile that knows and answers at the same time—such that we keep our eyes on them, ever questioning and ever-hopeful.

5

Humor, Me

A (Tentative) Conclusion

When I began this book, I envisioned telling a story about the "why" of racial authenticity inspired by Black comics' read of the events of September 11, 2001; Hurricane Katrina; Michael Richards's outburst at The Laugh Factory, L.A.'s legendary comedy club; Kevin Hart's meteoric rise to become a global superstar and modern-day trickster; and the election of "America's first Black president." But something else asserted itself during my writing process that demanded a different reckoning;[1] as I toiled to get words on the page, I experienced an onslaught of encounters that I deemed "strange and stranger." As a result, my writing stalled and my world as I knew it unraveled, but thankfully not before my scholarly curiosity about the "why" of racial authenticity (or real Blackness) and truth shifted into a bolder-faced stance about "a" real Black—or, what is decidedly Black about Blackness. The passage of time permits me to say a bit more about this, and so I will.

For reasons that remain unclear to me, I seemed to have slipped on the proverbial banana peel, upending myself in a tragic saga known to many anthropologists as "[what happens when] the anthropologist becomes data"—save in my case, I became a laughable subject.[2] This saga announced itself rather benignly, so benignly that it took a while for me to catch on. At first, folks I didn't know but who seemed to know me (or at least act like they did) erupted in soulful dance moves when they saw me. "Cool," I thought of this strange occurrence. "That's what's up and damn the stereotypes! Let's groove together!" But then, folks I knew and didn't know threw out what struck me as lyrics from my very own private notebooks; others—seniors, middle-aged educated adults, adolescents, and even children—seemed to replay as if they were actors in scenes from my most personal and private moments. "Could this be the magic of synchronicity?" I reasoned, tentative but hopeful. Soon, however, what I once felt was merely strange or synchronistic crescendoed into truly stran*ger* instances of social mobbing, outright taunting, sexual harassment, physical threat, and a barrage of racial micro-aggressions from folks of all hues.

To Be Real. Lanita Jacobs, Oxford University Press. © Oxford University Press 2023.
DOI: 10.1093/oso/9780190870096.003.0006

For at least a year, some of my students made a spectacle of looking at their phones, then me, and erupting in laughter. Mocking laughter also seemed to follow me to airports, academic conferences, grocery stores, restaurants, local coffee shops, and even sites of reprieve (e.g., USC Faculty and Staff Clinic, USC Digital Technology Services, university awards ceremonies, churches, walks in the park, writing retreats).[3] Never had I ever felt so visible and yet invisible. Never had I ever felt so disrespected and clueless at the same time! When I asked for occasional clarity in direct and indirect ways from folks I knew and trusted at the time, I was, shall we say, not at all "humored" with bold-faced clarity and, in fact, got laughed at in my face a few times.

I knew something had to give when the sound of Black laughter, particularly Black women's laughter, stopped being one of the most precious magical things in my world and, instead, morphed into a foreboding trigger. Without humor's relief or Black women's comedic comradery, I worried far less about epitomizing the "anthropologist as laughable data and spectacle" and more about becoming the "anthropologist who's come undone."[4]

At the advice of a dear and concerned friend, I consulted a therapist and a psychiatrist, but demurred when the prospect of medication came up; and I sought a new therapist or two when I felt my studied appreciation of racism as a form of gaslighting was not mutually shared. Committed to surviving, I heeded my therapists' counsel and doubled down on differentiating the truly "strange" from the merely "synchronous" or the undeniably "stranger."[5] I also started writing as if to God and myself in a single-spaced typed document that grew to over 150 pages in the span of three daunting years.

It helped. I finally realized that I was asking way too much of myself if I made the completion of my book contingent on my capacity to make sense of the inexplicable. What I needed to do instead—and, in fact, the only thing I could do—was to get comfortable with not fully understanding the motivations or the end game and live, teach, write, love, and literally breathe through it toward the next burst of writerly magic. I'm talking about occasional bursts of insight that can happen when we remain at our writing tables in faith that this excruciatingly slow-crawl effort will eventually lead us from one sentence to the next.

I also apparently needed to move from a beautiful historic home in one of L.A.'s last not-yet-gentrified Black communities. Only I didn't know it until I reached the apex of despair and re-encountered one of Zora Neale Hurston's greatest works: a literal move of her own. Hurston experienced a fall from grace in "community" after she was falsely accused by her Black landlady of molesting two young Black boys (the landlady was the mother of one of the boys). The black press printed the story even though the boys rescinded their allegations and Hurston was clearly out of the country at the time of their allegations. Even so, Huston became suicidal. She overcame feelings of communal abandonment and intra-racial betrayal, to say nothing of enduring racism and sexism simmering underneath it all, by writing, cooking, and feeling her way to wellness on a houseboat she named "Wanago." She also revised some assumptions or, rather, presumptions about "home" and "community," which is precisely what I needed to do. She likewise inspired me to literally move myself from a home I loved but couldn't protect from car crashes, "break-ins," fraudulent contractors, the specter of surveillance, plant immolation, verbal snipers on foot, and a few beautiful meddlesome kids. I moved to a cabin in the woods and a boat I named "Wanago II" in deference to Zora's writerly discipline and resilience.[6]

Zora wasn't the only scholar who seemed to speak directly to me like an intervention, helping me return to my book and slow-walk my way back to Black laughter and laughter more generally. One day, while revisiting the work of Franz Fanon, I discerned faint murmurs that helped me appreciate Michael Richards's comedic acumen and racist intent anew. I also drew strength from Fanon that helped me process the irony of my hypervisibility as a Black female humor scholar turned Black female spectacle. And although I admittedly chose "love" and "curiosity" to publicly address breaches of misinterpolation—well, I may have playfully put my hands around the necks of a few folks who "played me way too close"—I nonetheless *felt* Fanon when he resorted to biting humor to both save face and "serve" the mother who sought to placate him with a compliment after her young son racistly objectified him. When the woman's young son cried out, "Maman, look, a Negro; I'm scared!," and she tried to calm him and defuse the racist slight by saying, "Look how handsome the Negro is." Fanon retorted, "Kiss the handsome Negro's ass, madame!"[7]

Toni Morrison's (2019) *The Source of Self Regard*, and her insights concerning the whiting out of race in literary studies and canonical literary texts also resonated with me. This was especially so since prevailing dictates concerning the right, most-rigorous, or "authentic" way to study race in literary studies and beyond (e.g., anthropology, American Studies and Ethnicity) can sometimes end up effectively disciplining scholars whose vetting of race does not *merely* privilege, say, a constructionist and/or transnational or hemispheric lens. I'll quote Morrison at length:

> The world does not become raceless or will not become unracialized by assertion. The act of enforcing racelessness in literary discourse is itself a racial act.

Pouring rhetorical acid on the fingers of a black hand may indeed destroy the prints, but not the hand [my bolded emphasis here and elsewhere]. Besides, what happens, in that violent, self-serving act of erasure, to the hands, the fingers, the fingerprints of the one who does the pouring? Do they remain acid-free? The literature itself suggests otherwise. Explicit or implicit, the Africanist presence informs in significant, compelling, and inescapable ways the texture and shape of American literature. It is a dark and abiding presence that serves the literary imagination as both a visible and an invisible mediating force . . . in matters of race, silence and evasion have historically ruled literary discourse. **Evasion has fostered another, substitute language in which the issues are encoded and made unavailable for open debate. The situation is aggravated by the anxiety that breaks into discourse on race. It is further complicated by the fact that ignoring race is understood to be a graceful, liberal, even generous habit. To notice is to recognize an already discredited difference; to maintain its invisibility through silence is to allow the black body a shadowless participation in the dominant cultural body.** Following this logic, every well-bred instinct argues against noticing and forecloses adult discourse. It is just this concept of literature and scholarly *moeurs* (which functions smoothly in literary criticism, but neither makes nor receives credible claims in other disciplines) that has terminated the shelf life of some once extremely well-regarded American authors and blocked access to the remarkable insights some of their works contain. (2019, 142)

Morrison's lamentation about the erasure of race in literary studies as an act of grace recalls similar critiques leveled by linguistic anthropologists about their discipline's reluctance to center race in language studies—something *raciolinguistics* seeks to explicitly redress (see Preface). Morrison continues:

Thus, in spite of its implicit and explicit acknowledgement [by humanists and postmodernists], **"race" is still a virtually unspeakable thing, as can be seen in the apologies, notes of "special use," and circumscribed definitions that accompany it—not the least of which is my own deference in surrounding it with quotation marks. Suddenly [for our purposes, suddenly] "race" does not exist.** For three hundred centuries black Americans insisted that "race" was no usefully distinguishing factor in human relationships. During those same three centuries, every academic discipline, including theology, history, and natural science [—and anthropology—Jacobs's addition], insisted "race" was *the* determining factor in human development. When blacks discovered they had shaped or became a culturally formed race, and that it had specific and revered difference, suddenly they were told there is no such thing as "race," biological or cultural, that matters and that genuinely intellectual exchange cannot accommodate it. **In trying to** understand the relationship between "race" and culture, I am tempted to throw my hands up. It always seemed to me that the people who invented the hierarchy of "race" when it was convenient for them ought not to be the ones to explain it away now that it does not suit their purposes for it to exist. But there *is* culture, and both gender and "race" inform and are informed by it. Afro-American culture exists, and though it is clear (and becoming clearer) how it has responded to Western culture, the instances where and means by which it has shaped Western culture are poorly unrecognized or understood. I want to address ways in which the presence of Afro-American literature and the awareness of its culture both resuscitate the study of literature in the United States and raise that study's standards. (164)

Morrison's critique about Black erasure in literary studies[8] and the politics of academic legitimacy subtexting ardent claims about "race as a social construction" struck me as spot on—as spot on as Jackson's reminder in "A Little Black Magic" that

the rhetorical avoidance of race does not automatically buttress its antiessentialist cause. In fact, taking away race's vocal chords, the acoustic concreteness of its explicit bark, does not mean that one has defused its bite. If anything, race becomes more compelling in silence. (12005a, 394)

Whereas Jackson's work and concept of "racial sincerity" gave me healthy studied pause when I first considered putting the emphasis on "a" real Black, Morrison's writing pushed me to boldly embrace the notion of "a" real Black while settling up with some lingering hurts at home, in "community," academia, and beyond.

I also found answers, or rather a prompt to remember, in an essay I'd written at the start of my academic career. I wrote that "native" scholars have to be particularly attentive to the politics of representation when conducting and then translating research "at home." However, I apparently underestimated the enduring significance of this unoriginal observation when I landed in what felt like a season of gaslighting run amok. Ethnography, I now more profoundly know in my soul, is as wondrously intersubjective as it is fraught; anthropologists can "fail" and make missteps during and after fieldwork for which they can be demoted, disciplined (e.g., ridiculed), and silenced. They can also end up on the "wrong" side of "right" in the minds of their research participants when friendly exchanges or observations in the field translate to formal words on a page. Most important, ethnography makes no promises of enduring friendship or allegiance. Nor does Black humor or humor writ large.

Contrary to Steve Harvey's caution in *Why We Laugh: Black Comedians on Black Comedy*, that "something (e.g., compassion) always has to come before the joke," if something's funny, a comic will likely exploit it to excess reserving later regard for humor's wily stakes and consequences. I only wish I knew some of the jokes that coalesced around me so as to mobilize an inter-ethnic, class-diverse, laughing and winking base so that I might laugh as heartily as I have been laughed at (. . . or not). Until then, as I told a woman who barely stifled laughter while greeting me at a mindful writing workshop: "I'm sorry I didn't return your greeting a bit earlier. I prefer to know what I'm laughing at before I join in."

Today, I think, "Ha, anyhow." Because somewhere in the proverbial rabbit hole that delivered Alice into wonder,[9] I ran smack dab into the virtues of "a" real Black and found it worthy of comedy's invitation and seeming exclusion. Best, I realized anew that matters of truth and racial authenticity, a real Black, is worth fighting for—especially when one hears such bids in comics' nuanced contextualized appeals as a yearnful ethos, a celebration of that which is decidedly Black about Blackness that is often denied or even pathologized. Here, I recall how Black comics like Rod Man Thompson envisioned poor Black Hurricane Katrina victims disparagingly described in the news as "looters" as, instead, industrious (i.e., long-range thinking) entrepreneurs, thus empathizing and holding them as "fam." I also remember Black comics' fierce and, at times, gracious critique of Michael Richards and The Laugh Factory's short-lived n-word ban, specifically how their barbs indicting racist and racial disparities coloring their industry were purposefully aligned with "a" real Black positionality and communal stance.

When I look back, way back to the start of this study—well before I could even name "a" real Black so as to finally *see* Kevin Hart as a modern-day trickster—I again hear Ian Edwards's joke about "Arabs as the 'new nigger'" post 9/11. It wasn't just the sardonic premise of Edwards's joke and its capacity to stoke empathetic remembrance (not just "celebratory" distinction) that captivated me; it was also if not equally a Black female audience members' weary retort, "Finally," that made me give longitudinal chase to Black standup comedy's intersubjective reveals concerning the stakes of truth and bids to racial authenticity. I realized that these jokes, at times framed as cultural imperatives, are often rooted in the idea that Blackness warrants a stance. And this ideological, linguistic, discursive, spiritual, and communal stance is frequently vetted and lodged in the comedic parlance of truth, racial authenticity, and sincerity in pursuit of empathetic recognition and redress. Which is to say: when the shit hits the fan as it is now, and then again when things are calm and still, Black standup comics invite us all to name, celebrate, and even bracket "a" real Black as if our lives depended on it or privilege a real Black sans quotes in unabashed celebration or a priori acceptance. When comics pull this off and manage to stoke an "I *see* you" mutuality, life-saving empathy, and truth-facing accountability—despite recent scholarly treatises "against empathy," essentialism,[10] or Lacanian commonsense understandings of the spuriousness of any kind of "real" or "reality," well that's when some real magic happens. This magic can blessedly remind one of who one is and belongs to so as to heal all sorts of wounds. That's all I have to say and, frankly, it's all I can really say for now. But I do offer these parting words in keeping with a Conclusion's gift:

Who can say whether someone is "real" Black? "No one," right? But the real answer is this. We all *can*. And will. Indefinitely. As if our lives depend on it. For as long perhaps as we are beautifully and besiegingly Black.[11] As long as we both shall live. If we are to live more fully then, even in a moment of overlapping and compounding pandemics inclusive of covid-19, structural racism and White supremacy, rape, climate change, and on and on, then let us make room to celebrate, shout, and murmur about "a" real Black. Let us decide that there is something decidedly Black about Blackness and tenderly choose to put our emphasis in this blessed place wherein laughter—winking or otherwise—lifts, soothes, bears empathetic witness, grounds, and reminds us of who and whose we are and suggests, too, that at the end of the day, we're all in this beautiful mess together, and shared laughter can be a way to get us all through.

Notes

Introduction

1. Star 69 refers to "Last Call Return," a calling feature which, if dialed on a landline and some cell phones, calls back the last caller.

2. Some of the caricatured subjects of Chappelle's "When 'Keeping It Real' Goes Wrong" sketches are not a far cry from the "niggahs" Chris Rock castigates as the bane of hard-working Black folks' existence in his (1999) standup comedy film, *Bigger and Blacker*; for a rich discussion of Chappelle's distinction between "niggahs" and "Black folks," see Bambi Haggins, "Murphy and Rock: From the 'Black Guy' to The 'Rock Star,'" in *Laughing Mad: The Black Comic Persona in Post-Soul America*, 69–98 (London: Rutgers University Press, 2007), and chapters 1 and 3 of this book.

3. Dave Chappelle was tackled by Isaiah Lee, a twenty-three-year-old man carrying a weapon during a live standup comedy performance in May 2022 at Los Angeles.

4. Warnke (2005) further articulates the various reasons an interpretive approach is essential to understanding race and (then) gender in non-essentialist terms.

5. Comic "Earthquake" taught me to avoid taking notes in the front row (duh!) when he noticed me doing so and asked, from the stage, "Hey girl. What you doing?!" Later, when I finally moved to the shadows of the club, audience members (some of whom knew comics and promoters personally) would ask me the same thing in different form (e.g., "hey uh . . . what ya' got there?") when they noticed my pen moving. I understood. They were invested in the integrity of standup comedy; I'd sometimes share my business card with them so they could look me up or check my story.

6. Kevin Hart's (2016) *What Now* standup comedy film arguably comes in second if one counts his domestic and worldwide box office sales.

7. See Jacobs 2015.

8. See Hymes (1966, 1972), who coined the term "communicative competence" to refer to a speaker's grammatical knowledge of a language as well as their ability to use utterances appropriately in social contexts. Inspired by linguistic theory, Carrell (1997) posits that a "successful" joke depends, first, on folks' "joke competence" (i.e., their ability to recognize a joke as a "joke") and, second, on their "humor competence" (i.e., their perception of the joke as indeed a joke, one that may or may not be humorous.) Readers might also be interested in Lacoste et al.'s (2014) edited volume, *Indexing Authenticity: Sociolinguistic Perspectives*, which broadly examines how local meanings of authenticity are expressed in spoken and written language.

9. Eddie Murphy has since been reluctant to critique Cosby onstage. When asked to impersonate Cosby in 2015 at *Saturday Night Live*'s 40th Anniversary Show, "SNL 40," Murphy refused, saying he did not want to kick a man when he was down. I discuss the potential reasons why in this book's conclusion.

10. See Higginbotham 1994.

11. This is why my colleague Dorinne Kondo once described anthropology as a "corporeal epistemology" during one of my department's most impassioned faculty meetings.

12. See cross-disciplinary work regarding the "natives gazing and talking back" in academia by hooks (1989), Narayan (1993), Jacobs-Huey (2002), and Jackson (2008); see also Allen and Jobson (2016).

13. Actually, sharing excerpts of my fieldnotes wasn't quite "unprecented" for me. I also shared excerpted meeting notes (i.e., fieldnotes) with a group of Christian cosmetologists who met monthly for bible study in a Beverly Hills salon; sharing my notes was both a reciprocal gesture and an affirmative response to a cosmetologist's explicit request for them. In their mind, I was not just an "ethnographer" as much as an archivist for their organization; my notes, they reasoned, would serve both me and them. As a "native" anthropologist invested in the politics of reciprocity and accountability, I was all too happy to provide them.

14. Another reason comics called me the "writer" and not, say, an assistant professor (which I was at the time) was because I didn't stress this identity. Inspired by prior fieldwork and Black "native" anthropologists such as the late John Gwaltney and Zora Neale Hurston, I knew that approaching comics with a business card would probably do me a disservice by making me seem pompous, presumptuous, and, well, like a "researcher." Given the legacies of the Tuskegee Syphilis Study and many Black folks' subsequent and enduring qualms about being treated as guinea pigs by scientists, I made a habit of handing comics my business card upside down with a handwritten note and my cell phone number that was signed, simply, "Lanita." The one time I did neglect this practice and slid my card to a Black female comedian (Melanie Comarcho) in the shadows of the club, I learned a valuable lesson. She simply slid it back across the table at me. I learned what I had, in fact, suspected: that underscoring my professional title to gain access to comics could likely backfire and make me seem, as Gwaltney noted, like a woman "talking with a paper in my hand." It could also perhaps win me trust, such as when another comedian, Michael Colyar, slid my "Project Information" sheet approved by my institution's Institutional Review Board back at me across a restaurant table before an interview.

15. I'm again using the term "intersubjective" to highlight how comedy relies on both comics' and audiences' shared communicative competence and mutual investment in laughter for not only laughter's sake, but laugher as a means to resilience, speaking truth to power, declaring "I/we are here," etc.

16. See work by Abu-Lughod (1991), Baker (1994; 1998; 2010), Cole (1992), Gregory and Sanjek (1994), Epperson (1994), Jones (2005), Mukhopadhyay and Moses (1997), Harrison (1992, 1995, 1997, 1998a; 1998b , especially Harrison and Harrison (1999), Szwed (1969), Hartigan (2005), Kelley (1997), Michaels (1992), Rigby (1996), Shanklin (1994, 1998), Viseweswaran (1998, 2010) who differentially problematize anthropologists' preoccupation with culture versus race and relative silence about African American cultural specificities.

17. See Theodossopoulos 2013.

18. See Benson 2013; Theodossopoulos 2013, 353.

19. See also Jenkins 2005, Favor 1999, and Daniels-Rauterkus's (2020) brilliant and beautifully written book, *Afro-Realisms and the Romance of Race: Rethinking Blackness in the African American Novel.*

20. See also Stephens's (2009) highly relevant and gender-attuned piece, "What Is This Black in Black Diaspora?"

21. See Baudrillard 1995, 2017; Banet-Weiser 2012; Brown 2016.

22. See Cashmore 1997; Johnson 2003; LaBennett 2011; Lott 2013.

23. See James 1907, 1909, 1955; see also Bury (1986) who cites Thompson (1978, 210): "The character of the table is determined by the logic of the wood," occasioning insightful retorts by Nicolson and McLaughlin (1987, 1988) concerning the utility of social constructionism in an empirical case study.

24. For additional critiques of the limitations of postmodernism in anthropological analysis, see Trouillot, "Anthropology and the Savage Slot: The Poetics and Politics of Otherness," in *Recapturing Anthropology: Working in the Present,* ed. Richard G. Fox, 17–44 (Santa Fe, NM: School of American Research Press, 1991); Trouillot argues that postmodern anthropologists tend to look for to thus indict the proverbial "savage in the text" versus "address directly the thematic field (and thus the larger world) that made (makes) this slot possible, morosely preserving the empty slot itself" (40). Ortner (1995, 184) asks similar questions of poststructuralist theorists' attempts to document the way marginalized "subalterns" resist their oppression: "I am sympathetic with what they are trying to do, which is to introduce complexity, ambiguity, and contradiction into our [anthropologists'] view of the subject in ways that . . . must be done with politics and culture (and indeed resistance.) Yet the particular poststructuralist move they make toward accomplishing this goal paradoxically destroys the object (subject) who should be enriched, rather than impoverished, by this act of introducing complexity. I write with these provocations in mind, as well as Gayatri Spivak's subsequent qualms about her own call for "strategic essentialism" (see Ray 2009; Jackson 2005; and, especially, Spivak 1988)," given mounting concerns about the dangers of essentialism in an ever-changing world, in hopes that entering the essentialist "trap" of essentialism and playing in the trick bag that is race (damned if you do, damned if you don't) might nonetheless reveal why black comics and their diverse audiences routinely appeal to and question stances around "real Blackness."

25. Still, readers may be interested in scholars who do, including Benson and Stangroom (2006); Berman (2009[1970]; Blackburn (2005); Guignon (2004); James (1997[1909]), 1955); Lindholm (2013); Lynch (2001); Taylor (1991); and Trilling (1972), who notes that "authenticity" infers a "more strenuous moral experience than 'sincerity' does, a more exigent conception of the self and of what being true to it consists in, a wider reference to the universe and man's place in it, and a less acceptant and genial view of the social circumstances of life" (Trilling 1972,11).

26. Karen Sotiropoulos (2008) argues that racial authenticity was also something African American vaudevillians pursued with fraught ambivalence and a dogged insistence that there be something "strictly Negro" and hence, "real" during the "coon [song] craze" of the 1880s and 1890s.

27. See Richard Handler, "Authenticity," *Anthropology Today* 2:1 (February 1986): 2–4.

28. But see also work by scholars who insist on authenticity's utility and stalwart relevance when assessing music and art (e.g., Baugh 1988, Caruthers and Bierria 2011, Gilroy 1993, Hall 1997, Handler 1986, Jones 2010, Kajikawa 2009, Linnekin 1991, McLeod 1999, Moore 2002, as well as those who interrogate varied constructions of black authenticity with clear regard for what these notions of "real" Blackness may mean to African American participants and practitioners (e.g., Houston Baker 1979[1990]), Bey 2012, Gwaltney 1993, Haggins 2007, Hurston [1935] 1990, Jarrett 2007, Johnson 2001, Kelley 1997, Neal 2002, Retman, 2011, Shanklin 1998, Shelby 2005, Shotwell 2006, West 2005, and Morgan 2009).

29. See, for example, Harper 1996, and, of course,Hall 1992. Paul Gilroy's (1990) seminal essay, *Nationalism, History, and Ethnic Absolutism,* is also especially relevant .

30. See also Baker 1998a, 1998b, and 2010.

31. See also de Lauretis (1989), Case (1997, 1-2 and 11–12), Sutherland (1993), Goldberg (1997), McClaurin (2001a, 2001b), Rodriguez (2001), and Pasevich (2009) for additional riffs on what bids to authenticity afford African Americans and other marginalized groups.

32. Cultural critic Randall Kennedy (2011) also asserted in his critique of Touré's (2011) theory of post-Blackness: "When African-American artists, politicians or activists assert that they are going to 'keep it real' despite complaints that they are 'too black,' they are adopting a stance that is important to appreciate even if one disagrees with it. That stance, like the strategy of dilution, is no figment of the imagination. It is a choice that gives rise to different grades of blackness. That is why it is proper, Henry Louis Gates notwithstanding, to recognize that the music of James Brown at the Apollo is more authentically black than the music of the Supremes at the Copacabana." Kennedy's use of "stance" and "choice" in many ways reflects the tenor of this book; this is, this book's "stance" and "choice" emphasize the "why" of racial authenticity as a generative query for both understanding race and enduring notions of authenticity in African American culture. As Epperson (1994, 18) rightly notes, "While Gates agrees that 'race' is *only* a sociopolitical category, nothing more," he warns against the "lurking positivism in the *non sequitur* movement from 'socially constructed' to essentially unreal. In its most extreme from universal anti-realism—as embodied in discourse about death of the subject—sanctions a radical denial of the subjectivity of subaltern peoples at the precise moment when they are beginning to challenge the dominance of western White male subjectivity" Gates 1986, 1990; see also Harrison 1995, 1997 (4-6), 19987.

33. See again Stephens (2009), as well as Simien (2005) and Dawson (1994) for additional discussion of African Americans' "linked fates" and, per Spillers (1997), [shared] "interior intersubjectivity."

Chapter 1

1. See Scepanski (2021) who examines how the dynamic of tragedy + time informed televised comedy after key historical moments like the assassination of JFK, 9/11, and the Donald Trump presidency.

2. Quite a few scholars and writers have been swept up in the stories comedy can tell about particular historical moments, including Fox (1983), Hendra (1987), Hill and Weingrad (1987), Jenkins (1994), Watkins (1994; 2002), Stone (1997), Boskin (1997), Limon (2000), Shales and Miller (2002), Krutnik (2003), Nachman (2003), Kercher (2006), Lewis (2006), nirHaggins (2007), Thomas (2009), Zoglin (2009), nirRobinson (2010), Gournelos and Greene (2011), and Krefting (2014).

3. Enss Mitchell, who owns The Comedy Union and wrote for NBC at the time, was the first to return my initial call and letter to voice his strong opinions about 9/11. He told me that shortly after 9/11, he posted a sign discouraging (but not completely censoring) comics' discussion of the national tragedy. Much like "America's 9/11," his signage was unprecedented, since he valued comics' creative license to joke about anything, including 9/11. Mitchell was clear about his motivations and stance: he'd observed a few comics bomb and a few audience members leave for what they deemed to be distasteful discussions of 9/11;

Mitchell also had friends in New York who were still awaiting news about loved ones who were in the World Trade Center on the day of the attacks; Mitchell felt audiences' needed (and deserved) cathartic release in his club and hoped his sign would minimize impulsive and/or half-baked 9/11 humor that could ruffle audience members' already frazzled nerves.

4. See, for example, scholarly work on the role of laughter in everyday conversation (e.g., Duranti & Brennais 1986, Duranti 2013, Glenn 2003, Ochs & Capps 2001, and Scarpetta & Fabiola 2009), and humor, in particular (e.g., Chapman 1983, Carrell 1997, Smith 2005, Friedman et al. 2011, Batalion 2012, and especially Rayner 2012). I had to trust laughter as evidence of comedy's intersubjective dance throughout my fieldwork, even as I appreciated laughter's many potential affective forms and (dis)guises (e.g., laughter can be uncomfortable, wry, incredulous, superior, even oppressive [see, for example, Johnson 2003 (see Ch. 2, "Manifest Faggotry: Queering Masculinity in African American Culture"), Oring 2003 (see Ch. 4, "The Humor of Hate"), Santa Ana 2009, and Krefting 2014 (see her Conclusion, "How to Avoid the Laugh Last Laugh"). Also, while I did informally interview a few regulars and listened intently to audience responses, the ethnographic nature of my study, wherein you listen as unobtrusively as you can, left me no other choice. I couldn't well stop audience members while they were laughing to ask, "What are you specifically laughing at right now?" (Nor did I wish to poll them using surveys or other systematic means practiced by audience reception researchers.) Rather, I had to trust the dialogue I presumed was happening while, as I noted before, keeping my interpretations of what I'd heard from comics onstage and audiences, loose.

   By keeping "loose," I (again) mean I had to constantly get behind the energy of my own and others' expectations of what 9/11 humor could and should do for the masses, whether the comedy served to reinforce versus implode stereotypes, and how it compared in order to better assess what comics were doing in real time, on their own terms, before Black and brown audiences who weren't afraid to intone their agreement, disagreement, or equivocal responses. I also had to concede that sometimes laughter affirmed the joke but could also mark nervous laughter since laughter was itself "loose" that way; laughter, Chapman (1983) argues, can also serve to "reveal group allegiances, communicate attitudes, and heal in establishing and reaffirming dominance in a status hierarchy" (135). Figuring out precisely how and when was a wholly interpretive affair.

   I didn't let the indeterminacy of it all shake me given the incredible opportunity that stood before me: to observe how comics, together with club owners and audience members, negotiated the precarious line where funny begins and abruptly ends around the highly charged subject of America's 9/11, and further, explain why, for many comics, funny even trumps the political imperative of an expected critique, or at least must bow to it. That required close listening of comics onstage and backstage, interviews over time to better understand comics themselves and the motives behind particular joke threads, and a consummate vetting of my own perceptions via consistent ethnographic field notations.

5. Hear comic testimonies of heckles, the worst of which is often silence, in the (2007) documentary, *Heckler*, as well as Borns (1987), Knoedelseder (2009), Gregory (1990[1964]), Littleton (2006), Littleton and Littleton (2012), and Seguin (2012) to start.

6. One comic who also worked as a barber would not let this premise go; he mused time and time again that when Shaquille "Shaq" O'Neal, an American retired basketball player, wore Stacey Adams shoes made of alligator skin, he must've worn the whole alligator. (Shaq is 7'1" and wears a size 22.)

7. In July 2002, a White Inglewood Police Department officer, Jeremy Morse, was captured on tape beating Donovan Jackson, a black sixteen-year-old with special needs who was handcuffed at the time. Jackson and his family eventually won a $2.4 million discrimination lawsuit in 2005, but Morse and the other White officer involved, Bijan Darvish, were never charged and, in fact, managed to successfully sue the City of Inglewood for race discrimination *against them*; Morse received $1.6 million and Darvish was awarded $810,000 (John Esterbrook,. "Jury Awards Fired Calif. Cop $1.5M." CBS/Associated Press, January 19, 2005. Web).

8. Godfrey C. Danchimah Jr.'s stage name is, simply, "Godfrey."

9. See also relevant scholarship highlighting how anti-black racism served as one means through which European and Jewish immigrants became "American"—in real life and onscreen (Rogin 1992, Brodkin 1999, Roediger 2005, Ignatiev 2009). Incidentally, this option does not extend to all ethnic minorities, including Asian Americans who, despite "model" but not unproblematic comparisons to other racial and ethnic groups, are forever deemed "foreign" or questionable citizens at best in America (see Waters 1990, Tuan 1999, Lee 2004). Similarly, African American comics' ability to deploy anti-Arab/anti-Muslim rhetoric to uplift themselves is similarly constrained, since anti-Blackness rears its head (in ways Black comics themselves concede) are either more powerful and encompassing of (and therefore undergirding) anti-Arab racism.

10. Evan Lionel actually had trouble telling this joke at The Comedy Union while shooting his 2002 comedy album, *"Too Real for Ya'll.* When he tried to deliver the line, "We all love this country," a black female audience member interrupted him not once but four times with the words, "Nope!" After her third, "Nope!" Lionel asked the audience, "Whose outpatient is this?" After her fourth single-word intrusion, he switched things into high gear and eventually silenced her with one sound effect, "Gunk," to simulate the sound of silencing by way of genitalia.

11. Dominique Whitten's stage name is, simply, "Dominique."

12. The late Ralphie May, a White comic, was surprised and a bit relieved by the news. He joked that he was glad to learn the sniper was Black and Muslim because Blacks would've never let "us" (i.e., poor Whites) live it down. Then, he looked squarely at me and other Black audience members and said, "Yeah! I said it! Yeah!" in his typical unapologetic way.

13. Comics' riffs on this theme were abundant. For example, Shang quipped, "If it had been a plane going to Freaknik (a now-defunct annual spring break meeting in Atlanta, Georgia, comprised primarily of students from historically black colleges and universities), they [terrorists] would have said, 'We are going to Allah!' and we [Blacks] would've said, 'Naw niggah; we going to Atlanta. Sit your ass down. You're messing up the in-flight movie.'" In his (2003) standup comedy film, *Dysfunktional Family*, Eddie Griffin vouched that if Black folks had been on the plane, "shit [9/11] wouldn't a went down like that. . . . You know how long a nigga have to save up for a ticket to Boston to L.A. A nigga would've been on the plane talking about, 'We ain't making no motherfucking no u-turns! Fuck you talking about? Nigga, I saved up for these tickets for two years! All that motherfucker got is a box cutter?! Nigga, we grew up in the projects! We done been in a knife fight before! [*simulates a fight*] Niggah would've whooped his ass and cut him up with his own knife and walked right to the pilot's booth. [*knocks on the door*] 'Yeah, everything out here cool. Aw, they ain't fucking with nobody else. . . . Look, we was wonderin' if we could get some free drinks because people kind of nervous.'" Other comics, including Loni Love, joked that

the terrorists explicitly avoided Southwest Airlines (a company known for its low fares) because it wouldn't have enough gas to pull off the attacks.

14. Other comics also critiqued America's purported "loss of innocence" by hinting at its complicity in past and recent atrocities. Shang joked, quite poignantly, "Fuck Bush! We [America] funded the Taliban. If I buy you a knife and you stab me, *how can I be mad?!*" Kathy Westfield remarked that the police who are stopping Arab Americans (and some Indian Americans by mistake) say, "They [Arab Americans] need to go home but hell, we all need to go home because this land originally belonged to the Indian." Glenn B., a dark-skinned Indian comic fluent in African American English, took the stage wearing a gold head wrap and waving an American flag. Using an Indian accent, he quipped, "This is bull-shit. God damn it! I'm fucking Indian! Stop it. Can't we all get along? Stop the stereotyping. We are all fucking American you motherfucking Americans!" Marc Howard, an African American Muslim comic, cautioned black audiences not to put what happened on the faith (Islam) or religious community. Michael Colyar also cautioned, "We gotta be careful because folks been . . . only going after terrorists with dark skin. People get lumped . . . and we can't forget that the Asians [Japanese Americans] were put in concentration camps. Let's not embrace the fear. Call people and tell them you love them." Brandon Bowlin made similar observations of Latinos as "new Americans" who don the flag strategically to avoid racial profiling and xenophobia post 9/11. "They got flags in their cars so they won't get deported. . . . Latinos don't care about your black pride motherfucker. [*imitates a Latino man]* 'My last name is California motherfucker!'"

15. Brandon Bowlin was not the only comic who recognized the valor of the terrorists in decided contrast to reputed "real" black folks. African comic Godfrey C. Danchimah Jr., known simply as "Godfrey," joked, "I'm not impressed by American niggahs no more. Iraqi motherfuckers, them Middle Easterners! How do you beat a motherfucker that will blow themselves up?!"

16. Consider for example, how Ian Edward's joke, which designates Arabs as the "new nigger," implies a "real" or authentic "nigger"; said another way, if Arabs are the so-called "new niggers," then who, his joke asks by implication, is the original and/or "real" nigger? Incidentally, this question proved critical to a few comics when I shared my essay draft with them before publication in ways I'll soon share.

17. Ralphie May died in October 2017. He left a message for fans on his Twitter page: "I hope when I die people make jokes about me, don't cry for me. Life is great."

18. For example, when Arie Spears asked a primarily black audience how many were still shook up by the events of 9/11, only two people raised their hands. When Yoursie Thomas asked a black crowd, "How many niggas gonna fight," only three people raised their hands.

19. Lester Barrie, a pastor and comic, similarly imitated a conversation between a disgruntled Osama Bin Laden and an Al Qaeda operative after a failed terrorist strike at a location familiar to many blacks and Latinos in his audience. Bin Laden says to the operative, "I don't see anything! Did you drop the bomb?!" "Yes," he replies. "WHERE did you drop the bomb?" "I dropped the bomb at the corner of Florence and Normandie." (Florence and Normandie is the site of the infamous beating of White truck driver Reginald Denny during the 1992 Los Angeles riots.)

20. These scholars (see, for example, Early 1994, Jackson Jr. 2005a; 2005b, Crouch & Benjamin 2002, Fontenot Jr. et al. 2001, Bobo 2000, Allen Jr. 2002, Shelby 2005) dutifully chart Du Bois's disparate use of this Hegelian-inspired concept (i.e., double consciousness) over the course of his career. Beyond their attempts to situate and contextualize his use of the term

in a sociohistorical and political moment, many rightly ask, do all blacks occupy the same Du Boisian problematic? The quick answer is, of course, no, but this book is admittedly less invested in shoring up those terms as it is preoccupied with why, say, Dave Chappelle in *Killin' 'Em Softly* would appeal to and situate a Black Nigerian on a plane as a [Black] comrade who gets to enjoy the rare perk of racism by being viewed as a worthless hostage. (As Chappelle explains, both he and the Nigerian passenger understood what their fellow White passengers did not: "Terrorists don't take Black hostages.") This book is also preoccupied with why England-born, Jamaica-raised comic Ian Edwards, who is especially proud of and vocal about his Jamaican heritage, would embrace the term "Black" over "African American" to identify and coalesce Black folks throughout the world in his televised sets.

21. See Arana (2003).
22. See Jacobs (2016).
23. See Lamar (2015).

Chapter 2

1. I thank my graduate Research Assistant, [now] Dr. Imani Kai Johnson, and undergraduate Research Assistants Forest Trujillo, Laura Guzman, Miko Phillips, and Syan Cromwell for their help in especially this and other chapters.
2. See Dyson 2017.
3. In her (2011) memoir, *No Higher Honor: A Memoir of My Years in Washington*, Condoleezza Rice expressed considerable regret for her decision to take a vacation despite reports of Katrina's looming devastation. She called her decision to take a well-needed vacation "tone death" and said she told President Bush, "Mr. President, I'm coming back. I don't know how much I can do, but we clearly have a race problem." However, while serving as secretary of state, Rice consistently downplayed the role of race in her public statements during Hurricane Katrina, earning her considerable scorn from Black comics and many Black folks at the time. Comics spared no offense lambasting white and especially Black politicians and pundits they perceived as complicit in the err-apparent handling of the storm and thus, insincere and racially inauthentic. Rice did not fare well in this parsing of comic justice. A month after the storm, Comic "Sexy Marlo" told a small crowd at The Townhouse, a supper club in Los Angeles that often features standup comedy, karaoke, and live music and has since been renamed The Cork, "[One of the things that bother me] is that niggah Bush. I'ma kick his ass when I see him. Him and that hood rat Condi. I'm a kick her ass, too. They fucking. You know they fuckin." Then in a sacred-meets-the-profane moment that is neither rare in humor writ large nor Black standup comedy, she quoted a scripture from St. Matthew before adding, "Ain't no use of worrying. All we can do is pray." Later during the same show, legendary comic Paul Mooney rapid-fire quipped, "Bush don't give a shit about no niggahs except Condeleeza . . . and that's just at night." Never one to leave himself misunderstood, he added (per Sexy Marlo's insinuation), "Oh you know they're fucking. You know!" Questioning the legitimacy of America's search for weapons of mass destruction in Iraq and Afghanistan, Mooney added, "They ain't found a fuckin' firecracker!"
4. So, too, did a Black male student I'll never forget named Levi Powell. Back in 2013, during one of my African American Society and Culture lectures, I was especially candid about the care I took when discussing race and my ambivalence when doing so because I feared I sometimes left Black students hanging. With palpable love and regard, Levi looked at me

pointedly and said, "And you don't have to Lanita." I heard him then and I hear him now as I type these words.

5. See (again) Dyson 2017.

6. See, for example, Stephens 2009.

7. So says the Federal Emergency Management Agency (FEMA) and the National Oceanic and Atmospheric Administration (NOAA), according to "Hurricane Katrina Statistics Fast Facts," *CNN Library* (Augustj 28, 2017), Accessed: http://www.cnn.com/2013/08/23/us/hurricane-katrina-statistics-fast-facts/index.html, and Nathaniel Meyersohn, "The Costliest Natural Disaster in U.S. History," *CNN Money* (September 11, 2017), http://money.cnn.com/2017/09/11/news/costliest-natural-disasters/index.html.

8. See Wade 2015.

9. See Carr 2005 and Thevenot & Russell 2005. ; Thevenot & Russell's Hurricane Katrina coverage earned The 2006 Pulitzer Prize in Public Service.

10. See Amadeo 2019.

11. See Associated Press, "Report: U.S. Did Not Use Foreign Aid after Hurricane Katrina" (January 13, 2015), https://www.foxnews.com/story/report-u-s-did-not-use-donated-foreign-aid-after-hurricane-katrina), and Mayer et al.'s 2011 report titled, "Accepting Disaster Relief from Other Nations: Lessons from Katrina and the Gulf Oil Spill"; Mayer et al. state that nearly 400,000 Meals Ready to Eat (MREs) donated by the United Kingdom in September 2005 also went unused when government officials learned that the British MREs contained beef, which the US still banned at that time given the outbreak of "mad cow disease" in the UK during the mid-1990s.

12. To err is human but to breach is to err in beguiling yet ultimately insightful ways; herein lies the essence of what scholar Harvey Garfinkel (1967; Garfinkel and Rawls 2002 calls the "breach"; he adds, it's like going to McDonalds and requesting a Whopper (a burger you'd find at Burger King, an American fast food chain), or showing up as an uninvited guest to a house party and asking to take a shower. When breaches occur, they force speakers (and even witnesses) to stop and assess whether it was intentional, as in the case of a joke, or, unintentional (i.e., sincere) so that they can reconstitute a sense of normalcy. In this "bracketing process," they are reflecting on questions of accountability, intentionality, and normalcy in relation to everyday assumptions about what is "right" or "wrong" behavior, talk, etc.; see also Jacobs-Huey 2007).

13. In a clip that's funnier now than it was at the time, West ignored the teleprompter's script and declared this instead: "Bush doesn't care about Black people" as his segment co-host, Canadian-comedian Mike Myers, winced. When I show students this clip now, they laugh wryly given West's nervous delivery, their knowledge of West's mounting record of breached protocols, and Myers's palpable discomfort onscreen. Myers eventually settled up with his unforeseen role in what many now appreciate as West's laudatory "speaking truth to power"—set comically and dramatically against Myers's stunned expression. One month after the telethon, Myers and West lampooned the incident on *Saturday Night Live*; Myers also praised West some years later, "To have the emphasis on the look on my face versus the fact that somebody spoke truth to power at a time when somebody needed to speak? I'm very proud to have been next to him." See Grow 2014. .

14. Then-president George W. Bush did not immediately release troops from the war effort in Iraq to abet the Katrina recovery.

15. Chris Rock also thought of his own daughter while volunteering at a food bank in Houston, Texas, following Hurricane Katrina. Rock cried openly when he saw a young Black girl

who, despite having lost everything in the storm, seem comforted as long as she was near her father, a Katrina survivor. Both Rock and Luenell [Campbell] publicly struggled with the pain and hope of raising Black daughters in a land that does not always recognize their citizenship, let alone come to their aid when they are in duress.

16. Waitresses at The Comedy Union (where I conducted the majority of my videotaped observations) were essential in organizing fundraisers, literally enacting the ways comedy heals and even saves through appeals to sincerity, truth, and even racial authenticity. The club sold $3 orange wristbands that read, "Katrina. We are one" to help raise funds for Katrina victims. Several comediennes also wed sincerity and working-class testimony and sensibilities—themselves reputed markers of "real" Blackness rooted in struggle and hope—in witty and, at times demonstrative, calls to give. For example, comedienne "Sexy Marlo" regrettably told a crowd at what is now The Cork" a supper club in Los Angeles, that regularly features standup comedy, "I wish I could help but I gotta EBT card. I can send them a box of noodles." Melanie Comarcho was willing to give but a bit cynical: "I need to see where my money is going. I'm taking clothes [instead]."

17. Adeline Masquelier underscores this critique in her poignant and timely 2006 article: "Why Katrina's Victims Aren't *Refugees*: Musings on a 'Dirty' Word." Masquelier also notes, with tragic irony, that Katrina storm victims would have actually fared better in terms of relief had they applied as literal refugees.

18. I ask readers to indulge my orthographic liberties in the following transcription; I'm trying to inflect Williams's gifts of impersonation and caricature via my spelling choices.

19. Comic Relief USA president and founder Bob Zmuda apparently worked diligently and through a few missteps to ensure that Comic Relief 2006 was racially–sensitive and pitch perfect. To do so, he hired a "keep it real" consultant, hired locals, and worked hard on a Las Vegas set built to Lower Ninth Ward specs. He also spoke several times during the show to home in on the unfinished work of rebuilding New Orleans and other areas damaged by Katrina. Still, his efforts and a few comics' sets (e.g., Sarah Silverman; Billy Crystal's "Jazzman" routine which comedian and podcaster Tom Scharpling likened to Michael Richards's n-word laced rant at The Laugh Factory in November 2006), occasioned mixed responses. For example, see Rees 2006, Walker 2006, and Blevins 2016. .

20. See A. C. Thompson's (2008) award-winning piece, "Katrina's Hidden Race War," as well as Thompson 2009.

21. See Fussell et al. 2010.

22. This part—showing and seeing without co-opting—elides one of the "dangers" of empathy; in the wrong hands, empathy can be deployed toward nefarious or purely commercial ends and even rob those most in need of it if and when those who've done the work to personally identify with their experience walk off into the dawn, feeling better about themselves with not a peep from the folks they're leaving behind. Paul Bloom, a psychologist at Yale, underscores these and other dangers in his provocatively titled book (2016), *Against Empathy: The Case for Rational Compassion*. Other scholars teach us of the performativity and rhetorical nature of empathy's third cousin, sympathy, as it pertains to Muslims and Middle Eastern citizens and subjects post 9/11 (e.g., Abu-Lughod 2013, Al-Ali & Pratt 2009, Ansultany 2012, Jhally et al. 2006, Naber 2012, Shaheen 2012).

23. Duran Howard gave one of the best glosses any linguistic anthropologist could ever hope for when he joked about the distinction Black folks make between "this nigga" versus "that niggah there"; in the first instance, "this niggah" carried negative affective weight. Folks might be talking disparagingly about O. J. Simpson in the first but glowingly of President

Barack Obama in the latter. These interpretive possibilities aside, Wells's deployments of "niggah" and even more critical "this niggah" ultimately signal a call to empathy and critique that doesn't leave "This niggah with the TV" lying in the water with respectable Black folks safely ensconced everywhere else.

24. Other comics riffed on this popular premise. Comedienne Luenell [Campbell] quipped, "The guy runnin' down the street with the big ass TV? That nigga ain't looting; he's crazy. You clean motherfucker. The dope man ain't there!" before declaring, "Niggas need to migrate to the next town and take over—me and my whole nigga family. . . . I'm pissed! We all gone suffer from this." (This Shit Ain't Fo' Everybody Comedy Joint 9/5/05). On Comic Relief 2006, Tony Rock opened his set by joking, "I want to thank the brothers in the Ninth Ward for this TV screen that they stole during the hurricane," before distinguishing between righteous looting (for survival) and "real" looting. He added, "Nike don't make no scuba gear."

25. Hughes performs "whiteness" via a higher nasal-inflected register often used by Black comedians to "voice whiteness." Often, these performances associate such delivery with white duplicity, as well as earnestness, white conservatism, and white liberalism. Readers might likewise be familiar with rapper, writer, director Boots Riley's film, Sorry To Bother You, whose central character, Cassius "Cash" Green (played by Lakeith Stanfield), speaks in a comically hyper-performed "white" voice in his low-level telemarketing job. Comediennes Adele Givens and Amanda Seales have also joked about Black women's capacity to codeswitch or "talk white" in their dealings with white folks in order to gain respect, leverage power, and appear "professional." This skill, they and Riley suggest, is emblematic of resources born of Blacks' double consciousness and lived realities under white supremacy. Readers might also be interested in Aisha Harris's (2018) article, "When Black Performers Use Their 'White Voice."

26. Kapoor (2018) examines the 2012 extradition of five Muslim men—Babar Ahmad, Talha Ahsan, Khalid al-Fawwaz, Adel Abdul Bary, and Abu Hamza— from Britain to the United States to face terrorism-related charges; these racialized subjects were dehumanized, made non-human, both in terms of how they are represented and via the disciplinary techniques used to expel them. These cases illuminate and enable intensifying authoritarianism and the diminishment of democratic systems, and bear similarities to some of the political discourse and policies that abetted the evacuation of Black NOLA residents as "refugees" and "looters" in and after Hurricane Katrina.

27. Black comics appealed to racial authenticity in additional ways by personifying Hurricane Katrina as an angry Black woman or otherwise highlighting what was "real Black" about the storm and its victims. Lavell Crawford, Leslie Jones, and even Billy Crystal (on Comic Relief 2006) mined for humor by likening the storm itself to an "angry Black woman." Jones's jokes were among the funniest (Crystal's got pilloried); she jested, "They named the hurricane after a Black girl and their problem was calling her 'mild." "You can't call no Black girl mild. She gon' fuck everything up." (This Shit Ain't Fo' Everybody after Hours 9/5/05). Before delivering her (and for me pen-drop worthy) joke, "We refugees now after done built this motherfucker?" Melanie Comarcho felt Black female Katrina victims upheld a standard of appearance often associated with "real Blackness" when she quipped at an after-hours comedy spot, "They hair was whipped [i.e., well-coiffed]. Niggas didn't forget they gel in this tragedy." Storm allusions also found their way into comedic repertoires, particularly among comics trying to corral hecklers. At Mixed Nuts Comedy Club in the wake of Katrina (9/10/05), G'Thang tried to silence a female heckler by taking a shot at one of

the woman's fake ponytails. When she responded, "It's mine! I bought it!," G'Thang grew weary: "I am way too famous to be arguing with Aunt Pearl. Speedy [show host], you got a show out of control here! . . . I feel like throwing her in the water. I really feel like treating her (the audience member he'd called "Aunt Pearl") like a victim."

28. Hardy L. Jackson's testimony during an emotional interview with news reporter Jennifer Mayerle captured the hearts of many viewing audience members, including R&B singer Frankie Beverly (of "Maze") who relocated and bought Jackson a house in Atlanta. During his TV interview, Jackson mentions that he can't find his wife's body and also, that there are at least three other unidentified bodies stuck in the mud. The African American cameraman who filmed Jackson's interview (and later consoled the reporter) speculated that Jackson started dying when "he let his wife's hand go." Hardy, who lost his daughter to cancer, died on March 30, 2013, of a terminal illness. See WKRG News 5's report, "Hurricane Katrina: 10 Years Later, 2005–2015," https://www.youtube.com/watch?v=-zO2oXvW3Hg.

29. I wish readers could hear, feel, sense if only to better understand how and why Thompson makes people laugh *real*. Laugh like they haven't in a long time. Laugh until they cry. Laugh in the manner of what he, himself, boldly (and deservedly as winner of the 2003 Bay Area Black Comedy Competition Winner and *Last Comic Standing: Season Eight*) calls "that good funny" with riffs that provoke a crescendo of sidesplitting laughter.

30. Consider, for example, a couple of the late comics' signature jokes told in the height of the civil rights movement: "Segregation is not all bad. Have you ever heard of a collision where the people in the back of the bus got hurt?," and, "I sat in at a lunch counter for nine months. When they finally integrated, they didn't have what I wanted." In both jokes, Gregory's political critique is strategically lodged within irony, softening both his implicit critiques of segregation but also slyly hinting at controversial b-sides (e.g., "integration was a bust" in the lunch counter joke and "segregation is not all bad" in the joke about racial discrimination on public buses). Each of his jokes likewise relies on his listener's acuity for *indirectness* and capacity for capacious interpretation. For example, Gregory's joke about "segregation" would make the late-great anthropologist and writer Zora Neale Hurston laugh out loud, even though her own non-comedic, or rather, bold and public cynicism toward integration earned her considerable scorn and painful discipline from Black politicians and pundits.

31. See, for example, Christie Davies's (2011) book, *Jokes and Targets*.

32. Bel is particularly culturally astute here, riffing back, if readers remember, to Chris Spencer's (and other Black comics') recognition of the different ways Black folks grieve in times of tragedy. During the Iraq war, Chris Spencer told the Laugh Factory's *Chocolate Sundaes* audience, "It's a damn war going on and Black folks are the only ones going out [and] having a good time!"

33. Cartoonist Aaron McGruder's post-Katrina strips were less critical of the nation than his post-9/11 ones. He, too, seemed to center his critiques tough-lovingly and squarely on Black so-called "refugees" in his comic strips and his 2004-2014 TV Series, *The Boondocks*, which included an episode titled, "Invasion of the Katrinians" (Season 2, Episode 9; airdate December 10, 2007).

34. In her ethnographic study of white "road comics" in the Midwest and South-Central regions of the United States, Susan Seizer (2011) found that comics use swear words like "fuck" and "shit" consistently in idiomatic, non-denotational, and non-referential—which is to say non-literal—ways to "express the intensity of the speaker's own experience of awe, fear, or any other such wonderment" (210). Further, male and female comics' deployment enable them to convey "off the record" attitude and otherwise speak to audiences "from the heart";

that is, with intimacy and informality. The trick all comics, especially female ones, face is leveraging expletives in a way that doesn't consign them to the shtick of "blue comedy," or humor rife with curse words but lacking in craft and substance. Adele Givens, a hilarious Black comedienne from what she calls the "deep hood," exemplifies this by subverting and revising expectations of Black femininity in her racy 1990s *Def Comedy Jam* performance; in it, she cheekily describes herself as "a fuckin' lady" while effortlessly tackling subjects like sexual pleasure and desire. When a Black male attempted to heckle her about the size of her lips, she took him down a peg and owned the stage by quipping, "Yeah, I know they some big motherfuckahs. Ay—I know they some big motherfuckers. Yeah, . . . all my lips are big, motherfuckah." See clip here: https://youtu.be/TGi-ihN4EDA?t=218.

35. These rescues were spectacles of relief during Hurricane Katrina; when US agencies like FEMA and the Homeland Security Department failed to galvanize resources while the US Coast Guard used their own bodies and a basket-looking apparatus to lift folks off roofs and transport them to safer ground.

36. New Orleans residents balked in 2009 when Krewe of Orpheus selected Carlos Mencia to be a celebrity rider and performer in the city's annual Mardi Gras parade, leading its captain, Sonny Borey, to issue this public statement: "Our [K]rewe is very sensitive to the feelings of our community and the way our city is viewed."

37. The comment, "That's funny" or "You're funny" is also a way some speakers question others' sincerity; likewise, Mencia's use of "funny" winks b-sidedly, questioning the sincerity and consistency of Black folks' commitment to racial justice.

38. Mencia did not say anything other Black and brown comics weren't also saying about "Mexicans," whether undocumented immigrants or US citizens. For example, comic/actor George Lopez used his televised set at Comic Relief 2006 to figuratively and unapologetically "rep his set (i.e., *peeps*)," joking: "More Latino people would have been saved during Hurricane Katrina except when they saw us on the roof, they thought the rebuilding had already started." Lopez also predicted New Orleans would be rebuilt "stronger, safer, and better than it was before . . . with MY new FEMA, . . . which stands for, 'Find Every Mexican Available!' " (Similarly, Roseanne Barr quipped on Comic Relief 2006, "We could've solved two problems at once if we would've hired all the Mexicans that are in our country to rebuild Katrina 'cause that would've taken like three days and cost about $1,100. Rich people want that wall and it's to keep the Mexicans in!") Readers may notice that, unlike Mencia's joke, Lopez doesn't throw Blacks under the bus in order to recognize and salute Latino storm victims and NOLA rebuilders. Readers may also notice that, much like Mencia's joke, Lopez situates "Mexicans" as the central rebuilders, effectively absenting Black native New Orleanians from a future workforce committed to the port city's rebirth and preservation.

39. In New Orleans, more than 175,000 Black residents left in the year after Katrina; more than 75,000 never returned. According to the US Census Bureau's 2016 population estimates, there are 92,348 fewer African Americans living in New Orleans (Orleans Parish) compared to 2000. Contrastingly, the non-Hispanic white population has all but returned to its pre-storm total, and the small "Hispanic" population has grown by more than 30%. See also Icess Fernandez Rojas's (2015) article, "10 Years after Katrina, A Defined Latino Presence in New Orleans." This "defined Latino presence" is also under assault as many recent immigrants face harassment by police and immigration agents; see Alexia Fernández Campbell et al.'s (2014) article, "Is New Orleans Trying to Deport Undocumented Workers Now That Rebuilding Is Over?"

40. For more on this, see Stephen Benko's (2020) edited collection, *Ethics in Comedy: Essays on Crossing the Line*.

41. Even Rod Man Thompson, who revised the overwhelmingly negative read of Black looters who stole TVs and such by stressing their forethought and industriousness, followed his joke by saying, "Mexicans are resilient too. They'll try to sell you anything, including comforters without any plastic on them."

42. Tuan (1999) argues that the "model minority" myth is a trick bag indeed since those deemed "model" on the a-side can still remain "forever foreigners" and otherwise suspect on the b-side by virtue of having even been deemed "good" on the flip side (see also Naber 2012). Carbado and Gulati (2013) also note how race, in particular Blackness, shapes and distinguishes American identity and American citizenship; in particular, they remind us that anyone who fits the description of the naturalized American (i.e., white, blond, blue-eyed) can be "American" even if they're not citizens, while outliers—those with say Black, brown, or yellow skin—can be actual American citizens but never quite really seen as true "Americans" except by comparative default. In fact, American citizenship hinges and pivots around racial phenotype such that someone is deemed not just "white" but also "American" because somebody else is "Black"; someone is "American" because Blacks' "Americanness" is specious by default; we interpolate one another based on these explicit and implicit, state-sanctioned, and very much legally naturalized distinctions such that they become cemented, "real" in our cultural imagination. Who gets to be American and a citizen remains an intersubjective assessment and achievement that is oft contingent on disavowing Blackness and Black folk (see Brodkin 1999, Ignatiev 2009, Gualtieri 2009, Roediger 2005, Rogin 1992).

43. Chris Rock castigated Hollywood for its "race problem" in the *Hollywood Reporter* (December 3, 2014), saying, "It's a white industry. . . . But forget whether Hollywood is Black enough. A better question is: is Hollywood Mexican enough? You're in L.A., you've got to try not to hire Mexicans. It's the most liberal town in the world, and there's a part of it that's kind of racist—not racist like 'F— you, nigger' racist, but just an acceptance that there's a slave state in L.A. There's this acceptance that Mexicans are going to take care of white people in L.A. that doesn't exist anywhere else. I remember I was renting a house in Beverly Park while doing some movie, and you just see all of the Mexican people at 8 o'clock in the morning in a line driving into Beverly Park like it's General Motors. It's this weird town." He continued, "You're telling me no Mexicans are qualified to do anything at a studio? Really? Nothing but mop up? What are the odds that that's true? The odds are, because people are people, that there's probably a Mexican David Geffen mopping up for somebody's company right now. The odds are that there's probably a Mexican who's that smart who's never going to be given a shot. And it's not about being given a shot to greenlight a movie because nobody is going to give you that—you've got to take that. The shot is that a Mexican guy or a Black guy is qualified to go and give his opinion about how loud the boings are in Dodgeball or whether it's the right shit sound you hear when Jeff Daniels is on the toilet in *Dumb and Dumber*. It's like, 'We only let white people do that.'" https://www.hollywoodreporter.com/news/top-five-filmmaker-chris-rock-753223.

44. See relevant work by Dyson 2006, Gotham & Greenberg 2008, Lipsitz 2006, Owen 2011, Wailoo et al. 2010, along with documentaries by Spike Lee (2006) and Tia Lessin and Carl Deal (2008).

45. Even now, as I write these words, I mourn the loss of Victor McElhaney, a twenty-one-year-old African American student from Oakland, California, whose undergraduate career in

jazz studies was cut short by a failed robbery attempt in March 2019; he drummed with passion and wanted to change the world through music.

46. The backbeats abetting this turn are many, including Geertz's call for "thick description" and frank heed to the fact that anthropologists construct what Jackson would later call their own "ethnographic sincerity" by virtue of demonstrating that they had, of all things, "been there" in the field with their research participants. Jackson Jr. (2013) critically revisits Geertz's notion of "thick description" and the prospect of ethnographic innocence in his book, *Thin Description: Ethnography and the African Hebrew Israelites of Jerusalem.*

Chapter 3

1. American writer, poet, librarian, and civil rights activist Audre Lorde said something similar in February 1982 when she delivered the address, "Learning from the '60s," during the Malcolm X weekend celebration at Howard University: "There are no new ideas, just new ways of giving those ideas we cherish breath and power in our own lives." She also said something else that is extremely germane to this book's focus, especially as it relates to the many reasons that notions of "real" blackness must be interrogated as a matter of moral and communal praxis; I'll quote her at length:

> In the '60s, White America—racist and liberal alike—was more than pleased to sit back as spectator while Black militant fought Black Muslim, Black Nationalist badmouthed the nonviolent, and Black women were told that our only useful position in the Black Power movement was prone. The existence of Black lesbian and gay people was not even allowed to cross the public consciousness of Black America. We know in the 1980s, from documents gained through the Freedom of Information Act, that the FBI and CIA used our intolerance of difference to foment confusion and tragedy in segment after segment of Black communities of the '60s. Black was beautiful, but still suspect, and too often our forums for debate became stages for playing who's-Blacker-than-who or who's-poorer-than-who games, ones in which there can be no winners.

> The '60s for me was a time of promise and excitement, but the '60s was also a time of isolation and frustration from within. It often felt like I was working and raising my children in a vacuum, and that it was my own fault—if I was only Blacker, things would be fine. It was a time of much wasted energy, and I was often in a lot of pain. Either I denied or chose between various aspects of my identity, or my work and my Blackness would be unacceptable. As a Black lesbian mother in an interracial marriage, there was usually some part of me guaranteed to offend everybody's comfortable prejudices of who I should be. That is how I learned that if I didn't define myself for myself, I would be crunched into other people's fantasies for me and eaten alive. My poetry, my life, my work, my energies for struggle were not acceptable unless I pretended to match somebody else's norm. I learned that not only couldn't I succeed at that game, but the energy needed for that masquerade would be lost to my work. And there were babies to raise, students to teach. The Vietnam War was escalating, our cities were burning, more and more of our school kids were nodding out in the halls, junk was overtaking our streets. We needed articulate power, not conformity. There were other strong Black workers whose visions were racked and silenced upon some imagined grid of narrow Blackness. Nor were Black women immune. At a national meeting of Black women for political action, a young civil rights activist who had been beaten and imprisoned in Mississippi only a few years before, was trashed and silenced as suspect because of her white husband. Some of us made

it and some of us were lost to the struggle. It was a time of great hope and great expectation; it was also a time of great waste. That is history. We do not need to repeat these mistakes in the 80s.

2. I'd be lying if I said I had a firm hold on "a" real Black at that time. I didn't. I was tallying up Black comics' appeals to racial authenticity, sincerity, and truth using the prioritized and legitimacy granting constructionist paradigms in my respective fields (e.g., anthropology, American Studies and Ethnicity, humor studies) so I was still too busy to own "a" real Black as a *scholarly* stance. I eventually got there, though, joke by joke, theory by ever-evolving theory, and by feeling and writing my way toward a hook I could hold firm.

3. This includes even the most painstakingly wrought transcripts authored by members of a central tribe of mine, linguistic anthropologists; they would have a field day with this excerpt and likely turn up even more detailed transcripts toward a deep analysis of verbal and nonverbal language, extant contextual variables, and the like. Our disciplinary concession is that all transcripts are "partial" insofar as they are selective representations of verbal and non-verbal conversation inherently divorced from their original context.

4. TMZ is an American celebrity tabloid news website and tabloid based in Los Angeles and owned by the Fox Corporation.

5. Another veteran comic, Sinbad, was at The Laugh Factory the night of Richards's set and admitted to the show's host and media that he was shocked by what he saw; when pressed by the media for an opinion, he said comics should never resort to sexism or racism when decimating hecklers.

6. I initially wondered if this is one reason that Doss and his ethnically diverse party weren't dissuaded to leave by what Richards allegedly said off-camera when they first entered the club during his set [i.e., "All the stupid blacks and Mexicans are here"]; maybe they mistakenly thought he'd somehow transform this into comedic gold and thus gave him the benefit of the doubt. (Doss and his friend Frank McBride addressed my curiosity in their interview with Matt Lauer, saying they were busy giving their drink orders to a waitress at the time and a bit in shock, especially when Richards continued his racist verbal assault.)

7. This does not mean that language and humor scholars haven't tried to successfully delimit the nuances and socializing dynamics of audience laughter as well as laughter's many semiotic possibilities (e.g., Bergson 2005 [1911], Freud 1960, Apte 1985, Provine 2000, Glenn 2003, Weems 2014).

8. Speaking of "gifts," Richards has many, not only in the fields of entertainment but also born of his former medical training, a stint as a medic in the US Army, and schooling at the California Institute of the Arts, Los Angeles Valley College, and the Evergreen State College (from which he received a BA in drama). He's known among his peers in entertainment as a perfectionist, frequently if not always hitting his lines while cracking up stagehands and fellow actors in the process; he's said to sometimes chides fellow actors for flubbing their lines (or laughing at his expert execution of his) as they head into a "second-take."

9. I am aware that some readers, especially if they are comics, might pause at the use of the word "petty," especially since the complete annihilation of a heckler is an imperative, a right, heck, a responsibility to most comics—regardless of their fame level. When Doss rather calmly tells Richards, "That was uncalled for," Richards rhetorically asks or, rather, mimes Doss's question before cheekily answering, "What 'wasn't uncalled for'? It's uncalled for you to interrupt my ass, you cheap motherfuckAHS!" Petty entails "complaining about things that are not important" or "something relatively worthless or unimportant";

some readers might likewise feel that Richards's clout and performance cred should have protected him against this public spectacle of coming undone. But maybe "petty" is relative in this case. Clearly, Richards's stage time meant much to him, so much that he resorted to a retrograde form of racism (after Doss said his friend thought him to be unfunny) in order to regain the floor and a sense of racial superiority over Doss and others.

10. Readers should appreciate that this "cap" is tilted a bit to the side versus donned straight; I simply do not go "all in" by deploying all the conventions or even linguistic analyses available to me to represent and unpack this transcript. My reasons are many, including my foremost pursuit of a more accessible writing style. I want to write a book my mother and comics might read and understand.

11. See Rickford (1977) and Green (2002)

12. Here, a linguistic anthropologist might draw attention to Richards's deictic expression (i.e., his use of words or phrases—for example, "me" or "here") that cannot be understood without additional contextual information—in this case, the identity of the speaker ("me") and the speaker's location ("here"). That is, until the limitations of this Wikipedia-ish gloss run smack dab into the historical contingencies of race. Everyone in Richards's audience was likely familiar with who he was targeting by the word "nigger" and likewise shocked that he would do so on a public stage. They'd know for the same reasons that students in my diverse seminars in American Studies and Ethnicity and Anthropology chuckled when I quipped, "If somebody came in the class talking about, 'Death to niggers!,' we all know who'd be running out first!" The Wikipedia gloss likewise adds that "Words are deictic if their semantic meaning is fixed but their denotational meaning varies depending on time and/or place." Indeed, and this is why even Black comics like "Scruncho"—who present more encompassing reads of the signifier "niggah"—start with a qualifier that seeks to dislodge audience presumptions of who a "nigger" is from what, in the comic's mind, a "nigger" can actually be. Yancy (2012) poignantly adds that it's not just the imperative, "Look," that sullies the see, but "Negro," too, insofar as " 'Negro!' functions as a signifier that gives additional *urgency* to the command, 'Look' " (1). "Look, a Negro!" likewise culls illocutionary force from White fear and misrecognition since "the Negro in [the White child's imagination] is presumed to have "always already done something by way of being Negro (2)." Thus, Yancy notes of Fanon's experienced deduction, "To 'see' a Negro is to 'see' a nigger; it is to 'see' a problem—a problem deemed, from the perspective of Whites, onto-logical" (3).

13. In his gift of a book, *Look, A White! Philosophical Essays on Whiteness*, George Yancy (2012) cautions, "The white boy, though, is not a mere innocent proxy for whiteness. Rather, he is learning, at that very moment, the power of racial speech, the power of racial gesturing. He is learning how to think about and feel toward the so-called dark Other. He is undergoing white subject formation, a formation that is fundamentally linked to the object that he fears and dreads" (3).

14. Here, I remember Raoul Peck's (2016) ninety-four-minute film, *I Am Not Your Negro*, which envisions the book James Baldwin never finished. Before he died in 1987, he'd written only thirty pages of a book recalling the successive assassinations of his close friends and compatriots: Medgar Evans, Malcolm X, and Martin Luther King Jr. The book was to be called *Remember This House*, and it has since evolved into a critical meditation of race in America, re-envisioned by Peck, who seeks to finish Baldwin's book using Baldwin's original words and archival footage.

15. It occurs to me now, as I type this, that the gentleman laughing giddily here and throughout the rest of Richards's set may have been hip to Richards's attempted flip; that is, he may be laughing at Richards's audacious attempt to reframe his racist remarks into play while chiding his (apparently gullible) audience for deigning to take him seriously at all.

16. Their laughter nonetheless taunts Richards during his set and haunts him afterward. After his set, he told his friend, the late comic-legend Paul Mooney, that some non-Black audience members approached him after his set to comfort and assure him that they shared his views; ironically, Richards found this to be disturbing.

17. Especially relevant here is Chun (2020) and especially Bucholtz and Lopez's (2011) study of European American actors' performance of African American English (AAE) in Hollywood films (e.g., Warren Beatty [with African American actress Halle Berry] and Steve Martin [with African American actress and rapper, Queen Latifah]). Remember, Richards marshals aspects of AAE to exonerate himself and indict Black males in his audience. Bucholtz & Lopez show Beatty and Martin to be dabbling in a similar play insofar as their performances of AAE function as a form of "linguistic minstrelsy"—"a form of mock language that reinscribes stereotypes about African Americans and their language while participating in a longstanding and often controversial pattern of European American appropriation of Black cultural forms" (681). They add that much like Blackfaced minstrelsy (which must be distinguished from the "metaparodic" and "reflexive 'high' performance" of "neo-minstrelsy" (Coupland 2007) wherein White actors' deliberately seek to represent either Whiteness or (especially) blackness accurately), linguistic minstrelsy is "racially performative in the sense that [it] does not simply reflect but actively construct both blackness and Whiteness and thereby expose racial categories as socially contingent and, hence, changeable" (683) (cf. Nowatzki 2007). Bucholtz and Lopez hasten to point out that while this may seem to make for multiple analytically productive interpretations—including, say, decentering static notions of race or valorizing blackness versus stigmatizing it outright— the actual take-aways are actually quite limited – as limited, I'd add, as Richards' attempted racism redux; they note: "Despite the fact that the films examined in this study portray potentially subversive acts of racial crossing through language and valorize African American language and culture as superior in some ways to hegemonic linguistic and cultural forms, they habitually use these representations to restabilize White middle-class masculinity, the dominance of which has grown more and more insecure in recent decades" [683] (cf. Pfeil1995). Why? Beatty and Martin's portrayals—scaffolded by Black female actresses who both augment and obscure their ultimate purchase of "authentic" White masculinity—"feed a middle-class White male fantasy of gaining cultural cool through linguistic minstrelsy (700)" by appropriating the sounds and so-called gendered and sexual affects of (male) blackness. Richards also marshals aspects of AAE to restore his sense of White masculine superiority but he indemnifies it in a fledgling real-time performance of "neo-minstrelsy";—that is, as a smorgasbord that folds in comedic one-upmanship, moral reproof, and even self-parody for comedic vindication. In each case, White male (comic) actors' pursuit of personal transformation via linguistic minstrelsy is not wholly "innocent" and, in fact, may very well suggest something else a bit more pernicious. As Bucholtz and Lopez conclude: "The indexicalities of race, gender, sexuality, and class constructed in the films expose the insecure position of present-day White hegemonic masculinity. It is only by incorporating the essential qualities of young Black masculinity—toughness, sexual aggressiveness, rebelliousness—into their own identities that these characters become authentic White men. The logic of such narratives does not ultimately challenge the

dominance of Whiteness, but it suggests that the semiotic resources of blackness are necessary in order for Whiteness to claim authenticity and thereby retain its authority" (701).

18. The "mic drop" is an intentional and bodacious gesture in standup comedy; comics (and
even politicians like Barack Obama) first extend and then literally drop their microphones
after a killer set to signal their triumph onstage. It's possible, then, that Richards's weak
and weary "mic drop" at the end of his stage time was far more than a cheeky and ironic
sign of defeat given his wildly unsuccessful set; he may have been parodying this bodacious practice in standup comedy, as well as the failure of his own set, to discerning comics
in the room. He may have trumped the laughs and chides he knew were sure to come by
parodying his own spectacular comedic fail.

19. Again, I'm admittedly plumbing the surface of this dialogue; if I wrote merely as a linguistic anthropologist, I'd deploy discourse analysis toward an even deeper excavation of
Richards's attempted repairs. These "repairs," which rely on repetition, re-glossing (consider, for example, Richards's differential uses of "ass"), could source additional articles
on the sincerity and authenticity of comedic apologies. So, too, could Richards's apologies
(e.g., Ellwanger 2012).

20. See also Pérez (2022).

21. Readers might recall that one disgruntled audience member lobbed the critique "White
boy" at Richards during the height of the verbal fight. Yet I doubt that it hurt Richards
any more than their claim that he was not funny. In fact, Richards's retort ("SHUT UP!
Fifty years ago, we'd have you upside-down with a fucking fork up your ass!... . . . *Throw
his ass out. He's a NIGGER! He's a NIGGER!*") suggests as much. That is not to say that
these words do not wound. I'm sure they do in certain contexts. But Richards's vindictive
remarks were sure to trump their critiques for reasons Richards clearly emphasized, "You're
a nigger! . . . That's what happens when you interrupt a White man." Ian Edwards exploited
this very premise through a joke about poker where victory is predicated on the severity of
one's hand of racial slurs. He likens "nigger" to a full flush insofar as it wins every time when
compared to other racial slurs.

22. Bucholtz and Lopez's (2011) delineation of the machinations of "linguistic minstrelsy" is
particularly apt. They note: "As mock language, linguistic minstrelsy in [Hollywood] films
involve sociolinguistic processes of deauthentification, maximizing of intertextual gaps,
and indexical regimentation (684–685). With deauthentification, the the performance/
performer is exposed to the audience as 'fake' or engaged in 'mock language' (685). *(How,
readers may wonder, do performers pull this off?)* They concertedly 'miss their marks,' thus
'maximizing the intertextual gaps' between a performance and its source to produce a
parody of, say, Black characters/subjects and a meta-parody of white characters/subjects.
This play of minstrelesque performance entails what Bucholtz (2011a; see also 2011b) calls
a process of 'indexical regimentation' wherein the many semiotic possibilities available
through language are 'ideologically reduced to a much more limited and stereotypical set of
indexical meanings (e.g., the stereotypical 'wigger' or 'honky,' as well as 'hard, tough Black
thug' are among the many reductionist tropes that proliferate and color instances of linguistic minstrelsy in Hollywood films.) The authors' careful sociolinguistic tracing of linguistic minstrelsy's entailments (i.e., deauthentification, maximizing of intertextual gaps,
and indexical regimentation) in two films is revelatory; they reveal how such performances
might seem to merely transgress notions of racial essentialism when, in actuality, they
also serve to 'both reproduce and to undermine the symbolic dominance of hegemonic
white masculinity' (680). Bucholtz & Lopez thus add: "Linguistic minstrelsy is therefore,

to borrow Jane Hill's [2008] phrase, a key component of the 'everyday language of white racism' not only through its representation of blackness but also through its representation of whiteness (685)."

23. See also Molina-Guzmán (2018), Webber (2019), Benko (2020), and Sundén and Paasonen (2020).

24. I'm of course *signifyin'* when I call Richards's improvised heckler retort "mad improv"; on one hand, I'm marking the way anger riddled his heckler assault and broader set with White supremacist entitlement and intent; on the other hand, I'm saluting his capacity to immediately recognize his racist "violation" and try to flip it via "crazy" next-level lyrical improvisation. My use of "mad improv" is, incidentally, quite different from what humor scholar Bambi Haggins (2007) calls "laughing mad" in a book with the same title, *Laughing Mad: The Black Comic Persona in Post-Soul America*. Haggins's notion of "laughing mad" annunciates how Black humor and comedy attends to the many ways Black folks laugh, live, and breathe, sometimes (and even) through clenched teeth, in the face of White supremacy. It appreciates, as well, the ways Black folks' penchant for "laughing mad" to survive and bear mutual witness to Black pain and joy, the profane and the prophetic, and all complexities in between also "supplied laughter for (White) mainstream audiences when constructed through the narrowing and diminishing lens of minstrel tropes" (2). While Whites, like Richards, can co-opt aspects of Black language, lyrical expressions, and even trickster tropes, Black laughter remains an outward sign and signal of Black interiority, the thing that cannot be touched, fully understood, or stolen; Black laughter can thus seem like a tell-tale sign when, in fact, it can mask the inside feelings and motives of the person laughing. Black laughter both improvises and is improvisational.

25. Neither did *The Daily Show with Jon Stewart*'s "Senior Black Correspondent" Larry Wilmore, who joked in typical cheeky fashion that he didn't think Michael Richards was racist. In a sketch featuring him and straight man host Jon Stewart on November 30, 2006, he said, "Don't you see Jon. He's not a racist. He just had a one-night stand with racism. Yeah. And when he was done, he just kicked it to the curb. Real classy." Wilmore also quipped that Richards owed an apology not merely to the Black community ("My people have endured all sorts of brutality, but I've never heard of the upside-down anal fork. Jon, I don't know if he's threatening a brother or a turkey"), but also to racists ("[R]acism is a discipline just like any other. To step onstage and clumsily drop a few n-bombs. It doesn't show any respect for the craft of bigotry!")

26. Lesley Harbidge (2012) highlights such underrated dynamics of standup comedy in a chapter titled "Audienceship and (Non)Laughter in the Stand-up Comedy of Steve Martin." She argues, "It is appropriate to turn to the point of *laugher*, that physical and most gratifying manifestation of both intra-audience and performer-audience relations" which functions as "a truly concrete marker of the crucial bonds or contracts promoted and exploited in stand-up" (97); see also Jason Rutter (1997) and David Marc (1980). Martin's comedic stylings serve to socialize and instantiate what Harbidge calls "audienceship," replete with respectful silences or "(non)laughter" as audiences ever-familiar with Martin's comedic trove patiently and gleefully await, as if a collective, for his punch(line). Richards's set, however, occasioned another form of (non)laughter, if even "un-laughter," but not just that: he incited an explicit conversation between an audience whose collectivity and "we-ness" got so jarringly disturbed that they gave actual voice to their disparate yearnings and fraught reconciliations about the reasons abetting the show's early end.

27. See Smith (2005), as well as Benko (2021) and Sundén and Paasonen (2020).

28. Veteran comic, actor, and American radio personality Frazier Smith, who hosted that night, told Adam Ray and Brad Williams, hosts of the podcast "About Last Night," that this massive walkout was instigated by Doss who shouted angrily from the balcony, "I want everybody out of this club now! Now!" as if directing traffic. Talk about a heckler-upset! This declaration instantiates an audience's supreme authority by not only subverting Richards's White supremacist power play by effectively ending his set, but also by disrupting the club's bottom line (i.e., ticket sales) since Masada had to oblige disgruntled customers' demand for a refund. Also, Smith says he offered his own un-recorded quip after Richards's bad set: "I think we just saw Kramer morph into Mel Gibson!"

29. Why is race deemed "performative"? Because race as biological fact is a myth and might best be understood as something humans "do."

30. African Americans, to say nothing of Blacks in America, are undoubtedly a mixed bunch and any ethnographer worth their salt, including "native" ones like me, must concede this. Any Black humor scholar can safely assert that appeals to "realness" or racial authenticity litter the Black comedic archive almost like a through-line, preoccupation, and pervasive if not subversive and cheeky riff.

31. In his memoir, *Black Is The New White,* Mooney recounts an experience with censorship in loving tribute to his former pal, the late-great Richard Pryor: "Things keep happening that I want Richard to see, that I want Richard to react to. I am doing a *Showtime at the Apollo* episode when they actually stop the whole shit and censor my ass offstage. "Hey Richard," I say to his memory, "This ain't the old Apollo that we know." The theater is owned by Time Warner now and they don't like me criticizing a sitting president. It might interfere with their lobbying efforts in Washington.

    Fuck the Bushes. I hate the whole family. Like that mother of his, she looks like the guy on the Quaker Oats box. . . ."

    They pull my ass right off the stage. The whole show stops for a motherfucking hour over that shit. "What happened," I keep asking. "You offended an executive from Time Warner," somebody tells me. "What? Who?" I never get a straight answer and I resolve never to play the Apollo again until I am satisfied" (242–243).

32. See Texeira 2006.

33. Mooney's grace also seem to channel the epiphany of his friend, the late-great Richard Pryor, who, after returning from Kenya, publicly vowed onstage and in print never to use the n-word again in his sets to refer to Black folks. Pryor told *Ebony Magazine* in 1980: "While I was there, something inside of me said, 'Look around you, Richard. What do you see? I saw people. African people. I saw people from other countries, too, and they were all kinds of colors, but I didn't see any 'niggers.' I didn't see any there because there are no 'niggers' in Africa. Can you imagine going out into the bush and walking up to a Masai and saying, 'Hey nigger. Come here!?' You couldn't do that because Masai are not 'niggers.' There are no 'niggers' in Africa, and there are no 'niggers' here in America either. We Black people are not 'niggers,' and I will forever refuse to be one." Pryor's epiphany is richer still in light of his legendary *SNL* sketch with Chevy Chase on December 13, 1975. The sketch, titled "Racist Word Association" and "Dead Honky," is a job interview wherein the interviewer (Chase) asks the applicant (Pryor) to take a word association test that soon devolves into a racist-word association contest. Pryor is hilariously reactive, emanating at first surprise and then one-upmanship. When the interview says the word, "nigger," Pryor as the applicant responds "*Dead* honky." In this sketch, Pryor underscores the power and stakes of

racial slurs, including the n-word, even as he seeks to trump it by accentuating "honky" (a racial slur for White folks) with "dead."

34. Patrice O'Neal, a provocateur if not a comic's comic who died in 2011, joked on *The Opie and Anthony Show* radio show, "[Richards should've just said] 'I'm sorry. I usually do a better job of hindering [*sic*—hiding?] my disgust for other races, but I blew it under pressure.'" O'Neal also admitted that he didn't know Richards was a racist until he apologized on TV; to him, Richards's confession blew his "Kramer" shtick and reputation in the industry as a bit of a perfectionist (e.g., Richards is renowned for sometimes snapping at audience members and even fellow comics who flub their lines.) O'Neal was neither amused or terribly offended by Richards rant, and, in fact, purported that many blacks felt similarly, since Richards simply revealed the racism that "lies just beneath" most, if not all White actors from the '90s and even White pundits who rushed in to decry Richards's behavior as "abhorrent." O'Neal boldly offers up another query worth considering, namely, could the rush to decry Richards as racist and The Laugh Factory's n-word ban as a mistake miss subtler forms of racism enacted by liberal-seeming Whites in word, deed, and thought every day—while punishing Black comics for it and telling them it's for their own good?

35. Roseanne Barr's controversial pictorial parody of Hitler portrayed him in drag (as a housewife) holding a pan of burnt cookies of Jewish people. She claims she didn't see the insult in it since she, perhaps like a younger Brandon Bowlin, was trying to provoke queries about other genocides and atrocities. Still, one of her colleagues, the late Patrice O'Neal, called her on it during a radio show saying, "But it's kind of [offensive] though; the only thing that would've made it more offensive is if you'd made them skinny."

36. This is true for several reasons, not the least of which include the scale of this human atrocity and the fact that comedy must be damn good to pull off jokes that make victims the butt of the joke. Roseanne Barr staged herself in a pictorial joke that featured her dressed as Adolf Hitler taking burnt cookies resembling Jewish people out of an oven, and her career was decimated despite her public outcry and assertion to disbelieving comics that she was just "joking"—conscientiously so. As I'll soon discuss, Black comics suggest additional reasons that jokes about the Holocaust fall flat, including the role of Jews as privileged "White" citizens—which is to say always and already empathizable—as compared to Black Americans who are often denied empathy even when in duress (recall Hurricane Katrina humor here), and the powerful role of Jews in the Hollywood entertainment industry.

37. It bears noting that comics work hard to earn a spot on this club's popular Sunday show. Not only does the club rightly boast its title, but it's also a great launching pad for comics wishing to catch the eye of Hollywood scouts. As such, those who earn the right to grace its stage often must endure the careful scrutiny of club owner and former comic Jamie Masada. In the case of The Laugh Factory's Black or "urban" show, *Chocolate Sundaes*, comics must also pass muster with two additional groups: the first is the show's highly discriminating and vocal Black audience; the second is executive producer Leland "Pookey" Wigington Jr. and the longtime host at the time, Chris Spencer (who has since moved on to writing, producing, and TV roles, most notably *Real Husbands of Hollywood*, *White Famous*, and *Black Love*). Once they are featured, however, comics work even harder to finesse their routines, calibrating their hooks over time for just the right punch.

38. While reminiscent of Chatman's quip and rhetorical query ("After September 11, we wasn't niggers no more. We had <u>new</u> niggers! Now [that we know the Washington, DC, snipers were Black (and Muslim)], we niggers again. . . . How you gon' be niggers again?!"), R.T.'s joke is sardonic at best on multiple fronts. His joke collectivizes White folks and relies on

the assumption that the real or alleged sins of a lone White person (whether famous or not) might work in the same way that the sins (or alleged sins) of one Black person—whether high profile or a lay citizen (doesn't much matter)—can indict the entire Black community given Black folks' intersubjective lives and fates.) Such linked fates, tethered to race and racial marginalization, are part and parcel of communal appeals to what I'm calling "a" real Black, alongside more trenchant and, at times, divisive notions of racial authenticity ("real blackness.") R.T.'s joke is funny because it plays with and atop such opposing realities.

39. In my first book, *From the Kitchen to the Parlor: Language and Becoming in African American Women's Hair Care,* I discuss another comic's (Anthony B. "Scruncho" McKinley) implicit instructive in a joke wherein he differentiates between "real" niggahs and "fake niggahs" in a joke about hair. On its surface, his bit extends the tenets of Chris Rocks' celebrated and, for some, infamous distinction between Black folks and so-called "niggahs" but towards a decidedly different end. Whereas in *Bigger & Blacker,* Rock bemoans the way so-called "niggahs'" fuck it up for the rest of hardworking Black folks by, say, shooting in a recently opened theatre, leaving Black kids to jump around in a circle on one leg inside their homes given the lack of safety in their hoods, Scruncho's joke is less steeped in a politics of respectability and, like Rock's joke, is chiefly Black-facing; in other words, Scruncho also loves Black folks and could give a damn how performances of "real" blackness impact white peoples' perceptions of blacks – or of "real blackness" as performative for that matter. His comedic intervention, and I dare call it that, begins and ends with Black folks' communal and interactional marshaling of notions of "real" blackness that are tethered to how they identify their racial heritage (e.g., whether or not they claim Indian ancestry when asked to identify themselves), who they date (e.g., he espouses all women, in particular, to keep them a "real niggah" on their team, one who would've sneered in the face of a box cutter on that fateful 9/11 airline flight). Both Rock and Scruncho's jokes explicitly qualify Black folks' uses of the term and implicitly censor others; further, they sometimes invoke the term to connote people more generally, whether they be Black, White, (most often) men, with positive, negative, and sometimes decidedly communal affect. This is one reason why many comics, and Black comics, in particular, issued a literal and sardonic 'nigga' please' retort to the Laugh Factory's short-lived n-word ban.

40. Rodney Perry, who regularly hosted and headlined at The Comedy Union where I conducted most of my fieldwork, helped me understand why he and the aforementioned comics weren't even surprised by Richards's remarks; to them, Richards simply evinced his and other White and non-black comics for bringing hidden or backstage racism and anti-blackness frontstage in moments of weakness or sheer audacity. As we chatted in The Laugh Factory's balcony (a hangout for comics, celebrities, and special guests during live shows), he recalled performing at a major L.A. comedy club where he'd witnessed two White comics, one male and the other female, commit a faux pas similar to Richards's. In the White comedienne's joke, a White child asks her mother if what she sees is a gorilla and the mother tells her it is a (Black) pimp. (When he told me this, I couldn't help remembering Frantz Fanon's real-life experience on a train when a White boy sees him and becomes scared, even as I understand that the White comedienne's joke hinges on both racial stereotype and a universal disdain audience members may have for men who exploit women sexually for financial gain; in other words, Fanon's story beckons empathy for him as a stigmatized subject whereas the comedienne's punchline banks on the moral trade audience members will make between racial stereotype and the maligning of a [Black] male pimp who exploits women sexually for his primary gain.) Rodney added that the White

male comic who followed her further stoked the schtick by using the n-word repeatedly. All this made Rodney weary and angry; as he milled about backstage that night, he pondered whether it would be expedient to beat the male comic's ass. Ultimately, he decided against it since the comic's set wasn't captured on tape as Richards's was. Also, while toiling on this chapter, I also attended a show by a politically maligned but resilient White comedienne who ended her set with a joke about monkeys and gorillas that skirted, in my mind, too close to veiled racism, though I wasn't clear from the laughter and applause she received if others shared the same read.

41. I was "surprised" because I was somehow under the impression that I had effected an under-the-radar ethnographic stance; I apparently had not and don't know why I even privileged this "fly on the wall" stance as the "right" way to be in the field—something I'll say more about in my Conclusion.

42. Here, I'm admittedly taking liberties in my rather personal reference to former US secretary of state and national security advisor, Republican politician, political science professor, and avid pianist, golfer, and football fan Condoleezza Rice.

43. Consider, too, a joke I heard at an American Jewish Conference by a fellow conference goer with impeccable timing. Right before a keynote speaker began, he leaned over and quipped, "What did the Nazi say to the Black Jew? Get to the back of the train." I nodded and smirked, but later felt like *"WTF!"* when I could not extract any empathy in the joke's hook for either Jews or Black folks. Later, when I recounted this experience and the joke with filmmaker Ferne Pearlstein, I reared my head back and laughed. She did too. I felt differently about the joke by then and that she and I were at least laughing together in a mutually seeing kind of way. (Readers may be interested in her 2016 documentary, *The Last Laugh,* which asks comedians, Holocaust survivors, and anti-racism activists whether the Nazi death camps are an appropriate subject for humor.

44. See, for example, work by Waters 1990; Ignatiev 1995; Brodkin 1998; Roediger 1991, 2005; Gualtieri 2009; and an interesting caveat by Yang and Koshy 2016).

45. I also sense a through-line linking their dissent not just to Fanon but also to Ralph Ellison's widely quoted (1958) article, "Change the Joke and Slip the Yoke." I, like many others, initially took Ellison's comment to denote a trickster play wherein one "changed the joke/narrative" so as to slip out of its confining story. No, Ellison was saying something way more nuanced as Ellison himself (with his longtime pal and confidant, scholar Albert Murray [2001]) and Weate (2003) underscore. Ellison wrote "change the joke and slip the yoke" to speak back to Stanley Edgar Hyman and scream of the ways he got mis-interpolated and missed altogether in Hyman's review of his widely celebrated work, *Invisible Man.* Ellison writes (in response to Hyman's collegial suggestion) to change the joke that weighs on Hyman's mind and writing pen so that he might slip the yoke wrought by (de-)limited vision and a foreclosed analytical imagination. Hyman's review, it might be argued, is (de) limited by an inability to see both Ellison's brilliance and the canon that so clearly screams for recognition in Ellison's work; as such, Ellison (ironically) cannot even be seen by this reviewer (of *Invisible Man,* no less) who likely knows full well the canon that informs Invisible Man but can nonetheless only fix Ellison in his mind as a folktale pioneer and Black minstrel performers as proverbial trickster "spooks who sat by the [White, privileged] door." Reader: I'm about to take some liberties. "Let me remind you," Ellison seems to say to Hyman, "of the importance of contextual and genre-specification, right? Let me remind you of the ways authors, even those who are Black like me, can pull from many sources and tell a story about Black male invisibility. . . . which has this big reveal at the end right—seemingly

wrought by his own hands. Can you get to that? Can you even see that?" [Ellison's call to Hyman in the parlance of African American English and discourse styles, might likewise sound like this: "Why you always got to see a 'Negro' as a trickster? I have no problem with this ascription since I, too, am one ((just ask [Albert] Murray who won't tell you nothing, good friend that he is). I know what you mean by the trickster but please don't forget that we are all suspended in a trick bag of race and racism, and we all become tricksters as a result, lying to ourselves about each other and wearing masks, some of us voluntarily and some of us by necessity, to weather the trick. But in doing so, we miss the ways we are all made to be jokesters, ignorant to our inextricable connectedness, mutual self-actualization, and the ways we come to understand ourselves in relation to one another. By missing this, we essentially don masks so as to preempt any projections we may think White folks have of Black folks and vice-versa, missing each other all the while. The whole way out, then, is to change the joke—recognize our interconnectedness as well as our vibrant differences—don't paint me with a broad stroke and then bless your own heart please! That way we can slip the yoke, the trick bag of decontextualized and ahistorical accounts of race and race-making."] This seems to be Ellison's primary critique, one that also even sources his pain (and not just offense) when his Jewish friend and colleague mis-interpolates his work, Black folks, Black tricksters, Black pain even. And *this* feeling of having been misunderstood and woefully misread by a fellow colleague also seems to subtext Black comics' excoriating jokes about "real" blackness and Black comics' backstage queries about the likely fate of ANY comic who'd poke fun at Jewish holocaust victims in a spirit akin to Richards's angry and casual invocation of the enslavement and lynching of Black folks in the United States. Like Ellison, Black comics and their extended tribe are questioning Whiteness, White privilege, White supremacy and the well-intentioned n-word ban that suggest an allegorical relationship between Richards's racist use of the n-word and Black comics' creative, poetic, in-group, communal, and, at times, hyper-bracketed uses of "nigga" on public stages. They are also saying, essentially, "You missed me altogether Bruh. But how could you miss me when my pain and legibility is right in front of your face, conditioning even your racist riffs?!" That proffered, I can't help but wonder: so what then would it mean to "change the joke and slip the yoke" in Richards's case? It would mean that he changes the joke of White supremacy *for real this time* so as to slip its constraining and lie-abetting yoke. It would mean that he (Richards) calls the racist joke for what it is/was and even name, so as to better appreciate, its conditions of possibility (something da Silva [2007] brilliantly extols in regard to the global notion of "race")—perhaps a tall albeit redemptive order for a humorist. What could it also mean for us as readers to do the same thing in our assessment of Richards's rant and Black comics and their extended tribe's responses to it? It would mean appreciating Richards's improvisational work and black comics' capacity for grace, truth-speak however virulent, and comedic and linguistic agency toward something even better: a clearer understanding of the ways we are always and already-made jokesters by virtue of the trickery of race-making, the pernicious kind rooted in White supremacy that is forever masked and naturalized, so that it can slip that yoke altogether. For this essentially is what Ellison asks of Hyman and other readers: Blackface minstrelsy performers who are Black are not [the] only tricksters. So let's also not put Black tricksterdom on some vaulted and exceptional perch lest we forget Black folks are doing when they don blackface and also WHY they must even don it in the first place. Let us not forget that White folks don masks too, often of their own choosing or volition, sometimes without even seeing the difference between their and Black folks' respective deployments of the mask.

46. Take Michael Richards as a case and point. While he is recognized as a comedian and an actor, many Black comics also see him as White and famous and hence privileged with the opportunity to even *apologize* for his racist humor. Not only did Richards reject the opportunity Jamie Masada extended to him at The Laugh Factory, but he also seemed to undermine the sincerity of his public apologies by mocking the whole debacle in a recent *Driving in Cars* interview with host and friend Jerry Seinfeld. His "interview"—and I'll leave it to readers to explore it more fully—left me and perhaps other viewers wondering whether his dialogue with Jerry, complete with a visit to legendary boxer Sugar Ray Leonard's home (but decidedly *not*) was a joke (Jerry says it was not), was a way to reconcile his ultimate silencing and perhaps his inability to recover his social face in a redemptive way. For another take on this, check out Matthew Daube's 9/30/12 blog post, Stand-up Sunday: Michael Richards, Six Years Later, on "Humor in America: Ha! Intelligent Writing about Humor and Stuff."

47. He is also inferencing the complexities underscored in Laurence Mordekhai Thomas's bold attempt to interrogate the differences between American slavery, the Holocaust, and the conquest and murder of American Indians under settler colonialism in his book, *Vessels of Evil: American Slavery and the Holocaust*. Thomas's goal is not to compare these evils so as to suggest one is/was worse than the other, as much as to underscore the conditions of possibility that seeded and abetted such evil. Still, there are others who understand the scope and tenor of the provocative joke Brandon Bowlin once told and now finds problematic; some include Armenian and Jewish scholars and activists who find it analytically useful and politically expedient to ask how and why certain ethnic groups' experience with mass extermination and relocation by the state are not as widely understood or even acknowledged as, say, the experience of other groups or other atrocities such that their legitimate claims to historical and enduring harm are not even acknowledged, let alone mourned or properly redressed in the present. These discussions also include righteous calls to a proper accounting of the nuanced ways in which genocide and its enduring impacts affect the groups being compared and contrasted. Blessedly, they also include scholars such as USC history professor, Steven J. Ross, who call upon their very institutions to be transparent in their support of initiatives like #Black Lives Matter of hidden or shrouded histories concerning former university presidents who openly practiced anti-Semitism and anti-Blackness as a matter of university policy (see Ross 2020).

48. Much like this chapter evolved in response to comics' multi-faceted deliberations about Michael Richards and the n-word ban, so, too, did my initial draft of my 9/11 humor essay given some comics' concerns of my surface read of the "Arab as new nigger" premise. .

49. See Dance 1998 and Kennedy 2003.

50. Racism and White supremacy are admittedly flawed belief systems much like prejudice and bias; however, racism, especially in the United States, has and continues to be entrenched within powerful institutions, social structures, prevailing social discourses, and everyday policies that abet White supremacy and White dominance. Prejudice and bias, especially when practiced by the less powerful, are relatively less trenchant and consequential which, as Rodney's joke suggests, by no means suggests they are unproblematic. One need only consider why Black audiences laugh at Rodney's joke to understand the distinction here; many Black audience members DO in fact "remember the water hose" and also rightly suspect that Rodney Perry, a dark-skinned Black man of husky build, would never be allowed to tackle unsuspecting White people in grocery stores without swift punitive action, maybe even death.

51. Chris Rock (2014) wrote candidly about Hollywood as an essentially "White industry" in *The Hollywood Reporter*; Rock recounts the many challenges he and other black comics and actors face in an industry wherein Hollywood's gatekeepers are largely White (he did not say "and Jewish"); this is true, he said, even when and after Kevin Hart, who is African American, becomes the world's top-ranking comic and/or his or other black actors' and filmmakers' movies draw millions in revenue.

52. So, too, do comediennes Leslie Jones and Whoopi Goldberg who boldly asserted that the work of contending with Richards's outburst by policing their use of the n-word was not their load to carry. Jones began one of her sets at The Comedy Union in 2006 like this: "Fuck that niggah (Richards). He's rich and White. What am I gonna do about it?" Note how her use of the n-word absents blackness but not the word's negative sting. Also notice how she names racial and class privilege, namely Richards's White privilege and fame and fortune, as essential to her stance as an African American comedienne. Lawrence, one of club's security guards, felt similarly; when I asked him if he was at all bothered by the Richards controversy, he said, simply: "Why worry about that? What does that have to do with me?" Whoopi Goldberg also seemed to parody the n-word ban on *Funny or Die* in 2008, quipping, [*incredulously*] "Like the 'n-word!' That's what we have to call it now. [*audience laughs*] The 'n-word.' And everyone says . . . [*dramatic sober-voice*], 'Don't say it again! We should put a moratorium on it. Because it's a baaaad word. It's a word that raises all kind of connotations to people—and it's bad!' [*straight-voiced*] But see it's not bad to me because I don't know any and I've never been one," to wild applause from her diverse audience. Far from being apathetic, these comedic (and lay comedy stewards if one equally values Lawrence's viewpoint) assessments reflect an investment in their own individual and Black folks' collective communicative competence and creative agency—irrespective of White folks' linguistic missteps or appropriations.

53. See also Alemoru 2006.

54. Readers are welcome to search these apologies out on social media or consult Ellwanger (2012).

Chapter 4

1. Hart is, as he describes himself, "a big motherfuckin' deal" with a net worth of approximately $200 million in 2021 (according to Google); Hart also "dethroned Jerry Seinfeld" as the "highest paid comedian" in 2016 (according to Forbes.com).

2. See Beatty 2006; Dance 1978, 1998; Watkins 1999, 2002.

3. Joel Chandler Harris 1940; with Chase 1955 [2002]); see also important commentaries by Lester (1939 [1999]; xiv–xvi), Walker (2012), Watkins (1994), and Wolfe (1949 [1990]) for further contextualization of these and other Brer Rabbit tales.

4. Williams (1993), citing Baker (1990), notes that real-life Black tricksters became even more explicit about their lyrical subversion and performative trickery after freedom. This is likely why famed ethnographer Zora Neale Hurston (1935 [1990]) encountered African Americans in Eatonville, Florida, in the late nineteenth century still telling Brer Rabbit stories—this time as Brother John or "The brother in Black" who was essentially a shape shifter, moving betwixt human and animal form in his dealings with Ole Massa.

5. See Chude-Sokei (2006) and Forbes (2008).

6. See Williams (1995) and Wood (2014, 2021) to learn more about Mabley's "masked" humor and the 2014 HBO documentary *Whoopi Goldberg Presents Moms Mabley* to hear how Mabley masked her queer identity onstage but (certainly) not off. In the 1980s, Clarice Taylor, the veteran stage actress who played Bill Cosby's mother on *The Cosby Show*, staged *Moms*, written by Harlem-born playwright and author Ben Caldwell, that examined Mabley's veiled sexuality and the many personal tragedies that informed her humor and comic persona. For example, Taylor learned that Mabley was raped twice as a child and lost both of her biological parents in tragic accidents before joining a minstrel show at age thirteen.

7. The "chitlin' circuit" refers to the informal network of segregated nightclubs, theaters, and movie houses that Black entertainers toured before the civil rights movement.

8. Fellow comic Katt Williams described Hart as Hollywood's "puppet" (quickly adding, through no fault of Hart's own); Sony Studio's Screen Gems president Clint Culpepper deemed Hart a "greedy whore" for demanding compensation for promoting a movie via tweets, and Google turned up besmirched comic legend Bill Cosby's image in a search for Kevin Hart's net worth.

9. See Chude-Sokei 2006, as well as Forbes 2008, Smith 1992, Smith 2014.

10. To learn more about Jackie "Moms" Mabley, see Goldberg 2014, Williams 1995, Watkins 1999.

11. Harrison 1998a, Johnson 2001, Jackson 2005a, Jackson 2005b; see also Jones 2005, Livingston 1998, Nayak 2006, Young 2006, Young and Braziel 2006; gender also matters materially for men who are said to talk and "act like women" in the Islamic, Hausa-speaking region of northern Nigeria (see Gaudio 2014).

12. "Racial sincerity" is a concept coined by Jackson (2005b) in a concerted attempt to disrupt the essentializing assumptions of "racial authenticity" through the tactical use of sincerity; racial sincerity stresses Black performativity and subjectivity over fixed notions of Black authenticity.

13. When "Black" is understood in performative terms, even its usage in explanatory terms can (and "should") be bracketed by scare-quotes.

14. See Paul Laurence Dunbar's (1895) poem, "We Wear the Mask."

15. It bears noting that Hart live-streamed his reaction to the 2016 US election; his off-the-cuff shirtless remarks on YouTube sought to "uplift my people" (by "my people," Hart meant "everybody" and "the world") given what he described as the "mind-fuck," "mind-blowing," and "damn, who would've thought?!" nature of Donald Trump's presidential win. Hart added, "What was once a joke has now become a reality" and Americans, in particular, must stand "accountability for our country's destiny" using the "power of love and positivity" and ever-mindful of the hard-won gains of the civil rights movement. "I don't want to go backwards; I want to do those people justice. . . . I urge and beg you all to understand . . . what America is supposed to be and what we're supposed to be fighting for. . . . Regardless of your damn race, this is the time for you to stand up and really take responsibility and action for making your country better." Then, Hart expressed a color-blind and spiritual worldview (that subtly appreciated the challenges facing at-risk constituencies (e.g., Mexicans, Muslims) before taking a five-mile run.

16. Hart famously invested $700,000 of his own money on this standup comedy film and grossed over a $1 million profit. He has repeatedly invested in his projects, reaping million dollar profits every time.

17. *Live Comedy from the Laff House: Kevin Hart* (2006).

18. *I'm A Grown Little Man* (2009).

19. See Harper 1996, Johnson 2003, Neal 2013, Riggs et al. 1987.
20. *Laugh at My Pain* (2011).
21. *I'm A Grown Little Man* (2009).
22. *I'm A Grown Little Man* (2009).
23. *Let Me Explain* (2013).
24. *I'm A Grown Little Man* (2009).
25. *Seriously Funny* (2010).
26. *Seriously Funny* (2010).
27. Johnson likewise notes (2001: 3), "I wish to 'quare' 'queer' such that ways of knowing are viewed both as discursively mediated and as historically situated and materially conditioned. This reconceptualization foregrounds the ways in which lesbians, bisexuals, gays, and transgendered people of color come to sexual and racial knowledge. Moreover, quare studies acknowledges the different 'standpoints' found among lesbian, bisexual, gay, and transgendered *people of color* [my emphasis]—differences that are also conditioned by class and gender."
28. See also Marlon T. Riggs's (1987) film, *Ethnic Notions*, which traces the history and political consequences of such racist caricatures as the buffoonish "Sambo," deceitful "Zip Coon," sassy neck-rolling "Sapphire," hypersexualized "Jezebel," and the asexual and ever-subservient figures of "Uncle Remus" and "Mammy."
29. See Danielle's (2016) more recent interview with Kevin Hart.
30. The same point might be made of Hart's self-deprecating schtick. While self-deprecation is a common tool in all comics' wheelhouses—think Rodney's Dangerfield's self-deprecatory one-liner "I don't get no respect!"—Hart's laments about his routine run-ins with disrespect are freighted with the trace of race; which is to say, Hart's jokes about being a humbled or humiliated lover, father, spouse, etc. risk—and I do only mean "risk"—coming off as an artful redux of the Sambo (e.g., childish, emasculated) caricature. Hart's more recent standup comedy and interviews suggest that he is well aware of such dangers and their entailments. Namely, when he complains of disrespect in a manner that makes him seem literally and figuratively small, he wins effusive laughter and praise from adoring audiences who—this is me, Lanita, talking now—may or may *not* see him as a humbled *Black* man. However, when Hart waxes more seriously about his run-ins with disrespect in Hollywood or with fans and critics with long memories, the laughter is not as voluminous—perhaps because the specter of race and racism is explicitly acknowledged or strongly inferred.
31. Even humor scholars who, in struggling to honor the social constructionist understandings of Blackness, can't see Hart or a host of other comics (think Donald Glover, Key & Peele, Wayne Brady, Michael Carmichael) except to celebrate that they redefine or "queer" Black masculinity and Black comedy writ large (Gillota 2013). Few have imagined the ways even these comics might act as tricksters. To do so, we must always appreciate the racial landscape that he and other Black comics enter, as well as his intersubjectivity as an always-and-already Black man playing on his body politic with strategy and long-range vision. This does *not* mean we don't critique Hart's homophobic humor; rather, it means we consider how his deployment of decidedly heteronormative stances strategically shore up his always-and-already fraught (Black) masculinity in complicated and (not) unproblematic ways. Joanne R. Gilbert's (2004) rich analysis and female comedians' subversive performance of gendered marginality is teachable in this regard. She mines the comedic repertoires of comediennes like Phyllis Diller and Roseanne Barr and reveals how their self-deprecation onstage was and is but a rhetorical means to a strategic end insofar as they (both!) endeared

themselves to audience members while indicting sexism and feminist hypocrisy. Best, she suggests that instead of routinely asking, "Why do female comics self-deprecate," we'd do best to ask, "What is it about contemporary American culture that makes this time of 'marginal humor' "work" with diverse audiences?" Her provocation to appreciate comics and their routines as forever-situated and ever-reliant on audience interpretation is likewise teachable when unpacking Hart's self-deprecating "trickster" pose.

32. *I'm a Grown Little Man* (2009).

33. *Let Me Explain* (2013).

34. See (too) Bambi Haggins (2007, 2009: 221–227), who provides a masterful analysis of Chappelle's liberal and, at times, under-nuanced deployment of the n-word in several sketches of *The Chappelle Show*.

35. Hart effectively "kills" his scene-stealing cousin with unbridled homophobia by outing him as a (presumably straight) crack addict who "sucks dick" for drugs.

36. *Live Comedy from the Laff House: Kevin Hart* (2006).

37. *Laugh at My Pain* (2011).

38. *Seriously Funny* (2010).

39. Hart's mother, Nancy Hart, died of cancer in 2007, one year after his first comedy debut album, *Live from the Laff House: Kevin Hart*.

40. See Mason (2016, 53-54) wherein the author cites a poem titled "My Name," by the poet Kevin [John] Hart. The poem is about Hart's mother who was Jewish but kept this identity hidden:

> There is a silence words can't touch.
> And there's a name inside my name
> Though one my mother never said out loud
>
> She never said it, never once, although
> She knew there was another name
> That sleeps inside my name
>
> *Sleep now, old name,*
> *For no one wants to know of you*
>
> My mother, she is dead these dozen years
> And she is grown so small
> She sleeps inside my name when it is said
>
> I think she sleeps
> Within that other name as well, more deeply, far
> More quietly, turning only once or twice
> Inside that paradise
>
> *Sleep now, old love,*
> *It is too late to say a word to you*

41. "Light-skinned women usually have better credit than dark-skinned women. . . . Broke ass dark hoes . . . lol," "Dark skinned women take a punch @ da face better than light-skinned women . . . you soft as yellow bitches . . . lol"

42. "Attention all dark skin woman . . . . I am a fucking COMEDIAN, which means I tell jokes, stop being so damn sensitive. I'm joking jeeez. SMH."

43. Even by his own account, Hart is a trickster "born and bred." As a child, he used his "street smarts" (as opposed to book smarts) to dissuade his mother from disciplining him. Here's how he did it: he spread peanut butter on his behind to simulate poop and then tasted it. This caused his mother to cry, scream, and then pass out. Many years later, Hart's mother was hip to his game. She chided him for cursing, even though he was an adult. When he stood up for himself, cursing in the process, his mom screamed, "Let em go devil!" before flicking him with holy water. It burned, not because it was holy water but because it was bleach. Sounding very much like Brer Rabbit, Hart's mother then told him, *"Don't ever curse at me!"*

44. See also Mooney 2009; Sotiropolous 2008.

45. In *Laugh at My Pain* (2011), Hart joked that his dad frequently wore sweatpants sans underwear, creating a few embarrassing (and especially revealing) scenes during Hart's childhood.

46. Accordingly, Hart's (2017) book highlights the grit, gumption, and "heart"—essentially, everything-but-self-deprecation—required to transition from a comedy "grunt" and "hack" to a comedy icon. After barely graduating from high school and selling shoes, Hart honed his craft on New York's grueling (and comic-authenticating) stages, built a base too huge for Hollywood scouts to ignore while touring colleges and "thugged the fuck out" clubs where intimidating crowds would shout, "Go home Kevin," "Stand up Kevin" (referring to his height), or "Fuck you Kevin!" the minute he got onstage. Hart surmises, "I was finding my pain points and transforming them into something that could touch and maybe even help other people. An entertainer makes you laugh, I realized, but an artist makes you understand" (195).

47. Hart also leverages Halle Berry's star power (alongside African American actor Don Cheadle) in a funny Bond-sketch that precedes and follows Hart's standup. When "Money [Halle] Berry" asks "Little Bond" (i.e., Hart) after a daring escape, "So what now?", Hart responds, "Now? Well, now we do the same thing on a global scale." Then, he turns to the camera as if to speak directly to viewers and says, "I think it's time to show the world how funny Kevin Hart is." Just before credits roll, a Black-female sounding voice yells, "Kevinnnnnnnnnnnn"—recalling the many disciplining Black women in his life. It would seem, then, that Black women also and quite symbolically get the final word.

48. This domestic and global tour culminated in a (2019) *Netflix* film titled, *Kevin Hart: Irresponsible.*

49. I use the word "twin refusals" since Hart not only refused to apologize as a matter of principle, but he also passed on his lifelong dream of hosting the Oscars.

50. Kevin Hart's most recent starring role in *Fatherhood* (2021) helps too. Spoiler Alert: If wearing a dress proved controversial in his past work, it becomes an endearing achievement in this empathetic and empathizing movie. (Especially since "Maddy," played deftly by Melody Hurd, ends up wearing the pants—literally and proverbially—at her private Catholic school while he dons a kilt. Their clothing choices during the film's abrupt finale are queer-ally adjacent. Why? Both daughter and Dad have managed to change an archaic school policy mandating that all girls wear skirts; "Maddy" does her part by literally shedding blood after being taunted for wearing "boy's underwear" and falling off the jungle gym, and Hart's character ["Matthew Logelin"] assists by doing the very best a widowed Black father can do).

51. Hart actually quips that former football player turned comic-actor, activist, and bodybuilder Terry Cruz or the nerdy character "Carlton Banks" (played by Alfonso Lincoln

Ribeiro Sr.) from the '80s TV sitcom, *Fresh Prince of Bel Air*, would better fit the bill; Hart's "suggestion" slyly implicates the legitimating affordances of racial authenticity (or allegiance to "a" real Black) by way of pointed contrast.

52. When Hart invites his friends over for brick oven pizza, they essentially ask, "What's arugula and why is it even on the pizza?!"

53. It must be noted that sincerity and authenticity dance in cancel culture's machinations as well, not merely in Hart and other Black comics' humor discussed thus far. Why? We tend to presume that folks who wage seen + unseen takedowns against routine and/or unaccountable perpetrators of sexual harassment and violence, homophobic humor, etc., are sincerely seeking justice; either way, their capacity to "cancel" or otherwise silence a perp ultimately serves to "authenticate" a certain vision of justice. Sincerity and authenticity thus intermingle or, more precisely, co-constitute each other in consequential (i.e., authenti*cating*) ways.

54. See Sewell 2013.

Chapter 5

1. My desire to write about President Barack Obama humor was also deflected by a series of article and book-length treatments on this very subject (e.g., Alim & Smitherman 2012, 2020; Gillota 2013; Li 2011; 2015; Hughley 2017; Nixon 2019). For a brief moment, I also considered concluding with a discussion of Rachel Dolezal; she was a biologically blond, blue-eyed White girl whose infamous brush with fame came when in adulthood, she passed and identified as Black (after suing for reverse discrimination at a historically Black university). Then I realized that this episode was not central to what I was observing; however, the comic disciplining she received by way of Black Twitter offers testament to the way racial authenticity is not merely a game or a divisive anti-scientific (e.g., retrograde) banter. It is a way of shoring up understandings and boundaries—heck, signaling "a" real Black that can't be assumed, taught, aesthetically wrought, or imbibed.

2. Granted, this winking assessment misses the ways anthropologists are always and already products of our fieldwork and research findings, and it also misses the ways that Black female anthropologists doing work in "native" communities are inescapably hypervisible, despite their best efforts to achieve a "fly on the wall" stance. I now wonder why in the first place I ever even privileged a distant observer stance in this ethnographic study of comic performers? Especially when there were calls almost from the beginning to get curious about this or that or immerse self in the actual projects and lives of comics and their beloveds. Especially—too—because there are ways I was thrust into the center of my own telling which is certainly among the possibilities in the intersubjective dance that is ethnographic fieldwork.

3. When I, along with several senior male faculty, were inducted into the USC chapter of the Honor Society of Phi Kappa Phi in 2018, I wasn't sure if it was a joke or whether to put it on my resumé. The entire ceremony was tinged with laughter in a way that subverted my expectations of faculty decorum and civility. We were never actually "pinned" as is the ceremonial custom. But after the ceremony was over, I went onstage and dug out a few pins and handed them out to my illustrious and prolific colleagues.

4. Actually, I'm not sure I evaded either of these occupational hazards since, in addition to becoming literal humor studies fodder, I also came undone while naked in a gym locker room

after a scary "near-death" episode involving my mother; did someone record me during my phone chat and then send it all over the land?, I wondered. Or was it the day when a young kid yelled, "I took a picture of your coooochiieeee (i.e., vagina)" while passing my home on his way to school as I bent down to pick up the morning paper? Ha! (For rueful-real.) I used to deem such instances as constituting the very worst things that could happen to a Black female professor. Now, having faced racism and disrespect all up in my and other Black scholars' faces and having witnessed, along with my beloved college students, the words on my PowerPoint slides literally shift and transform before our literal eyes (real-time hack job?), I think it's all simply par for the course; or, rather, it is a tragic possibility given the constellation of rampant anti-Blackness, sexism, racial micro (and what seem like macro!) aggressions, to say nothing of entrenched elitism, cronyism, and institutional gatekeeping in society and academia.

5. Among the more confusing murmurs I received during this time came from a colleague who suggested that I had somehow upset the "Beyhive" (Beyoncé's fan club) or multiple strangers and acquaintances who insisted that I had a twin that was not my real biological twin—and they were right! One day, I saw my very own doppelganger at a gym I used to frequent, and she looked more like me than my own twin sister. When discussing my challenges dealing with racial micro-aggressions on campus, including at a Black graduation ceremony I hosted, I also had a college administrator do the Harlem Shake (a dance) before laughingly telling me, by way of a response, "If you come for L.A., L.A. will come for you." Caught by surprise, I suddenly laughed aloud. But rather than finding it funny, I found it all confusing since I simply don't think I sufficiently "matter" to Beyoncé or her virulently protective fan base to warrant what felt like such coordinated disinvitation, nor had I necessarily "come for L.A." I *have* been incessantly curious about Blackness in L.A. and have likewise conducted much of my ethnographic research here for the past two decades.

6. So, too, did Lama Rod Owens who confessed in his collaborative book, *Radical Dharma: Talking Race, Love, and Liberation* (Williams, Owens, [with] Syedullah 2016): "Personally, I've been the recipient of meanness. You have no idea what's going on, you don't know the language, you don't know the cause but you want to learn, and that meanness, where you're told you're a part of the problem, that's like progressive radical elitism. We get too old for that sometimes. It's not productive. I need to be part of spaces where I feel loved. And I don't feel loved in some of these spaces. Me leaving these spaces is self-care" (142–143). Lama Owens said something else I find utterly teachable and likewise share with my students alongside my own murmurs concerning "a" real Black: "The problem is not Whiteness or Blackness. The problem is the way in which we relate to those identities. It isn't inherently a problem to be White. The problem is that we have a whole way of relating to that identity that is the suffering itself, which is one of the things that dharma has an awfully good lens on. It's not inherently a problem that I'm anything, but the way that I relate to that often as a result of a collective social identity and social way of relating to it—that's actually where the problem lies. There's nothing wrong with any of us. And there's nothing wrong with any of who we are or who we were born as and what skin and what gender and what parts we have. That's why I want to keep pointing out that there's a construct happening. Just like ego is a construct. It's something that's out there. And then we have all of these challenges and heaps of suffering that are induced by how we relate to that ego, or that socially induced "identity"— that projection of ourselves" (130).

7. Readers may be interested in how Neetu Khanna (2020) unearths a resonant chord from Franz Fanon abetted by her excavation of the "visceral logics"—or the embodied

experience and political feeling—of the Progressive Writers' Association (PWA) in India between the 1930s and 1950s.

8. See also Terrion Williamson's (2017) Morrison-inspired work.

9. Here, I'm referencing Lewis Carroll's (1865 [2014]) children's novel, *Alice's Adventures in Wonderland*. The story begins when Alice, a seven-year-old girl, notices a White clothed rabbit with a pocket watch running past her and follows it down a rabbit hole. There, she encounters a fantasy land replete with human-like animals and other-worldly threats and challenges. That is, until her sister wakes her up from what has been a dream.

10. See David Brooks's (2021) essay troubling essentialism in the *New York Times* titled, "Here's The Mind-Set That's Tearing Us Apart."

11. Here, I rush to underscore that by "besiegingly," I in no way mean to imply that being Black is a problem a priori. Being Black contains and abets what Marlon Riggs and other Black voices suggest in their gospel riff session at the start of the film, *Black Is . . . Black Ain't*, tremendous possibilities and amazing extents. Here's how they tell it in a call-and-response riff session that picks up where the imagined Black preacher in Ellison's *Invisible Man* leaves off (note to Reader: I've removed verbal overlaps and callbacks between speakers):

> Marlon Riggs: I'll say, Black is and Black ain't! Black is and Black ain't. Black is blue! Black is red! And Black is tan! And Black is light.
>
> Yvette Flunder: Black will get you. And Black will leave you alone. Black can get you over. And Black can set you down. Black can let you move forward, and Black will make you stumble around.
>
> Djola Bernard Branner: BLACK is sooooo high. And Black is so low. Black can say yasssssssss. And Black can say no.
>
> UNKNOWN: Oh yeah!
>
> Linda Tillery: Black can be your best friend!
>
> UNKNOWN: Oh, yes!
>
> Linda Tillery: Be cozy as the night!
>
> UNKNOWN: Tell it!
>
> Linda Tillery: Black can do you in! Make you fuss and cuss and fight!
>
> Marlon Riggs: Black is Black.
>
> UNKNOWN: Preach it now!
>
> Marlon Riggs: And Black is Blue.
>
> UNKNOWN: Tell the truth!
>
> Marlon Riggs: Black is Bright!
>
> UNKNOWN: Black is brown!
>
> Marlon Riggs: [looks into camera] Black is YOU!

Riggs and other performers sing the *lived* and corporeal Black body electric; they bespeak the extraordinary diversity and possibilities of Blackness in a way that necessarily embraces shadow and is graciously capacious to perhaps include us all. But not in a way that abets an "I am now Black" stance of cultural appropriation or racial pantomime as much as a curiosity and an invitation to, per Yancy (2012), dwell within Black folks' looking glass toward a soulful reckoning of the many "why's" of "a" real Black, conditioned but not entirely (Zora Neale Hurston consistently reminds us!), by larger structures and systems entrenched in anti-Blackness and White supremacy.

Bibliography

Abu-Lughod, Lila. "Writing against Culture." In *Recapturing Anthropology: Working in the Present*, edited by Richard G. Fox, 137–162. Santa Fe, NM: School of American Research Press, 1991.

Abu-Lughod, Lila. *Do Muslim Women (Still) Need Saving?* London: Harvard University Press, 2013.

Al-Ali, Nadje and Nicola Pratt. "Iraqi Women Before the Invasion." In *What Kind of Liberation: Women and the Occupation of Iraq*, 21–54. London: University of California Press, 2009.

Alemoru, Olu. "N-Word Meltdown Sparks Comic Boundaries Debate." *The Sacramento Observer* (December 7, 2006): C6–C7.

Alim, H. Samy. "Who's Afraid of the Transracial Subject? Raciolinguistics and the Political Project of Transracialization." In *Raciolinguistics: How Language Shapes Our Ideas about Race*, edited by H. S. Alim, J. Rickford, and A. F. Ball, 33–50. New York: Oxford University Press, 2020.

Alim, H. Samy. "Introducing Raciolinguistics: Racing Language and Languaging Race in Hyperracial Times." In *Raciolinguistics: How Language Shapes Our Ideas about Race*, edited by H. S. Alim, J. Rickford, and A. F. Ball, 1–32. New York: Oxford University Press, 2020.

Alim, H. Samy and Geneva Smitherman. *Articulate While Black: Barack Obama, Language, and Race in the U.S.* New York: Oxford University Press, 2012.

Alim, H. Samy and Geneva Smitherman. "Raciolinguistic Exceptionalism: How Racialized 'Compliments' Reproduce White Supremacy." In *The Oxford Handbook on Language and Race*, edited by H. S. Alim, A. Reyes, and P. V. Kroskrity, 472–498. New York: Oxford University Press, 2020.

Alim, H. Samy, Angela Reyes, and Paul V. Kroskrity. *The Oxford Handbook on Language and Race*. Oxford: Oxford University Press, 2020.

Alim, H. Samy, John Rickford, and Arnetha F. Ball, eds. Raciolinguistics: *How Language Shapes Our Ideas about Race*. New York: Oxford University Press, 2016.

Allen, Ernest Jr. "Du Boisian Double Consciousness: The Unsustainable Argument." *Massachusetts Review* 43:2 (Summer 2002): 217–253.

Allen, Jafari Sinclaire and Ryan Cecil Jobson. "The Decolonizing Generation: Race and Theory in Anthropology since the Eighties." *Current Anthropology* 57:2 (2016): 129–148.

Alsultany, Evelyn. *Arabs and Muslims in the Media: Race and Representation After 9/11.* New York: New York University Press, 2012.

Amadeo, Kimberly. "Hurricane Katrina Facts: Damage and Costs." *The Balance* (September 8, 2019): https://www.lamar.edu/_files/documents/resilience-recovery/grant/recovery-and-resiliency/hurric2.pdf.

Apte, Mahadev L. *Humor and Laughter: An Anthropological Approach*. London: Cornell University Press, 1985.

Arana, Marie, ed. "Gloria Naylor [Interview]." In *The Writing Life: Writings on How They Think and Work: A Collection from the Washington Post Book World*, 259. New York: PublicAffairs, 2003.

Baker, Houston A. Jr. "Black Folklore and the Black Literary Tradition." In *Long Black Song: Essays in Black American Literature and Culture* (18–41). Charlottesville: University Press of Virginia, 1990.

Baker, Lee D. "The Location of Franz Boas within the African-American Struggle." *Critique of Anthropology* 14:2 (1994): 199–217.

Baker, Lee D. "Over a Cliff or into a Brick Wall." *Anthropology Newsletter* 39:1 (1998a): 16–17.

Baker, Lee D. *From Savage to Negro: Anthropology and the Construction of Race, 1906–1954.* Los Angeles: University of California Press, 1998b.

Baker, Lee D. "Fabricating the Authentic and the Politics of the Real." In *Anthropology and the Racial Politics of Culture* (66–116). Durham, NC: Duke University Press, 2010.

Banet-Weiser, Sarah. *Authentic™: The Politics of Ambivalence in a Brand Culture.* New York: New York University Press, 2012.

Batalion, Judy, ed. *The Laughing Stalk: Live Comedy and Its Audience.* Anderson, SC: Parlor Press, 2012.

Baudrillard, Jean. *The Gulf War Did Not Take Place,* translated by Paul Patton. Bloomington: Indiana University Press, 1995.

Baudrillard, Jean. *Simulacra and Simulation,* translated by Sheila Faria Glaser. Ann Arbor: University of Michigan Press, 2017.

Beatty, Paul, ed. *Hokum: An Anthology of African-American Humor.* New York: Bloomsbury, 2006.

Benko, Stephen A., ed. *Ethics in Comedy: Essays on Crossing the Line.* Jefferson, NC: McFarland, 2020.

Benson, Michaela. "Living the 'Real' Dream in la France profonde? Lifestyle Migration, Social Distinction, and the Authenticities of Everyday Life," *Anthropological Quarterly* 86:2 (Spring 2013): 501–525.

Benson, Ophelia and Jeremy Stangroom. *Why Truth Matters.* New York: Continuum, 2006.

Bergson, Henri. *Laughter: An Essay on the Meaning of the Comic.* Mineola, NY: Dover, 2005 [1911].

Berman, Marshall. *The Politics of Authenticity: Radical Individualism and the Emergence of Modern Society.* London: Verso, 2009 [1970].

Bey, Dawoud. "Swagger," in *Black Cool: One Thousand Streams of Blackness,* ed. Rebecca Walker, 147–154. Berkeley, CA: Soft Skull Press, 2012.

Blackburn, Simon. *Truth: A Guide.* Oxford: Oxford University Press, 2005.

Blevins, Joe. "Tom Scharpling Destroys Billy Crystal's Cluelessly Racist 'Old Jazzman' Routine." *AV News* (April 25, 2016). Accessed: https://news.avclub.com/tom-scharpling-destroys-billy-crystal-s-cluelessly-raci-1798246562.

Bloom, Paul. *Against Empathy: The Case for Rational Compassion.* New York: HarperCollins Publishers, 2016.

Bobo, Lawrence D. "Reclaiming a Du Boisian Perspective on Racial Attitudes." *Annals of the American Academy* 568 (March 2000): 186–202.

Borns, Betsy. *Comic Lives: Inside the World of American Stand-up Comedy.* New York: Simon & Schuster, 1987.

Boskin, Joseph. *Rebellious Laughter: People's Humor in American Culture.* New York: Syracuse University Press, 1997.

Brodkin, Karen. *How Jews Became White Folks and What That Says about Race in America.* London: Rutgers University Press, 1999.

Brooks, David. "Here's The Mind-set That's Tearing Us Apart." *New York Times* (October 7, 2021).

Brown, Chris. *Scenes, Semiotics and the New Real: Exploring the Value of Originality and Difference.* Basingstoke, UK: Palgrave Macmillan, 2016.

Bruce Baugh, Bruce. "Authenticity Revisited," *Journal of Aesthetics and Art Criticism* 46:4 (Summer 1988): 477–487.

Bucholtz, Mary. "Race and the Re-embodied Voice in American film." *Language and Communication* 31 (2011a): 255–265.

Bucholtz, Mary. *White Kids: Language, Race, and Styles of Youth Identity.* Cambridge: Cambridge University Press, 2011b.

Bucholtz, Mary and Qiuana Lopez. "Performing Blackness, Forming Whiteness: Linguistic Minstrelsy in Hollywood Films." *Journal of Sociolinguistics* 15:5 (2011): 680–706.

Bury, Michael R. "Social Constructionism and the Development of Medical Sociology." *Sociology of Health and Illness* 8:2 (1986): 137–169.

Butler, Judith. "Gender Is Burning." In *Bodies That Matter: On the Discursive Limits of "Sex"* (381–395). New York: Routledge, 1993.

Campbell, Alexia Fernández, Mauro Whiteman, and National Journal. "Is New Orleans Trying to Deport Undocumented Workers Now That Rebuilding Is Over?", *The Atlantic* (October 27, 2014): Accessed: https://www.theatlantic.com/politics/archive/2014/10/is-new-orleans-trying-to-deport-undocumented-workers-now-that-the-rebuilding-is-over/431406/.

Carbado, Devon W. and Mitu Gulati. *Acting White? Rethinking Race in Post-Racial America.* Oxford: Oxford University Press, 2013.

Carr, David. "More Horrible Than the Truth: News Reports," *New York Times* (September 19), 2005: http://www.nytimes.com/2005/09/19/business/media/more-horrible-than-truth-news-reports.html

Carrell, Amy. "Joke Competence and Humor Competence." *HUMOR: International Journal of Humor Research* 10:2 (1997): 173–185.

Carroll, Lewis. *Alice's Adventures in Wonderland.* New York: Millennium Publications, 2014.

Caruthers, Jakeya and Alisa Bierria. "Stay with Me: Reflections on Michael Jackson, Sound, Sex, and (Racial) Solidarity," *Journal of Popular Music Studies* 23:1 (2011): 125–132.

Case, Sue-Ellen. *The Domain-Matrix: Performing Lesbian at the End of Print Culture.* Bloomington: Indiana University Press, 1997.

Cashmore, Ellis. *The Black Culture Industry.* New York: Routledge, 1997.

Chapman, Antony J. "Humor and Laughter in Social Interaction and Some Implications for Humor Research. In *Handbook of Humor Research*, vol. 1, *Basic Issues*, edited by Paul E. McGhee and Jeffrey H. Goldstein, 135–157. New York: Springer-Verlag, 1983.

Chude-Sokei, Louis. "Migrations of a Mask." In *The Last "Darky": Bert Williams, Black-on-Black Minstrelsy, and the African Diaspora*, 46–81. Durham, NC: Duke University Press, 2006.

Chun, Elaine W. "The Meaning of Ching-Chong." In *Raciolinguistics: How Language Shapes Our Ideas about Race*, edited by H. S. Alim, J. Rickford, and A. F. Ball, 81–98. New York: Oxford University Press, 2020.

Clark, Ashley. "Burning Down the House: Why the Debate over *Paris Is Burning* Rages On," *The Guardian*, June 24, 2015.

Cole, Johnnetta B. "Forward: The South in the U.S. in the South." In *African Americans in the South: Issues of Race, Class, and Gender*, edited by Hans A. Baer and Yvonne Jones, vi–xii. Athens: University of Georgia Press, 1992.

Coupland, Nikolas. *Style: Language Variation and Identity.* Cambridge: Cambridge University Press, 2007.

Crouch, Stanley and Playthell Benjamin. *Reconsidering the Souls of Black Folk: Thoughts on the Groundbreaking Classic Work of W.E.B. Du Bois.* London: Running Press, 2002.

da Silva, Denise Ferreira. *Towards a Global Idea of Race.* London: University of Minnesota Press, 2007.

Dance, Daryl Cumber, ed. *Honey, Hush: An Anthology of African American Women's Humor.* New York: W. W. Norton, 1998.

Dance, Daryl Cumber. *Shuckin' and Jivin': Folklore from Contemporary Black Americans.* Bloomington: Indiana University Press, 1978.

Danielle, Britini. Boss Up: An Interview with Kevin Hart. *Ebony*, October–November 2016, 88–95.

Daniels-Rauterkus, Melissa. *Afro-Realisms and the Romance of Race: Rethinking Blackness in the African American Novel*. Baton Rouge: Louisiana State University Press, 2020.

Davies, Christie. *Jokes and Targets*. Bloomington: Indiana University Press, 2011.

Dawson, Michael C. *Behind the Mule: Race and Class in African-American Politics*. Princeton, NJ: Princeton University Press, 1994.

De Lauretis, Teresa. "The Essence of the Triangle, or Taking the Risk of Essentialism Seriously: Feminist Theory in Italy, the U.S., and Britain." *Differences* 1:2 (1989): 3–37.

Du Bois, W. E. B. *Darkwater: Voices from within the Veil*. New York: Dover, 1999 [1920].

Du Bois, W. E. B. *The Souls of Black Folk: Essays and Sketches*. New York: Vintage Books, 1990 [1903].

Dunbar, Paul Laurence. "We Wear the Mask." In *The Norton Anthology of African American Literature*, edited by Henry Louis Gates Jr. and Nellie Y. McKay, 918. New York: W.W. Norton, 2004 [1892].

Dundes, Alan. *Mother Wit from the Laughing Barrel: Readings in the Interpretation of Afro-American Folklore*. Jackson: University of Mississippi, 1990 [1973].

Duranti, Alessandro and Donald Brenneis, eds. "The Audience as Co-Author: An Introduction." Special Issue, "The Audience Is Co-Author." *Text* 6:3 (1986): 239–247.

Duranti, Alessandro. *Linguistic Anthropology*. New York: Cambridge University Press, 2013.

Dyson, Michael Eric. *Come Hell or High Water: Hurricane Katrina and the Color of Disaster*. New York: Basic Books, 2007.

Dyson, Michael Eric. *Tears We Cannot Stop: A Sermon to White America*. New York: St. Martin's Press, 2017.

Early, Gerald, ed. *Lure and Loathing: Essays on Race, Identity, and the Ambivalence of Assimilation*. New York: Penguin Books, 1994.

Ellison, Ralph. "Change the Joke and Slip the Yoke." *Partisan Review* 25:1 (1958): 212–222.

Ellison, Ralph and John F. Callahan, eds. *Trading Twelves: The Selected Letters of Ralph Ellison and Albert Murray*. New York: Vintage Books, 2001.

Ellwanger, Adam. "Apology as Metanoic Performance: Punitive Rhetoric and Public Speech." *Rhetoric Society Quarterly* 42:4 (2012): 307–329.

Epperson, Terrence W. "Race and the Disciplines of the Plantation." *Historical Archaeology* 24:4 (1990): 29–39.

Epperson, Terrence W. "The Politics of Empiricism and the Construction of Race as an Analytical Category." *Transforming Anthropology* 5:1–2 (1994): 15–19.

Fanon, Franz. *Black Skin, White Masks*, translated by Charles Lam Markmann. New York: Grove Press, 1967.

Favor, J. Martin. "Discourses of Black Identity: The Elements of Authenticity," in *Authentic Blackness: The Folk in the New Negro Renaissance*, 1–23. London: Duke University Press, 1999.

Fernandez Rojas, Icess. "10 Years after Katrina, A Defined Latino Presence in New Orleans," *NBC News* (August 29, 2015). Accessed: https://www.nbcnews.com/storyline/hurricane-katrina-anniversary/10-years-after-katrina-defined-latino-presence-new-orleans-n417026.

Fontenot, Chester J. Jr. and Mary Alice Morgan, with Sarah Gardner, eds. *W.E.B. Du Bois and Race: Essays Celebrating the Centennial Publication of* The Souls of Black Folk. Macon, GA: Mercer University Press, 2001.

Forbes, Camille F. *Introducing Bert Williams: Burnt Cork, Broadway, and the Story of America's First Black Star*. New York: Basic Civitas, 2008.

Fox, Ted. *Showtime at the Apollo: 50 Years of Great Entertainment from Harlem's World Famous Theatre*. New York: Holt, Rinehart, and Winston, 1983.

Freud, Sigmund. *Jokes and Their Relation to the Unconscious*. New York: W. W. Norton, 1960.

Friedman, Sam, Brett Mills, and Tom Phillips, eds. "Editor's Introduction: Foregrounding the Comedy Audience." *Participations: Journal of Audience and Reception Studies* 8:2 (2011): 120–127.

Fussell, Elizabeth, Narayan Sastry, and Mark VanLandingham. "Race, Socioeconomic Status, and Return Migration to New Orleans after Hurricane Katrina." *Population and Environment* 31.1–3 (2010): 20–42.

Garfinkel, Harvey. *Studies in Ethnomethodology*. Upper Saddle River: Prentice-Hill, Inc., 1967.

Garfinkel, Harold and Anne Warfield Rawls. *Ethnomethodology's Program: Working Out Durkheim's Aphorism*. Lanham, MD: Rowman & Littlefield Publishers, 2002.

Gates, Henry Louis Jr. "Critical Remarks." In *Anatomy of Racism*, edited by David Theo Goldberg, 319–332. Minneapolis: University of Minnesota Press, 1990.

Gates, Henry Louis Jr. "Introduction: Writing 'Race' and the Difference It Makes." In *Race, Writing, and Difference*, edited by Henry Louis Gates Jr., 1–20. Chicago: University of Chicago Press, 1986.

Gaudio, Rudolf P. "'Acting Like Women, Acted Upon': Gender and Agency in Hausa Sexual Narratives." In *Queer Excursions: Retheorizing Binaries in Language, Gender, and Sexuality*, edited by Lal Zimman, Jenny Davis, and Joshua Raclaw, 170–194. New York: Oxford University Press, 2014.

Gilbert, Joanne R. *Performing Marginality: Humor, Gender, and Cultural Critique*. Detroit, MI: Wayne State University Press, 2004.

Gillota, David. "Black Nerds: New Directions in African American Humor." *Studies in American Humor* 3:28 (2013): 17–30.

Gilroy, Paul. "Nationalism, History, and Ethnic Absolutism." *History Workshop* (Autumn 1990): 30–120.

Gilroy, Paul. "'Jewels Brought from Bondage': Black Music and the Politics of Authenticity." In *The Black Atlantic: Modernity and Double Consciousness*, 72–110. London: Verso, 1993.

Glenn, Phillip. *Laughter in Interaction*. Cambridge: Cambridge University Press, 2003.

Goldberg, David Theo. *Racial Subjects: Writing on Race in America*. New York, Routledge, 1997.

Goldberg, Whoopi. *Whoopi Goldberg Presents Moms Mabley: The Original Queen of Comedy*. HBO Studios (72 minutes), 2014.

Gotham, Kevin Fox and Miriam Greenberg. 2008. "From 9/11 to 8/29: Post-Disaster Recovery and Rebuilding in New York and New Orleans." *Social Forces* 87(2): 1039–1062.

Gournelos, Ted and Viveca Greene, eds. *A Decade of Dark Humor: How Comedy, Irony, and Satire Shaped Post 9/11 America*. Jackson: University Press of Mississippi, 2011.

Green, Lisa J. *African American English: A Linguistic Introduction*. London: Cambridge University Press, 2002.

Gregory, Dick, with Robert Lipsitz. *Nigger: An Autobiography*. New York: Pocket Books, 1990.

Gregory, Steven and Roger Sanjek, eds. *Race*. New Brunswick, NJ: Rutgers University Press, 1994.

Grow, Kory. "Mike Myers Supports Kanye West's Katrina Statement, Years Later." *Rolling Stone* (May 22, 2014). Accessed: https://www.rollingstone.com/culture/culture-news/mike-myers-supports-kanye-wests-katrina-statement-years-later-81099/.

Gualtieri, Sarah. *Between Arab and White: Race and Ethnicity in the Early Syrian American Diaspora*. Los Angeles: University of California Press, 2009.

Guignon, Charles. *On Being Authentic*. London: Routledge, 2004.

Gwaltney, John Langston. *Drylongso: A Self Portrait of Black America*. New York: New Press, 1993.

Haggins, Bambi. "In the Wake of 'The Nigger Pixie': Dave Chappelle and the Politics of Cross Over Comedy." In *Satire TV: Comedy and Politics in a Post-Network Era*, edited by Jonathan Gray, Jeffrey P. Jones, and Ethan Thompson, 233–251. New York: New York University Press, 2009.

Haggins, Bambi. *Laughing Mad: The Black Comic Persona in Post-Soul America*. New Brunswick, NJ: Rutgers University Press, 2007.

Hall, Perry A. "African-American Music: Dynamics of Appropriation and Innovation." In *Borrowed Power: Essays on Cultural Appropriation*, edited by Bruce Ziff and Pratima V. Rao, 31–51. New Brunswick, NJ: Rutgers University Press, 1997.

Hall, Stuart. "What Is This 'Black' in Black Popular Culture?" In *Black Popular Culture: A Project by Michele Wallace*, edited by Gina Dent, 21–33. Seattle, WA: Bay Press, 1992.

Handler, Richard. "Authenticity," *Anthropology Today* 2:1 (February 1986): 2–4.

Harbidge, Lesley. "Audienceship and (Non)Laughter in the Stand-up Comedy of Steve Martin." In *The Laughing Stalk: Live Comedy and Its Audiences*, edited by Judy Batalion. Anderson, SC: Parlor Press, 2012.

Harper, Phillip Brian. "What's My Name?: Designation, Identification, and Cultural 'Authenticity.'" In *Are We Not Men? Masculine Anxiety and the Problem of African-American Identity*, 54–73. Oxford: Oxford University Press, 1996.

Harris, Aisha. "When Black Performers Use Their 'White Voice,'" *The New York Times* (July 10, 2018); Accessed: https://www.nytimes.com/2018/07/10/movies/when-Black-performers-use-their-white-voice.html.

Harris, Joel Chandler and Richard Chase. *The Complete Tales of Uncle Remus*. Boston: Houghton Mifflin, 2002 [1955].

Harris, Joel Chandler. *Uncle Remus, His Songs and His Sayings, by Joel Chandler Harris*. New York: D. Appleton-Century, 1940.

Harris, Joel Chandler. *Uncle Remus: His Songs and His Sayings*. New York: D. Appleton, 1881 [1928].

Harrison, Faye V. "The Du Boisian Legacy in Anthropology." *Critique of Anthropology* 12:3 (1992): 239–260.

Harrison, Faye V. "The Persistent Power of 'Race' in the Cultural and Political Economy of Racism." *Annual Review of Anthropology* 24 (1995): 47–74.

Harrison, Faye V. "Anthropology as an Agent of Transformation: Introductory Comments and Queries." In *Decolonizing Anthropology: Moving Further Toward an Anthropology for Liberation*, edited by Faye V. Harrison, 1–15. Arlington, VA: American Anthropological Association, 1997a.

Harrison, Faye V. "Racism," in The Dictionary of Anthropology, edited by Thomas Barfield, 394–396. Oxford: Blackwell, 1997b.

Harrison, Faye V. "Expanding the Discourse on Race." *American Anthropologist* 100:3 (1998): 609–631.

Harrison, Faye V. and Ira E. Harrison, eds. "Introduction: Anthropology, African Americans, and the Emancipation of Subjugated Knowledge," 1–36. In *African-American Pioneers in Anthropology*. Chicago: University of Illinois Press, 1999.

Hart, Kevin, with Neil Strauss. *I Can't Make This Up: Life Lessons*. New York: Simon and Schuster, 2017.

Hartigan, John Jr. "Culture against Race: Reworking the Basis for Racial Analysis." *South Atlantic Quarterly* 104:3 (2005): 543–560.

Hendra, Tony. *Going Too Far: The Rise and Demise of Sick, Gross, Black, Sophomoric, Weirdo, Pinko, Anarchist, Underground, Anti-Establishment Humor*, 1987.

Higginbotham, Evelyn Brooks. *Righteous Discontent: The Women's Movement in the Black Baptist Church, 1880–1920*. Cambridge, MA: Harvard University Press, 1994.

Hill, Doug and Jeff Weingrad. *Saturday Night: A Backstage History of Saturday Night Live*. New York: Vintage Books, 1987.

Hill, Jane H. *The Everyday Language of White Racism*. Malden, MA: Blackwell, 2008.

hooks, bell. "Postmodern Blackness," 23–31. In *Yearning: Race, Gender, and Cultural Politics*, Boston, MA: South End Press, 1990.

hooks, bell. "Is Paris Burning?," 145–156. In *Black Looks: Race and Representation*. Boston, MA: South End Press, 1992.

hooks, bell. *Talking Back: Thinking Feminist Thinking Black*. Boston: South End Press, 1989.

Hughley, D. L. with Michael Malice. *Black Man, White House: An Oral History of the Obama Years*. New York: William Morrow/HarperCollins, 2017.

Hunt, Darnell M. "Making Sense of Blackness on Television." In *Channeling Blackness: Studies on Television and Race in America*, ed. Darnell M. Hunt, 1–24. Oxford: Oxford University Press, 2005.

Hurston, Zora Neale. *Mules and Men*. New York: HarperCollins, 1990 [1935].

Hymes, Dell H. "Two Types of Linguistic Relativity." In *Sociolinguistics*, edited by William Bright with C. H. Van Schooneveld, 114–158. The Hague: Mouton, 1966.

Hymes, Dell H. "On Communicative Competence." In *Sociolinguistics: Selected Readings*, edited by J. B. Pride and Janet Holmes, 269–293. Harmondsworth: Penguin Books, 1972.

Ignatiev, Noel. *How the Irish Became White*. London: Routledge, 2009 .

Jackson, John L. Jr. "A Little Black Magic." *South Atlantic Quarterly* 104:3 (2005a): 393–402.

Jackson John L. Jr. *Real Black: Adventures in Racial Sincerity*. Chicago: University of Chicago Press, 2005b.

Jackson John L. Jr. "An Ethnographic Filmflam: Giving Gifts, Doing Research, and Videotaping the Native Subject/Object." *American Anthropologist* 106:1 (2008): 32–42.

Jackson, Jr., John L. *Thin Description: Ethnography and the African Hebrew Israelites of Jerusalem*. Cambridge: Harvard University Press, 2013.

Jacobs, Lanita. " 'The Arab Is the New Nigger': African American Comics Confront the Irony and Tragedy of 9/11." In *A Decade of Dark Humor: How Comedy, Irony, and Satire Have Shaped Post-9/11 America*, edited by T. Gournelos and V. Greene, 47–56. Jackson: University Press of Mississippi, 2011

Jacobs, Lanita. "On 'Making Good' in a Study of African American Children with Acquired and Traumatic Brain Injuries." In *Mutuality: Anthropology's Changing Terms of Engagement*, edited by Roger Sanjek, 249–258. Philadelphia: University of Pennsylvania Press, 2015.

Jacobs, Lanita. "Truth and Authenticity in African American Standup Humor," Guest Lecture, American Studies 285: African American Popular Culture, University of Southern California, September 22, 2016.

Jacobs-Huey, Lanita. "The Natives Are Gazing and Talking Back: Reviewing the Problematics of Positionality, Voice, and Accountability among 'Native' Anthropologists." *American Anthropologist* 104:3 (2002): 1–14.

Jacobs-Huey, Lanita. "Black/'Urban' Standup Comedy: A Performance by Brandon Bowlin." *Theatre Journal* 55:3 (2003): 539–541.

Jacobs-Huey, Lanita. Gender, Authenticity, and Hair in African American Standup Comedy. In *From the Kitchen to the Parlor: Language and Becoming in African American Women's Hair Care*, 71–88. Oxford: Oxford University Press, 2006.

Jacobs-Huey, Lanita. "Learning through the Breach: Language Socialization among African American Cosmetologists." *Ethnography* 8(2): 171-203, 2007.

James, William. *Pragmatism: A New Name for Some Old Ways of Thinking*. New York: Dover Publications, 1907 [1995].

James, William. *Pragmatism and Four Essays from "The Meaning of Truth."* New York, Meridian, 1955.

James, William. *The Meaning of Truth*. New York: Prometheus Books, 1997 [1909].

Japtok, Martin and Jerry Rafiki Jenkins. "What Does It Mean to Be 'Really' Black? A Selective History of Authentic Blackness." In *Authentic Blackness: "Real" Blackness: Essays on the Meaning of Blackness in Literature and Culture*, edited by Martin Japtok and Jerry Rafiki Jenkins, 7–65. New York: Peter Lang, 2011.

Jarrett, Gene Andrew. *Deans and Truants: Race and Realism in African American Literature.* Philadelphia: University of Pennsylvania Press, 2007.

Jenkins, Candice M. "Decoding Essentialism: Cultural Authenticity and the Black Bourgeoisie in Nella Larsen's *Passing*," *MELUS* 30:3 (2005): 129–154.

Jenkins, Ron. *Subversive Laughter: The Liberating Power of Comedy.* New York: Free Press, 1994.

Jhally, Sut., Jeremy. Earp, and Jack G. Shaheen. Reel Bad Arabs How Hollywood Vilifies a People. Northampton, MA: Media Education Foundation, 2006.

Johnson, E. Patrick. "'Quare' Studies, or (Almost) Everything I Know about Queer Studies I Learned from My Grandmother." *Text and Performance Quarterly* 21:1 (2001): 1–25.

Johnson, E. Patrick. *Appropriating Blackness: Performance and the Politics of Authenticity.* Durham, NC: Duke University Pres, 2003.Jones, Richard A. "Race and Revisability." *Journal of Black Studies* 35:5 (May 2005): 612–632.

Jones, Siân. "Negotiating Authentic Objects and Authentic Selves: Beyond the Deconstruction of Authenticity," *Journal of Material Culture* 15:2 (2010): 181–203.

Kajikawa, Loren. "Eminem's 'My Name Is': Signifying Whiteness, Rearticulating Race," *Journal of the Society for American Music* 3:3 (2009): 341–363.

Kapoor, Nisha. *Deport, Deprive, Extradite : 21st Century State Extremism.* London: Verso, 2018.

Kelley, Robin D.G. "Looking for the 'Real' Nigga: Social Scientists Construct the Ghetto." In *Yo' Mama's Disfunktional! Fighting the Culture Wars in Urban America*, 16–42. Boston: Beacon Press, 1997.

Kennedy, Randall. *Nigger : The Strange Career of a Troublesome Word.* 1st ed. New York: Pantheon Books, 2003.

Kennedy, Randall. "The Fallacy of Touré's Post-Blackness Theory." *The Root*, August 11, 2011. http://www.theroot.com/articles/culture/2011/08/whos_afraid_of_postblackness_tours_p ostblackness_theory/.

Kercher, Stephen E. *Revel with a Cause: Liberal Satire in Postwar America.* Chicago: University of Chicago Press, 2006.

Khanna, Neetu. *The Visceral Logics of Decolonization.* London: Duke University Press, 2020.

Knoedelseder, William. *I'm Dying Up Here: Heartbreak and High Times in Stand-up Comedy's Golden Era.* New York: PublicAffairs, 2009.

Krefting, Rebecca. *All Joking Aside: American Humor and Its Discontents.* Baltimore, MD: Johns Hopkins University Press, 2014.

Krutnik, Frank, ed. *Hollywood Comedians: The Film Reader.* London: Routledge, 2003.

LaBennett, Oneka. *She's Mad Real: Popular Culture and West Indian Girls in Brooklyn.* New York: New York University Press, 2011.

Lacoste, Véronique, Jakob Leimgruber, and Thiemo Breyer, editors. *Indexing Authenticity: Sociolinguistic Perspectives.* Berlin: De Gruyter, 2014.

Lamar, Kendrick. "Alright." *To Pimp a Butterfly.* Aftermath Entertainment, 2015.

Lee, Rachel C. "'Where's My Parade?' Margaret Cho and the Asian American Body in Space." *Drama Review* 48:2 (Summer 2004): 108–132.

Lee, Spike, Director. *When The Levees Broke: A Requiem in Four Acts.* 40 Acres and a Mule Filmworks, 2006 (255 minutes).

Lessin, Tia and Carl Deal, Directors. *Trouble the Water.* Zeitgeist Films, 2008 (93 minutes).

Lester, Julius. *Uncle Remus: The Complete Tales.* New York: Dial Books, 1999 [1939].

Lewis, Paul. *Cracking Up: American Humor in a Time of Conflict.* Chicago: University of Chicago Press, 2006.

Li, Stephanie. *Signifying without Specifying: Racial Discourse in the Age of Obama.* New Brunswick, NJ: Rutgers University Press, 2012.

Limon, John. *Stand-up Comedy in Theory, or, Abjection in America.* London: Duke University Press, 2000.

Lindholm, Charles. "Authenticity, Anthropology, and the Sacred." *Anthropological Quarterly* 75:2 (2002): 331–338.

Lindholm, Charles. "The Rise of Expressive Authenticity." *Anthropological Quarterly* 86:2 (Spring 2013): 361–395.

Linnekin, Jocelyn. "Cultural Invention and the Dilemma of Authenticity." *American Anthropologist* 93:x (1991): 446–449.

Lipsitz, George. "Learning from New Orleans: The Social Warrant of Hostile Privatism and Competitive Consumer Citizenship." *Cultural anthropology* 21(3): 451–468, 2006.

Littleton, Darryl. *Black Comedians on Black Comedy: How African-Americans Taught Us to Laugh*. New York: Applause Theatre and Cinema Books, 2006.

Littleton, Darryl and Tuezdae Littleton. *Comediennes: Laugh Be A Lady*. Milwaukee, WI: Applause Theatre and Cinema Books, 2012.

Livingston, David N. "Representation and Authenticity: A Rereading." *Transactions of the Institute of British Geographers* 23:1 (1998): 13–19.

Lott, Eric. *Love and Theft: Blackface Minstrelsy and the American Working Class*. Oxford: Oxford University Press, 2013.

Lynch, Michael P., ed. *The Nature of Truth: Classic and Contemporary Perspectives*. London: MIT Press, 2001.

Marc, David. *Comic Visions: Television Comedy and American Culture*. Boston, MA: Unwin Hyman, 1980.

Masquelier, Adeline. "Why Katrina's Victims Aren't Refugees: Musings on a 'Dirty' Word." *American Anthropologist* 108(4): 735–743, 2006..

Mayer, Matt A., James Carafano, Jena Baker McNeill, and Richard Weitz. "Accepting Disaster Relief from Other Nations: Lessons from Katrina and the Gulf Oil Spill." *The Backgrounder* 2519 (February 17, 2011): 1–12. https://www.heritage.org/homeland-security/report/accepting-disaster-relief-other-nations-lessons-katrina-and-the-gulf-oil.

McClaurin, Irma, ed. "Introduction: Forging a Theory, Politics, Praxis and Poetics of Black Feminist Anthropology," 1–23. In *Black Feminist Anthropology: Theory, Politics, Praxis, and Poetics*. London: Rutgers University Press, 2001a.

McClaurin, Irma, ed. "Theorizing a Black Feminist Self in Anthropology: Toward an Autoethnographic Approach," 49–86. In *Black Feminist Anthropology: Theory, Politics, Praxis, and Poetics*. London: Rutgers University Press, 2001b.

McLeod, Kembrew. "Authenticity within Hip-Hop and Other Cultures Threatened with Assimilation." *Journal of Communication* 49:4 (Autumn 1999): 134–150.

Michaels, Walter Benn. "Race into Culture: A Critical Genealogy of Cultural Identity." *Critical Inquiry* 18 (Summer 1992): 655–685.

Mintz, Lawrence. "Standup Comedy as Social and Cultural Mediation." *American Quarterly* 37:1 (1985): 71–80.

Molina-Guzmán, Isabel. *Latinas and Latinos on TV: Colorblind Comedy in the Post-Racial Network Era*. Tucson: University of Arizona Press, 2018.

Mooney, Paul. *Black Is the New White: A Memoir*. London: Gallery Books, 2009.

Moore, Allan. "Authenticity as Authentication," *Popular Music* 21:2 (May 2002): 209–223.

Morgan, Marcyliena. *The Real HipHop: Battling for Knowledge, Power, and Respect in the L.A. Underground*. Durham, NC: Duke University Press, 2009.

Morrison, Toni. *The Source of Self-Regard: Selected Essays, Speeches, and Meditations*. New York: Knopf Publishing Group, 2019.

Mukhopadhyay, Carol C. and Yolanda T. Moses. "Reestablishing 'Race' in Anthropological Discourse." *American Anthropologist* 99:3 (1997): 517–533.

Naber, Nadine. *Arab America: Gender, Cultural Politics, and Activism. Arab America: Gender, Cultural Politics, and Activism*. New York: NYU Press, 2012.

Nachman, Gerald. *Seriously Funny: The Rebel Comedians of the 1950s and 1960s.* New York: Pantheon Books, 2003.

Narayan, Kirin. "How Native Is a 'Native' Anthropologist?" *American Anthropologist,* New Series 95: 3 (1993): 671–86. http://www.jstor.org/stable/679656.

Nayak, Anoop. "After Race: Ethnography, Race and Post-race Theory." *Ethnic and Racial Studies* 29:3 (2006): 411–430. DOI: 10.1080/01419870600597818.

Neal, Mark Anthony. *Looking for Leroy: Illegible Black Masculinities.* New York: New York University Press, 2013.

Neal, Mark Anthony. "'You Remind Me of Something': Toward a Post-Soul Aesthetic." In *Soul Babies: Black Popular Culture and the Post-Soul Aesthetic,* 1–22. New York: Routledge, 2002.

Nicolson, Malcolm and Cathleen McLaughlin. "Social Constructionism and Medical Sociology: A Study of Vascular Theory of Multiple Sclerosis." *Sociology of Health and Illness* 10:3 (1988): 234–261.

Nixon, James. "You Think I'm Joking": Examining the Weaponized Comedy of President Obama's Stand-up Addresses at the White House Correspondents' Association Dinner." *Studies in American Humor* 5:1 (2019): 103–123.

Ochs, Elinor and Lisa Capps. *Living Narrative: Creating Lives in Everyday Storytelling.* Cambridge, MA: Harvard University Press, 2001.

Oring, Elliott. *Engaging Humor.* Chicago: University of Chicago Press, 2003.

Orser, Charles E. Jr. The Challenge of Race to American Historical Archaeology. *American Anthropologist* 100:3 (September 1998): 661–668.

Ortner, Sherry B. "Resistance and the Problem of Ethnographic Refusal." *Comparative Studies in Society and History* 37:1 (January 1995): 173–193.

Owen, Graham. "After the Flood: Disaster Capitalism and the Symbolic Restructuring of Intellectual Space." *Culture & Organization* 17:2 (2011): 123–127.

Pasevich, Matthew. "Why Authenticity Matters." Doctoral Dissertation, University of Chicago, 2009.

Pérez, Raúl. *The Soul of White Jokes: How Racist Humor Fuels White Supremacy.* Stanford, CA: Stanford University Press, 2022.

Perrino, Sabina. "Race, Humor, and Politics: Racialized Joke-Telling and Anti-Immigrant Politics in Northern Italy." In *The Oxford Handbook on Language and Race,* edited by H. S. Alim, A. Reyes, and P. V. Kroskrity, 423–446. New York: Oxford University Press, 2020.

Pollack, Mica. *Colormute: Race Talk Dilemmas in an American School.* Princeton, NJ: Princeton University Press, 2005.

Provine, Robert R. *Laughter: A Scientific Investigation.* New York: Viking, 2000.

Ray, Sangeeta. *Gayatri Chakravorty Spivak: In Other Words.* London: Wiley-Blackwell, 2009.

Rayner, Alice. "Creating the Audience: It's All in the Timing." In *The Laughing Stalk: Live Comedy and Its Audiences,* edited by Judy Batalion, 28–39. Anderson, SC: Parlor Press, 2012.

Rees, David. "Billy, It Would Have Been So Much More Powerful and Moving If You Had Just Gone All The Way And Used Burnt Cork." *Huffpost* (November 19), 2006. Accessed: https://www.huffingtonpost.com/david-rees/billy-it-would-have-been-_b_34444.html

Retman, Sonnet H. *Real Folks: Race and Genre in the Great Depression.* Durham, NC: Duke University Press, 2011.

Rice, Condoleezza. *No Higher Honor: A Memoir of My Years in Washington.* New York: Broadway Books, 2011.

Rickford, John. "The Question of Prior Creolization in Black English." In *Pidgin and Creole Linguistics,* edited by Albert Valdman, 190–221. Bloomington: Indiana University Press, 1977.

Rigby, Peter. *African Images: Racism and the End of Anthropology.* Oxford: Berg, 1996.

Riggs, Marlon T. *Ethnic Notions.* Berkeley, CA: California Newsreel, 1987.

Riggs, Marlon T., Nicole Atkinson, and Christiane Badgley. *Black Is . . . Black Ain't: A Personal Journey through Black Identity*. Berkeley, CA: California Newsreel, 2004.

Robinson, Peter M. *The Dance of the Comedians: The People, the President, and the Performance of Political Standup Comedy in America*. Boston: University of Massachusetts Press, 2010.

Rock, Chris. "It's a White Industry." *Hollywood Reporter*, December 3, 2014, https://www.hollywoodreporter.com/news/top-five-filmmaker-chris-rock-753223.

Rodriguez, Cheryl. "A Homegirl Goes Home: Black Feminism and the Lure of Native Anthropology," 233–257. In *Black Feminist Anthropology: Theory, Politics, Praxis, and Poetics*. London: Rutgers University Press, 2001.

Roediger, David R. *Working toward Whiteness: How America's Immigrants Became White, the Strange Journey from Ellis Island to the Suburbs*. New York: Basic Books, 2005.

Roediger, David R. *The Wages of Whiteness: Race and the Making of the American Working Class*. London: Verso, 1991.

Rogin, Michael. "Blackface, White Noise: The Jewish Singer Finds His Voice." *Critical Inquiry* 18:3 (Spring, 1992): 417–452.

Rosa, Jonathan and Nelson Flores. "Unsettling Race and Language: Toward a Raciolinguistic Perspective." *Language in Society* 46:5 (2017): 621–647.

Rutter, Jason. "Stand-up as Interaction: Performance and Audience in Comedy Venues." Dissertation, University of Salford, 1997.

Santa Ana, Otto. "Did You Call in Mexican? The Racial Politics of Jay Leno's Immigrant Jokes." *Language in Society* 38 (2009): 23–45.

Scarpetta, Fabiola and Anna Spagnolli. "The Interactional Context of Humor in Stand-up Comedy." *Research on Language and Social Interaction* 42:3 (2009): 210–230.

Scepanski, Philip. *Tragedy Plus Time: National Trauma and Television Comedy*. Austin: University of Texas Press, 2021.

Seguin, Nile. "Hecklers: A Taxonomy." In *The Laughing Stalk: Live Comedy and Its Audiences*, edited by Judy Batalion, 186–188. Anderson, SC: Parlor Press, 2012.

Sewell, Christopher J. P.. "Mammies and Matriarchs: Tracing Images of the Black Female in Popular Culture, 1950s to Present." *Journal of African American Studies* 17:3 (2013): 308–326.

Shaheen, Jack G. *Reel Bad Arabs : How Hollywood Vilifies a People, Third Edition*. New York: Olive Branch Press, 2012.

Shales, Tom and James Andrew Miller. *Live from New York: An Uncensored History of Saturday Night Live*. New York: Little, Brown, 2002.

Shanklin, Eugenia. *Anthropology and Race*. Belmont, CA: Wadsworth, 1994.

Shanklin, Eugenia. "The Profession of the Color Blind: Sociocultural Anthropology and Racism in the 21st Century." *American Anthropologist* 100:3 (1998): 669–679.

Shelby, Tommie. *We Who Are Dark: The Philosophical Foundations of Black Solidarity*. London: Harvard University Press, 2005.

Shotwell, Alexis. "Commonsense Racial Formation: Wahneema Lubiano, Antonio Gramsci, and the Importance of the Nonpropositional." In *Race and the Foundations of Knowledge*, edited by Joseph Young and Jana Evans Braziel, 46–62. Chicago: University of Illinois Press, 2006.

Simien, Evelyn M. "Race, Gender, and Linked Fate." *Journal of Black Studies* 35:5 (May 2005): 529–550.

Smalls, Krystal A. "Race, Signs, and the Body: Towards a Theory of Racial Semiotics." In *The Oxford Handbook on Language and Race*, edited by H. S. Alim, A. Reyes, and P. V. Kroskrity, 233–260. New York: Oxford University Press, 2020.

Smith, Candis Watts. *Black Mosaic: The Politics of Black Pan-Ethnic Diversity*. New York: New York University Press, 2014.

Smith, Eric Ledell. *Bert Williams: A Biography of a Pioneer Black Comedian*. Jefferson, NC: McFarland, 1992.

Smith, Jacob. "The Frenzy of the Audible: Pleasure, Authenticity, and Recorded Laughter." *Television and News Media* 6:1 (2005): 23–47.

Smith, Patriann. "(Re)Positioning in the Englishes and (English) Literacies of a Black Immigrant Youth: Towards a 'Transraciolinguistic' Approach." *Theory into Practice* 58:3 (2019): 292–303.

Smitherman, Geneva. *Talkin and Testifyin: The Language of Black America*. Detroit: Wayne State University Press, 1986.

Sotiropoulos, Karen. "The 'Coon Craze' and the Search for Authenticity." In *Staging Race: Black Performers in Turn of the Century America*, 81–122. Cambridge, MA: Harvard University Press, 2008.

Spears, Arthur K., ed. *Race and Ideology: Language, Symbolism, and Popular Culture*. Detroit: Wayne State University Press, 1999.

Spillers, Hortense J. "'All The Things You Could Be by Now if Sigmund Freud's Wife Was Your Mother': Psychoanalysis and Race." In *Female Subjects in Black and White: Race, Psychoanalysis, Feminism*, edited by Elizabeth Abel, Barbara Christian, and Helene Moglen, 135–158. Berkeley: University of California Press, 1997.

Spivak, Gayatri Chakravorty. *In Other Words: Essays in Cultural Politics*. New York: Routledge, 1988.

Steiner, George. *Real Presences*. Chicago: University of Chicago Press, 1989.

Stephens, Michelle. "What Is This Black in Black Diaspora?" *Small Axe* 13:2 (2009): 26–38.

Stone, Lauri. *Laughing in the Dark: A Decade of Subversive Comedy*. Hopewell, NJ: Ecco Press, 1997.

Sundén, Jenny and Susanna Paasonen. *Who's Laughing Now? Feminist Tactics in Social Media*. Cambridge, MA: MIT Press, 2020.

Sutherland, Marcia. *Black Authenticity: A Psychology for Liberating People of African Descent*. Chicago: Third World Press, 1993.

Szwed, John F. "An American Anthropological Dilemma: The Politics of Afro-American Culture." In *Reinventing Anthropology*, edited by Dell Hymes, 153–181. New York: Pantheon Books, 1969.

Taylor, Charles. *The Ethics of Authenticity*. London: Harvard University Press, 1991.

Texeira, Erin. "Kramer Aftermath: Paul Mooney Renounces the N-word after Michael Richards' Rant." *Time Herald-Record* (November 29, 2006).

Theodossopoulos, Dimitrios. "Laying Claim to Authenticity: Five Anthropological Dilemmas." *Anthropological Quarterly* 86:2 (2013): 337–360.

Thevenot, Brian and Gordon Russell. "Rape. Murder. Gunfights." *NOLA.com/The Times-Picayune* (September 26), 2005.

Thomas, Mike. *The Second City Unscripted: Revolution and Revelation at the World-Famous Comedy Theater*. New York: Villard, 2009.

Thompson, A.C. "Katrina's Hidden Race War." *The Nation* (December 17, 2008).

Thompson, A.C. "The Nation: Katrina's Race War Four Years Later." *NPR* (August 31, 2009). Accessed: https://www.npr.org/templates/story/story.php?storyId=112399477.

Touré. "Who's Afraid of Post-Blackness? What It Means to Be Black Now." New York: Free Press, 2012.

Trilling, Lionel. *Sincerity and Authenticity*. London: Harvard University Press, 1972.

Tuan, Mia. *Forever Foreigners or Honorary Whites: The Asian Ethnic Experience Today*. London: Rutgers University Press, 1999.

Turner, Patricia. *I Heard It through the Grapevine: Rumor in African-American Culture*. Berkeley: University of California Press, 1993.

Van de Port, Mattijs. "Registers of Incontestability: The Quest for Authenticity in Academia and Beyond." *Etnofoor* 17:1–2 (2004): 7–22.

Visweswaran, Kamala. "Race and the Culture of Anthropology." *American Anthropologist* 100:4 (1998): 981–983.

Visweswaran, Kamala. *Un/common Cultures: Racism and the Rearticulation of Cultural Difference.* London: Duke University Press, 2010.

Viveros, Joy. "Black Authenticity, Racial Drag, and the Case of Dave Chappelle." In *Authenticity Blackness, "Real" Blackness: Essays on the Meaning of Blackness in Literature and Culture,* edited by Martin Japtok and Jerry Rafiki Jenkins, 139–153. Oxford: Peter Lang, 2011.

Wade, Lisa. "Who Didn't Evacuate for Hurricane Katrina? A Picture of Those Left Behind." *Sociological Images* (August 24, 2015). https://thesocietypages.org/socimages/2015/08/24/an-iconic-image-of-government-failure-courtesy-of-hurricane-katrina/.

Wailoo, Keith, Karen M. O'Neill, Jeffrey Dowd, and Roland Anglin, eds. *Katrina's Imprint: Race and Vulnerability in America.* London: Rutgers University Press, 2010.

Walker, Alice. "Uncle Remus, No Friend of Mine." *Georgia Review* 66:3 (2012): 635–637.

Walker, Dave. "Oh, What a 'Relief' It Was—HBO's Katrina 'Comic Relief' Hit (Almost) All The Right Marks." *NOLA.com/The Times-Picayune* (November 22, 2006) [updated July 24, 2015]. Accessed: http://www.nola.com/tv/index.ssf/2006/11/oh_what_a_relief_it_was_-_hbos.html.

Warnke, Georgia. "Race, Gender, and Antiessentialist Politics." *Signs* 31:1 (Autumn 2005): 93–116.

Waters, Mary C. *Ethnic Options: Choosing Identities in America.* Los Angeles: University of California Press, 1990.

Watkins, Mel, ed. *African American Humor: The Best Black Comedy from Slavery to Today.* Chicago: Lawrence Hill Books, 2002.

Watkins, Mel. *On the Real Side: Laughing, Lying, and Signifying—The Underground Tradition of African American Humor that Transformed American Culture, from Slavery to Richard Pryor.* 2nd ed. Chicago: Lawrence Hill Books, 1999.

Weate, Jeremy. "Changing the Joke: Invisibility in Merleau-Ponty and Ellison." *Philosophia Africana* 6:1 (2003): 5–21.

Webber, Julie A., ed. *The Joke Is on Us: Political Comedy in (Late) Neoliberal Times.* New York: Lexington Books, 2019.

Weems, Scott. *Ha! The Science of When We Laugh and Why.* New York: Basic Books, 2014.

West, Tim'm T. "Keepin' It Real: Disidentification and Its Discontents." In *Black Cultural Traffic: Crossroads in Global Performance and Popular Culture,* edited by Harry J. Elam Jr. and Kennell Jackson, 162–184. Ann Arbor: University of Michigan Press, 2005.

Williams, Elsie A. *The Humor of Jackie Moms Mabley: An African American Comedic Tradition.* New York: Garland, 1995.

Williams, John A. and Dennis A. Williams. *If I Stop, I'll Die: The Comedy and Tragedy of Richard Pryor.* New York: Thunder's Mouth Press, 1993.

Williams, Angel Kyodo, Lama Rod Owens, with Jasmine Syedullah. *Radical Dharma: Talking Race, Love, and Liberation.* Berkeley: North Atlantic Books, 2016.

Williamson, Terrion. *Scandalize My Name: Black Feminist Practices in the Making of Black Social Life.* New York: Fordham University Press, 2017.

Wolfe, Bernard. "Uncle Remus and the Malevolent Rabbit." In *Mother Wit from the Laughing Barrel: Readings in the Interpretation of Afro-American Folklore,* edited by Alan Dundes, 524–540. Jackson: University Press of Mississippi, 1990 [1949].

Wood, Katelyn Hale. "Laughter in the Archives: Jackie 'Moms' Mabley and the Haunted Diva." *QED* (East Lansing, MI) 1:3 (2014): 85–108.

Wood, Katelyn Hale. *Cracking Up: Black Feminist Comedy in the Twentieth and Twenty-First Century United States.* Iowa City: University of Iowa Press, 2021.

Yancy, George. *Look! A White: Philosophical Essays on Whiteness.* Philadelphia: Temple University Press, 2012.

Yang, Philip Q. and Kavitha Koshi. "The 'Becoming White' Thesis Revisited," *The Journal of Public and Professional Sociology* 8:1 (2016): 1–25.

Young, Robert. 2006. "Putting Materialism Back into Race Theory: Toward a Transformative Theory of Race, 32–45. In *Race and the Foundations of Knowledge*. Chicago: University of Illinois Press.

Young, Joseph and Jana Evans Braziel, eds. "Cultural Amnesia and the Academy: Why the Problem of the Twenty-first Century Is Still the 'Problem of the Color Line,'" 1–31. In *Race and the Foundations of Knowledge*. Chicago: University of Illinois Press, 2006.

Zoglin, Richard. *Comedy at the Edge: How Stand-up in the 1970s Changed America.* New York: Bloomsbury, 2009.

Index

For the benefit of digital users, indexed terms that span two pages (e.g., 52–53) may, on occasion, appear on only one of those pages.